Hope you like our "personality"

With love

"Gert"

1/30/61

Nashville

Personality of a City

BY THE SAME AUTHOR:

Nashville

Personality of a City

by

ALFRED LELAND CRABB

THE **BOBBS-MERRILL** COMPANY, INC.
A SUBSIDIARY OF HOWARD W. SAMS & CO., INC.
Publishers · INDIANAPOLIS · NEW YORK

To

S<small>ARA</small> G<small>ARDNER</small> C<small>RABB</small>

granddaughter of Nashville

CONTENTS

Nashville

Personality of a City

1

THE BEGINNINGS

CREATION DAY dawned bright and fair in that particular area of the universe which in the long passage of time was to become the Nashville country, and all of the participating forces smiled with pride for the part they had in the assignment. But it was to be a task past the understanding of man. Mankind can never understand the labor required for the creation of anything. He can adapt with speed perhaps, but for him creation is terrifyingly slow. The geologic ages passed. The region was roughed in with choice materials and ready for the final shaping. More geologic ages passed, and the forces of that special shift set diligently to work building the mountains, digging the rivers, leveling out the low places, and getting the lands set aside for forests ready for the seeding. The slow, slow centuries passed, and all was ready for the coming of man. The preparation for that arrival had been no casual matter. It was surely an important being for whom Nature had undergone all those incredible eons of incredible toil.

But man was in no hurry to make his entrance even though the stage had been made ready. His appearance was all that was needed to set the great drama into action. We do not know, of course, the year that the first man strode across the stage that awaited him. Nor do we know who he was nor whence he came. We think that he was small of stature, and of a reddish copper color. There is proof that he was reasonably expert at making things with his hands. We know that he was here and that he left, to arouse the wonder of later men, some remarkable mounds filled with the remarkable things he had made. It is not known how long he stayed, nor what became of him, nor when. Very likely, in terms of years or centuries, he disappeared gradually. He disappeared, leaving only those mounds and those artifacts and a great question mark to remind later men that he once played the principal role on this very stage.

Again the primeval silence closed in, unbroken by human sound. And then, almost suddenly, redder and larger men converged on the section from many directions. These men, by a series of coincidences, have been christened Indians. They penetrated a large part of the inland country, and claimed all the land as their own. They fought tribal wars, made treaties and then fought more wars.

Late in the sixteenth century white men began coming into the section. The first who came were mere explorers. They looked about, made a few notes and moved on. Two centuries later the eyes of white men lingered longer, more contemplatively. They began to regard specially favored places with the notion that they would make good home sites. They looked upon the land in personal terms, and seemed to feel some obligation to christen what they saw and to catalogue it in some vague way. Some of them manifested a special aptness in the fine art of christening.

One historic bit of christening occurred in 1748. An adventurous group of Virginia gentlemen rode through a fine valley in the southwestern part of the state to discover what sort of country lay beyond their wonted horizon. The outline of some western mountains took form against the western haze. The leader of the party was Dr. Thomas Walker. One of his favorite noblemen must have been the Duke of Cumberland. So he gave the name "Cumberland" to the mountains. They rode on and in time came to a great gap in the mountains. Dr. Walker christened it "Cumberland Gap." The Duke of Cumberland was being made immortal that day. The party made its way down the tortuous side of the mountain, and at its foot they came to a beautiful river. Dr. Walker made the series complete by naming it the "Cumberland River." The beauty in the name has pleased the people from that day to this.

And yet there is a massive irony in the colonists' acceptance of those christenings. The Duke of Cumberland, favorite son of George II, was in charge of the English troops at the battle of Culloden. The battle was a massacre, told of in tragic story and heartbreaking song. Dr. Walker was surely aware of the Duke's consequent reputation among the Scottish people. The Butcher, they called him, and with reason. One may be excused to regard somewhat oddly the Scotch-Irish settlers' willingness to accept it. The poetry of the name must have obscured its bloody associations.

But those were red letter christenings in the new country. The mountains have been towering in men's lives and imaginations ever since. Almost since that day the river has been spilling over with romance and song, with war and industry. Its source is in what is now Harlan County, Kentucky. For more than 300 miles it twisted and turned so as to fit its channel to the uneven lay of the land. It flowed for most of those miles to the southwest, then turned to the northwest. The marks of the travail of its finding its course are still upon it. But in its own geologic time it reached the freedom of the Ohio. The Cumberland is a river of infinite bends. It literally twists and thrusts its way through the mountains. The mountains and foothills dwindle into knobs, and through them the river dodges and bends as it falls gently into a great central basin. Where the folds of the river are thickest and amplest, there now is Nashville.

THE GREAT ARRIVAL

Nashville now is 181 years old. That isn't old at all when compared with the nation's senior cities, such as Boston, New

York, Philadelphia, Richmond, Charleston, Mobile, New Orleans. On the other hand, it is a bit hoary when compared with Birmingham, Dallas, San Francisco, even Chicago. The darkest days of the Revolution had been lived through when Nashville was settled, but not all the dark days. The treason of Benedict Arnold was then nine months in the future, the fall of Charleston five months. On the day that the Founders arrived at the Bluffs, a little later called Nashville, a red-haired lad named Andrew Jackson was in the midst of his brief schooling at Waxhaw Academy, in Lancaster County, South Carolina. His teacher was Dr. James Stephenson, who later was to live and teach and preach and die in Jackson's section of Tennessee.

Nashville was founded by a large body of Scotch-Irish pioneers from the Watauga settlement in the eastern part of what is now Tennessee. The founding was under the leadership of two remarkable men, James Robertson and John Donelson. It was of itself and in its effects one of the nation's epic events. Very favorable reports of the attractiveness and desirability of the country along the middle stretches of the Cumberland River had reached the eastern settlements, particularly Watauga. Those reports had caused some flurries of excitement among the pioneers of the Virginia valley. The Wataugans were in the mood to move. Some political developments had bothered them. Also, the Indians were always threatening, and sometimes their threats turned into grim reality. Furthermore the very term, the west, had come to have the drawing power of the lodestar. In that direction lay their opportunity. But they needed more proof than vague reports. So, in the early summer of 1779, they commissioned James Robertson, of renown as a scout, woodsman and diplomat among the Indians, to go to the western country and bring back a full report of what he found. In the early fall Robertson returned and reported his choice to be the land lying in the folds of the Cumberland River. There was, he told them, much fine bottom land in the section. The timber was the best he had ever seen. There were flowing springs that yielded both salt and sulphur. The particular site he had chosen was on the south bank of the river at a place he called "the Bluffs."

His report was so convincing that approximately 500 men, women and children committed themselves to seek homes at the place Robertson had chosen. The men, and the women no less, knew perfectly well that the move would involve extreme peril. So their plans were made with the utmost care and in full detail. It was, by their plans, to be a sort of pincers movement into the western wilderness, one fork moving through the woods, the other by the waters. The women and children were used to hardships, but not enough to undertake the winter journey on foot, across the mountains and through 300 miles of uncharted forests. It was their decision to build boats and take all but the most rugged of the men down the Holston to the Tennessee, down the Tennessee to the Ohio, up the Ohio to the Cumberland, up the Cumberland to the Bluffs. There, so the plan ran, they would meet those who had gone on by land. The boats would be built to carry, in addition to the emigrants, the furniture, the tools, the field and garden seeds, and the few but precious heirlooms owned by the settlers. Captain John Donelson, who had had a great deal of experience in water travel, was chosen to direct the building of the boats and to command the trip by water. The younger men and the livestock would make the trip through the woods under the leadership of James Robertson.

Robertson's party started early in November. There were about 200 of the men, twenty horses, fifteen cattle and a flock of sheep. Food and other things immediately necessary would be carried on packhorses. Robertson led the men northward into Virginia, then westward along the trail later known in history as the Wilderness Trail. They crossed the mountains at Cumberland Gap. Then, for days, they traveled a slanting course up into Kentucky. At Carpenter's Station, a few miles south of Crow's Station, now Danville, they turned their course southwestward, and moved on through the upper Green River country and across the Barrens. The weather was fair and they encountered fewer troubles than they had expected.

One night they went to sleep at the Double Springs, three miles east of the present city of Bowling Green. It was a fair and pleasing night, but the next morning they awoke to a frozen and troubled world. It was bitter cold and snowing. It was then that they began to hurry. Their food for man and beast was about used up, and travel was slow and exhausting. The main problem in all minds was getting across the Cumberland when they reached it. Robertson's recommendation had been to build the stockade and cabins on the southern bank. The men themselves could get across, but the stock was another matter. They found the problem solved for them. The river was frozen solidly enough for the stock to be taken across on the ice. Only three times is there record of the river having been frozen to such a depth. They killed a great bear and roasted it for their Christmas dinner.

The next day they began work on the cabins, making ready for the arrival of the boats. They finished the stockade and at the first sign of spring began to plan for the crops. They could get the ground ready but they couldn't plant it till the boats arrived with the seeds.

The redbud flowered and faded and the dogwood whitened the thickets and woodlands. Why didn't the boats come? John Donelson's last words, as they were leaving Fort Patrick Henry, had been to expect the boats about the middle of February. March came and blew itself away. Why didn't the Cumberland River answer the questions they asked it? Whenever they stopped for a moment from the cabins they were building or the ground they were making ready for the planting, they turned their eyes down the Cumberland. April came, and anxiety, almost terror, was etched on every face. Rivers could prove treacherous routes of travel.

John Donelson was finding it slow work getting the boats finished, a whole month slow. It had been good weather for the boatbuilders at Fort Patrick Henry, now Kingsport, but the finishing lingered. At last the final seam was watertight. Early in the morning of the first day of winter a man went the rounds spreading the word among the people that Mr. Donelson wanted them to come to the landing right after the midday meal. Food was swallowed hurriedly and the people gathered at the riverside. It was freezing cold, but they were used to that. They had lived through many freezing winters, and now something likely of massive consequences in their lives was about to happen. Mr. Donelson came walking rapidly, and the chatter ceased suddenly with his appearance. He told them simply that the departure would be at that hour the following day. He cautioned them as to the loading of the boats. All care should be used in placing the food, the ammunition, the guns, the clothing where they would keep dry. For the second time he went over the warning as to the care of the field and garden seeds. Those seeds would be of first importance in the new country.

Though it was very cold Captain Donelson took off his hat. "We are not coming back," he said in his deep voice. "We are going to a new country and we are going to stay there. We are going to build our homes there and live there till we die. After that the children will live there." He put his hat back on. "Be ready to leave at this time tomorrow."

The children slept a little that night, the men and women very little indeed. There was too much to do, and it was so cold that they put most of the cover on the children. The next morning they started to work early. They carried the last of the furniture to the boats, and also the food and cooking things. The boatbuilders made last minute examinations to see whether there might be any hidden defects. They could not afford any weaknesses where they were going. At the best there would be enough danger without adding anything unnecessary.

In the early afternoon they floated away from the landing. It was a stirring sight, the winter sun shining coldly on the river and fields and mountains. Thirty boats, large and small, drifted slowly down the Holston River. Captain Donelson's boat, the *Adventure*, floated in the lead. Those on the boats took long looks, tinged with sadness, back at the fort, back at the familiar scenes of the countryside. They drew deep, sad breaths. This was farewell to Watauga. Not many ever expected to see it again, not many ever did.

That was the beginning of a thousand-mile journey by water. Trouble set in almost at the beginning. That night the Holston froze solidly. They were only three miles from their starting place. And there, for six dismal weeks, they awaited a thaw. Their supply of food ran dangerously low, so low that it was plain that they would have to forage for food from then on. Not often again, on that long journey, were they to be free from the pangs of hunger.

But there were other foes to menace them. There was always the great threat of the Indians. Smallpox broke out on a boat carrying twenty-nine people. As a measure of safety it was placed at the rear of the procession. The Indians captured it, and there is no record as to the fate of those on board, though the inference is plain enough.

The most frightening day of all was the one spent running Muscle Shoals, a veritable torrent more than thirty miles in length. Those pioneers had faced death often enough before, but in that rush of water it seemed nearer than ever before. It was almost a miracle that there were so few casualties. The *Adventure* carried forty-eight people, besides considerable furniture and supplies. And yet the worst injury was a broken rib suffered by one woman. There were bruises but those were routine matters. After they reached the quiet water below the shoals the journey seemed safe enough.

They reached the Ohio on the twentieth of March. But that was in degree a mixed pleasure. The journey from that time on would be upstream. The prospect of that was so appalling to some of the most weary ones that they continued on down the rivers to Natchez and New Orleans. The rest braced themselves and took a firmer hold on poles and sweeps. Twelve back-breaking miles later they came to the mouth of the Cumberland. No riverman today can quite understand how they managed the rest of the journey. But they did. The currents of the spring flood beat against them, but in the end yielded to devoted purpose and pioneer muscle.

On the twenty-fourth of April the lookout whom James Robertson kept posted on the bluff above the stockade saw the prow of the *Adventure* nosing around the bend almost a mile down the river. He blew such a mighty blast on his horn that many of the settlers had reached him by the time the echoes quieted. Then he was blowing again. Everybody scrambled and fell down the side of the bluff to the water's edge, and there, bright-eyed, moist-eyed, waited to welcome wives and children and friends.

For a week they stopped work and celebrated the reunion with feasting and song and preaching and just being together again. The weather was then as fair as it had been cruel during the winter. The sun was kind, and the gentle breezes filled with the good cheer of spring.

When the reunion was over the people turned their ways into the routines of the reality about them. They assembled and formed the laws for the government of the new settlement, a document known as "The Cumberland Compact." It has been little publicized but it carried a remarkable understanding of justice and rights and restraints. When they had finished writing and signing that, they settled down into the business of finishing and moving into their houses, of planting and tending their crops, of making preparations against the ever-threatening forays and raids of the Indians, of promoting as best they could the ways and means of pioneer life.

AT HOME

That was the beginning of Nashville. At first it was called the Bluffs, and then, for three years, Nashborough. The legislature of North Carolina changed the name to Nashville in 1784. Both Nashborough and Nashville were christened for General Francis Nash, a hero of the Revolution. The episode of founding is related here for two reasons. It was one of the sturdiest exploits of the nation's history; and in considerable degree it explains Nashville today.

Of those founding families, arriving 180 years ago, there are not fewer than 7,000 direct descendants here now, in Nashville or close about. It seems unlikely that any other city in the country has such a substantial connection with its beginning. Metropolitan Nashville is literally sprinkled with the posterity of James Robertson (sixty-two grandchildren), of John Donelson, of Robert Cartwright, of Abel Gower, of John Rains, of Thomas Thompson, of John McMurtry, of John Cockrill, of William Crutchfield. Through them the influence of the Founders has dwindled surprisingly little in the shaping of the community's trends.

Those who came in the second wave of settlers were of like strength and permanence. Robert Coleman Foster came from Bardstown, Kentucky, in 1792. There has beeen a Robert Coleman Foster here ever since, sometimes no fewer than three.

James Alexander Porter reached Nashville from Ireland by way of Philadelphia in 1793. He flourished in the linen business and built the Porter home, Riverwood, today one of the city's show places. The Porters have been potent factors in the life of Nashville ever since he rode into the settlement with his bride, acquired on the journey, sitting proudly behind him on his horse. Later, a Porter of the second generation, showing special fitness for the law, was advised by General Andrew Jackson to settle in the bayou section of Louisiana, there being in the Teche country special need for lawyers of training and legal capacity. Young Alexander Porter took the General's advice and located at Franklin, Louisiana. In time he became judge, and then United States senator. He built his home, Oaklawn, a few miles out of Franklin. It was then and is now of considerable magnificence. The posterity of James Alexander Porter has composed an important phase of Nashville citizenry.

David McGavock came to Nashville from Rockbridge County, Virginia, in 1794. He established here a dynasty of culture and canniness. For a century the McGavocks were perhaps the section's leading family. It remains strong and durable.

Felix Grundy reached Nashville in 1804. He left Bardstown, Kentucky, for two reasons: partly because of the fine reports sent back by the Fosters, partly because he felt that Kentucky was not of size to contain both him and Henry Clay. There are surely as many as 300 of Grundy's posterity here now.

And as the *Adventure* fought its way upstream, inch by inch, the currents of history strove against the currents of the Cumberland. One of the boat's passengers was John Donelson's twelve-year-old daughter, Rachel, who a dozen years later married a young lawyer, newly arrived in the settlement, named Andrew Jackson. And that of itself added a dominant phase to the career of Nashville.

There were many things to brighten the eyes of James Robertson when he first surveyed the terrain in 1779. The multiple folds of the Cumberland and the twisting creeks made a great deal of good bottom land, and bottom land bore a clear meaning to any canny Scotch-Irishman. All about the river and streams were forests filled with the finest timber he had ever seen. Good timber was always a brightener of pioneer eyes. The streams without doubt were filled with fish and the woods with game. In a low place, back a little from the river, were mineral springs, salt for curing and cooking, and sulphur to heal the ills of the flesh. The wild things well knew the worth of those springs. The ground was smooth and hard from the paths which they had worn to reach them, deer, bear, buffalo and the smaller creatures.

There was no way to know in any detail the past of the place. The small, copper-hued men had been there, great numbers of them apparently. There was a small burial place on what is now Capitol Hill, a larger one near the Sulphur Spring, one on Brown's Creek on the southern margin of the city and perhaps the most important one of all at Old Town, eighteen miles to the south. It remains an enigma as to who were buried in those ancient graves. The Indians of the James Robertson era were not so careful with their dead. They were, however, zealous enough in their possession of the land to cause the Nashville settlers a great deal of trouble for more than a quarter of a century. The land as far south as the Cherokee (now the Tennessee) River had been ceded to the whites at the treaty of Stanwix in 1768. But as time passed the southern Indians denied the validity of that cession. By 1780 the Indians, urged on by the British in the north and east, and by the Spanish in the south and west, were challenging the settlers' right even to a single acre of land.

The settlers of Nashville paid dearly. But it was their land. The bleak journey from Fort Patrick Henry had been undertaken with that idea firmly fixed. It was theirs by the Stanwix treaty; it was theirs by an informal understanding with the state of North Carolina (made formal by the legislature of 1783). Further support was added their claim by a somewhat shadowy arrangement with Richard Henderson of the Transylvania Company. It was their land and they intended to hold it against any and all odds. Their epic journey had not been made whimsically. It had been for them a one-way trip. They had no thought of going back, or of relinquishing their land. But they were made to pay again and in blood for their homes. James Robertson lost two brothers and two sons by Indian raid or ambush. Within the first four years of the settlement's life sixty-four died at the hands of the Indians.

But Indians were not the only foes that menaced them. It seemed at times that both nature and human nature were bent on thwarting the existence of the settlement. The crops at first yielded poorly. The creeks and rivers rose and flooded at inopportune times. Wild beasts raided the unfenced crops. The first winters were starving times, and freezing times as well. There was a great deal of sickness, and graveyards began to be formed and filled.

John Donelson took up land on Stone's River, ten miles above Nashville. There he built temporary camps, and in one of them was born the settlement's first child, christened Chesed, after its maternal grandfather. But Captain Donelson became so disturbed that he left before the year was up. In the autumn the family moved to Casper Mansker's Station, twelve miles north of the settlement. After a little while there the family moved on to Harrodsburg, in Kentucky.

That move came to have, and is still having, a remarkable influence on the career of Nashville. The family fared better at Harrodsburg, but somehow the Cumberland country remained pleasantly in their minds. So much so that when the captain made a return trip to Nashville for some negotiations with the Indians he looked about and found a fine tract of land in what is now the Hermitage section. He made a formal claim for it, and even laid the foundations for a blockhouse and stockade before he returned to Kentucky. Very soon after his arrival at Harrodsburg he was sent to Richmond, Virginia, on some urgent pioneer matters. On his return home he made arrangements to move back to Tennessee. When everything was ready he went ahead on horseback. The family followed with such of their household goods as were transportable. In southern Kentucky, somewhere near the present town of Glasgow, the great pioneer was killed. It was never known whether he died at the hands of Indians or border white ruffians. After his burial was completed the family came on to Mansker's Station, and remained there while the stockade, begun by Donelson on his earlier trip, was being completed. When it was finished the family moved to it. Happily it was on the "Kentucky Road," and only three miles distant from the protection that Mansker's Station could offer.

Let us now turn back a bit and consider the neatness with which Destiny can plot its affairs. In the year 1788 a young man named John Overton left Louisa County, Virginia, bound on horseback for the famed Kentucky town of Lexington. But Lexington was not destined to become the home of John Overton. That young man was later to loom large in the affairs of Nashville, as well as the rest of the country. As he journeyed to Lexington, he carried along a few clothes and a large lawbook, and nothing else. His brother who had already gone on to Lexington had written him a letter saying that the town was a favorable place for a bright young lawyer to begin his practice. But John Overton, for some reason, did not find it a favorable place. Perhaps there were too many bright young lawyers there ahead of him. So, after a brief stay, he gathered up his lawbook, mounted his horse and rode on down to Harrodsburg. There is no record as to why he chose Harrodsburg, though in a very good sense it was a wise choice.

Then, apart from the desirability of Harrodsburg, another significant phase entered the situation. On the day of his arrival he secured lodging in the home of the Robards family. Living in the home at the time were Lewis Robards, son of the home, and his new bride, the former Rachel Donelson. Overton found these friendly enough, though he did have some concern for the bridegroom's ways. Rachel must have talked to Overton a great deal about Nashville. Though the settlement was grim and desolate when she left it, some inner vision of its promise must have been hers. There is indeed a large possibility that her enthusiasm for the place must have set the young lawyer on the road again, bound for Nashville. There is no documentary evidence that Rachel Robards directed him to her mother's stockade on the Kentucky Road, but it seems more than merely reasonable. If she did, her directions were to echo and re-echo for a long time. The Widow Donelson accepted the young man as a lodger and assigned him to one of her cabins. His cabinmate was another young lawyer named Andrew Jackson, just arrived from North Carolina.

The long line of sequences flowing from that arrangement fills a great many pages of our national history. It was the beginning of a long and potent friendship, one that the strains and tensions of pioneer leadership never interrupted. It may very well have been that the friendship begun in Mrs. Donelson's cabin started one of the young men on a journey that almost forty years later reached the White House. And his companion on that journey, though stopped by death just short of the White House, was the young woman who had recommended her mother's stockade to John Overton. That story will be mentioned somewhat later.

Nashville's first decade was filled with privation, with drudgery, with bereavement. But it was a time filled with high glimpses too. Such people could, given time, defeat such desolation. And they did. Crops fared better in fields enclosed by fences, and fences went up constantly. Babies, and adults not much less, fared better when there was milk to drink, and soon the settlers, besides the cows they were raising, began to bring in more from a distance. The settlers put in many back-breaking days and months and years building crude roads to the outside. Horses—they brought twenty with them—became a vital part of the section's life. And so the foundations were being laid even then for making Tennessee a great center for the raising of horses, particularly fine horses.

The mercantile life of Nashville began in 1786 when Lardner Clarke arrived from Philadelphia with ten horses laden with calico, linen goods and coarse woolens. Before that the men had depended in great degree on the skins of wild animals for their clothing, the women on the cloth they could weave from the materials they had. It was noted that after Mr. Clarke opened his store there was an added brightness in the dresses the Presbyterian ladies wore to hear Dr. Craighead preach, and the Methodist ladies to hear Dr. Ogden.

Nashville's pioneer physician was Dr. John Sappington. Soon, Sappington's pills, compounded of equal parts of mystery and sugar coating, were considered the proper panacea for most of the ills of pioneer flesh. Dr. Sappington himself delivered the pills, supervised their taking and observed the benefits which almost inevitably followed.

TENNESSEE GROWS INTO STATEHOOD

The hardships which were the main routine of their daily lives may have dimmed the settlers' dreams a little, but not much. They toiled like any slaves during the day, but whenever there were little intermissions, or perhaps at night, their thoughts ranged on ahead. Word reached them of the statehood achieved by Vermont, and a little later by their neighbor Kentucky. That news was most challenging, and the desire for statehood by the people of Nashville and of the other settlements took form in their minds and hopes. It was James Robertson who, as the main counselor of the people of the Cumberland country, directed the forming and phrasing of their application for admission to the sisterhood. There was delay and considerable discussion, but on June 1, 1796, Tennessee became the sixteenth state of the Union. John Sevier, a man of infinite variety and great competence, was chosen to serve as the state's first governor. The capital was placed at Jonesboro, though it was reasonably certain that a shift would soon be made.

The nineteenth century was under way before any full

understanding was caught of Nashville's real promise. It was a settlement in the wilderness, at the best a pioneer village. It seems unlikely, however, that any metropolis of the nation had its foundation laid by sturdier people. They were the cream of the sections from which they came: Watauga, the Valley of Virginia, South Carolina, the eastern parts of North Carolina, the Bardstown section of Kentucky and, early in the nineteenth century, a few of fine quality from New England.

The first and second tides of migration to reach Nashville had in them those virtues which endow permanence. The settlers were predominantly Scotch-Irish, certainly one of the most important of all the nation's founding groups. Their names are on all of the pioneer documentaries, and their ways are today Nashville's main characteristic. Their industry shared eagerness with their thrift. They understood land in all of its varying values. They knew which crops to grow and how to grow them. They knew which stock to raise for the most profit.

From some source they had gathered remarkable glimpses of the homes in which they wished to live. They chose sites with an almost uncanny sense of fitness. They built their homes slowly, amply and with pleasing commitment to grace and dignity. Happily, there remain enough of the houses of the first half of the nineteenth century for observers today to regard their excellence almost with wonder. It was the way of the founding Scotch-Irish to build good houses, and in them to live the best lives they could afford. The owners wished to share the charm of their homes with their friends. The food, homely at first, in short time became excellent in quality and distinctiveness. By 1820 the fame of Nashville's dining rooms was established and widespread. Of that excellence further statements will be made later on.

Nashville is composed of many parts. It is a city of many phases. In terms of geography and population it is the assembling of the formally bounded section—that within the city's limits—and of its various suburban areas into one working and living unity, though at times governed by differing legalities. Nashville has many suburbs, each one created by some special fitness, each one differing in its own right, but all bearing a close kinship to the city. Each has its own separateness, and yet with its own dependence upon the parent group. Each one has its own personality, yet all bear the flavors of the city's uniqueness.

As an instance, Belle Meade is a suburb of Nashville. It is about six miles to the southwest, and lies along the highway leading to Memphis. Belle Meade is the poetic name of the house built by William Harding. It was later the home of General William H. Jackson, who married one of the Harding daughters. The life lived in Belle Meade before the Civil War was in many ways a brilliant one. The war laid a heavy hand on it, leaving it desolate, but it gradually regained its splendor. For a full generation the place had more prestige raising blooded horses than any other in the country. The great barn, 200 feet behind the mansion, is reminiscent of the glory of those years. In 1887 President Grover Cleveland and his bride spent two days of their honeymoon there. Later, President Taft was to make a pleasing visit to Belle Meade, and the bathtub, hurriedly ordered from Cincinnati specially to accommodate his bulk, fascinates visitors today. Now the house is a shrine sponsored by the Tennessee Society for the Preservation of the Antiquities.

Around this historic center a great many homes have been built, most of them of excellent quality. The wealth of the Belle Meade community is impressive, and the houses suggest a liberal use of that wealth, spent in good taste. The men belong to the professions or are in business. Their offices and stores are in Nashville. There they carry on their practice, sell their wares, or direct such services as they have to offer. But their homes are in Belle Meade, so are their schools and churches. They are suburban people, but in a definite sense they are a vital part of the city of Nashville. They are separate in that they conduct a considerable part of their own affairs, fire department, police department, etc. They even have their own mayor and governing officers. In some ways Belle Meade directs its own life. But it is a part of Nashville. Take away Nashville and Belle Meade would tend to disappear. Belle Meade has more wealth than any other unit of the Nashville family, but each of the other suburbs adds its own color and meaning to the totality of Nashville.

But Nashville is the metropolitan center of a much larger area than those lying about the city's margins. In a very definite sense Nashville serves as a pattern for Gallatin and Fayetteville, and an impressive tier of small and middle-sized fine towns extending from the south central part of western Kentucky into northern Alabama. Those towns contribute greatly to Nashville's size and quality and commerce. But the contribution is by no means a one-way affair. Nashville responds by shaping itself according to their standards and by reflecting their personalities in its life. This story—a true one—illustrates the matter.

A lady of one of Clarksville's first families married and moved to Nashville. But she never forgot Clarksville, and she talked about it a great deal, always favorably. One day, twenty-five years later, she was still talking about Clarksville, still favorably. A friend inquired somewhat waspishly, "If Clarksville is so fine, why did you ever leave it?"

"Nonsense," said the lady crisply, "I didn't leave it. I brought it with me."

There are a great many ladies, and gentlemen, living in Nashville who brought their home towns with them.

The personality of Nashville is compounded of many phases. The long continuity of its citizenship is one. There are several thousand citizens of metropolitan Nashville who are direct descendants of the place's founders, arriving in 1780. And that adds a thick and tough stratum of conservatism to the city's life. Another phase is the kinship Nashville has always felt to war. Probably the city's favorite topic of conversation is the Civil War. That episode was a great breeder of talk in an already articulate city. Its partisan sense has been dulled until there is not much edge left. Usually the theme of the discussion fits within the what-might-have-been category.

For instance, if Jefferson Davis had appointed Bedford Forrest commander of the Army of Tennessee instead of John Hood . . . Or if the builders had used more sense in the construction of Fort Henry it wouldn't have fallen, in which case Fort Donelson wouldn't have fallen, in which case Nashville wouldn't have fallen, in which case the South wouldn't have fallen. That one is good for three hours of uninterrupted discussion.

The people of Nashville are gifted with imaginations which respond vigorously to the challenge of the Civil War. The town bears about itself the reminiscence of battlesmoke. It is filled with mementos of battle, with portraits of war heroes, with abstracts of Revolutionary war grants, with traditions and legends, with battle markers, with diaries kept by gallant men in gray. And this leads us directly to the next chapter.

2

NASHVILLE: WHERE THE BATTLE FLAGS ARE UNFURLED

THE WORD *Mars* is found frequently in the literature of Nashville. It adds a classic touch to a favorite topic. Mars was the Roman god of war. There is, to be sure, a planet named Mars, and from some talk lately a suburban status may presently be arranged for it. But the Mars used here bears the sound of conflict.

Nashville has been a martial city during much of its history. It seems doubtful whether any other city in the nation has been so intimately and continuously associated with war. Nashville has had full participation in every war since it was a mere stockade. Indeed, it was a war which brought that stockade into existence. The ways of the people have been conditioned and their thoughts shaped by war since the beginning. There are many families in Nashville who can claim valid blood connection with every war in which the nation has engaged. When the trumpets have sounded Nashville has always answered.

THE AMERICAN REVOLUTION

In a very direct way the Revolution was the major motive for the founding of the settlement. The first settlers came from Watauga on the western fringe of the lands overrun by the British. They knew very well that they couldn't escape the

Indians by a westward move. They could, however, greatly widen the gap between them and the Redcoats. They could, in the security that the distance provided, establish another colony in defense of the Patriots. Furthermore, the west was most alluring. It stirred brave visions and fond hopes. The challenge of the west added motive to that of the Revolution.

The expedition was in a sense a bit of splintering off from the main body of the war. The leaders and many of the men were intimate with the Revolution. James Robertson had taken part in it before it was spelled with a capital *R*. He fought at the battle of Alamance, which served as a dress rehearsal for Lexington. For several years he had known and greatly admired General George Washington. It was on the basis of that acquaintance that Washington later appointed him as a commissioner to the Indians, which turned out to be one of the wisest of the President's appointments. John Donelson had fought at the battle of Kanawha, which also helped prepare the stage for the oncoming conflict. John McMurtry came with Robertson, established his claim for land, built his cabin and then went back east to join the colonial forces and fight for his right to that land and that cabin. So did Thomas Thompson; so did John Rains; so did others whose names unhappily we do not have.

But the bulk of Nashville's Revolutionary patriots did not come with Robertson and Donelson. They came in 1784, and they kept on coming till after the new century set in. There is record of twenty-four men of Nashville who were granted pensions for service in the Revolution, and twenty-three others who served but were given grants of land instead. The settlement of Nashville had its roots in the Revolution, indeed very hardy roots.

There are now twelve chapters of the Daughters of the American Revolution, in Nashville, with a membership of 760. There is one chapter of the Sons of the Revolution. All of these hold regular meetings, and the Spirit of 'Seventy-Six breathes in their programs.

THE WAR OF 1812

No war is ever completed with the signing of a treaty of peace. Not all of its issues can be adjusted so simply, nor all of its costs paid for so conveniently; not all of its questions can be answered so readily, nor all of its effects so promptly brought under control. There has been too much violence, too much dislocation of men's thinking and living to be simply resolved. The Revolution nominally was brought to its conclusion by the treaty of Paris, signed September 3, 1783. Actually, the various matters involved were left so incomplete that another war had to be fought to take care of unfinished business, as well as some new business which had reared its ugly head.

The War of 1812 rested heavily on Nashville. It opened on several fronts, politically and geographically. By 1812 the United States had a great many ships engaged in carrying its products to European ports. England and France were in a state of war, alternately hot and cold. England didn't want our goods to reach France, and France didn't want them to reach England. England made a show of generosity by permitting our goods to be landed in France, provided that the ships carrying them first put in at an English port, registered the cargo and paid a heavy tax. That brought great hardships in this country, and very specially in New England. Then England began stopping our ships and impressing our seamen.

But perhaps its worst offense against us was its continued encouragement to the Indians to harass the settlers on the frontiers. General Andrew Jackson and James Robertson occupied themselves with raising troops for the struggle then imminent. Robertson's company was made up of veterans from the Revolution and sons of the veterans. The war began but no call was issued for those volunteers. Time dragged futilely

33

ahead. Late in the year 1812 a feeling of special uneasiness began to pervade the nation's capital. The British had achieved successes in Canada and on the northern lakes. That success, it was feared, would bring on an invasion of the coast lying along the Gulf of Mexico. Such a pincers movement would place the country in grave jeopardy, the brunt falling upon the South. Governor Blount was ordered to send 1,500 men to aid in the defense of New Orleans, if the need should develop.

Again time dragged, and it was January 7, 1813, before the expedition set out under General Andrew Jackson, Colonel John Coffee and Captain William Carroll. The troops marched overland to Natchez, arriving there in about five weeks. For two weeks they remained there impatiently awaiting orders. The orders proved to be short and crisp and dismally anti-climactic: Disband the troops at once. General Jackson refused to obey until money was forwarded for the pay and subsistence of the men. In the end he was forced to lead the men back to Nashville at his own expense.

On that forlorn homeward march he was awarded the immortal title, "Old Hickory." A soldier had become so ill that he was unable to continue the march. Jackson let the man have his horse, and he himself walked along with the men. One of the soldiers took a look at the General trudging along with his men and called out, "Take a look at Andy Jackson, jest a reg'lar piece of old hickory." The metaphor caught the men's fancy. They used it all the way home and gave it to posterity.

Again time dragged on, and the inaction inflamed the people of Nashville. Send Old Hickory into action and get the war over with, was the general comment. But Old Hickory's call came surprisingly and shockingly. In September 1813 word reached Nashville of a terrible massacre committed by the Creek Indians upon almost 600 whites at Fort Mims in southern Alabama. At that time Jackson was slowly recovering from a bullet fired into him by Jesse Benton in a fight on the city square. Though barely able to ride, he placed himself at the head of more than 4,000 troops and marched into Alabama. It was his belief, shared by the people of Nashville, that the Indians had been incited to the outrage by the British. Later that was found to be the case, though there was some indirectness involved and some assistance lent by the Spanish. Jackson's savage attack on the Indians left them irreparably weakened. He moved his forces on to Mobile and then to New Orleans. His military sense told him that the next battle of the war would be there.

His military sense, as usual, proved reliable. The British were keenly aware of the strategic worth of New Orleans, and were investing it with all the speed they could summon. Jackson, gaunt and grim and wasted from the Benton bullet, rode at the head of his army into New Orleans. His soldiers were mainly from Tennessee, but a considerable sprinkling of them were Kentuckians. The main body of the Kentuckians was to follow.

Jackson didn't know then, and couldn't know in those uncommunicative days, that Napoleon Bonaparte had escaped from his exile on Elba and was raising an army to resume his struggle against England. Nor could he know that England, under the stress of that threat, had made overtures to the United States. Nor could he know that a treaty had been signed at Ghent on Christmas Eve, 1814. Of these developments the British forces investing New Orleans were also unaware. So the battle of New Orleans was to be fought by two countries technically at peace. General Jackson was eager to get the campaign over with. It had been a long time since he had seen his wife, his home or his neighbors.

The American troops immediately settled down to the dilemma and drudgery of making ready against an attack which all agreed would come soon. But from what quarter? New Orleans was a sorely exposed city, but no one knew the conditions of its exposure. The British were coming; that much was known. But would they come by Lake Borgne, east of the city, or by Barataria Bay, south of the city, or would they sail boldly up the Mississippi?

Almost all of his life Andrew Jackson had studied terrains and approaches, and the various ways by which land can lend itself to military strategy. It had been a sort of passion with him. In the meantime, after the immemorial ways of the place, the General was wined and dined, at least as often as he felt that he could safely accept. Panic broke out in the city. He managed to allay it, but kept himself prepared for its recurrence. He struggled constantly with the problem of the route the British would take. He was certain that the river would help shape the battle, but would the British come directly up the river from the Gulf? Crisis was in the air.

Jackson sent a peremptory message to Coffee at Baton Rouge to bring his troops to the city with all speed. "Hurry, don't sleep till you get here." Orders to all commanding officers poured in volleys from the Marigny House, where he was making his town headquarters, commanding some to converge hurriedly on New Orleans, others to hold fast to their assignments as already issued.

Then, in an odd manner, fortune smiled on Old Hickory. The Baratarian pirates, commanded by the brothers Jean and Paul Laffite, had grown fat off the commerce of the Gulf but at last had come to grips with the Federal authorities. In fact, some of them were already in jail. It was the nature of the Laffites and their men to want a part in every battle near enough for them to get in. It is even possible that they were developing some fondness for the new nation. So Jean Laffite called on General Jackson, and the two men had a talk. It is certain that General Jackson did not offer Jean Laffite any money for his help, but at any rate, the pirate came out on the side of the Americans. It is not known what the convincing argument was. Laffite's statement was that if they had violated the laws of the country they wished all the more to assist in its defense. That added close to 1,000 fierce fighters to Old Hickory's army.

The handling of the army was keeping the General busy, but he added another item to the fullness of his day, a careful and systematic study of General Edward Pakenham, in command of the British forces. It would be helpful to know as much as he could about the man. Pakenham had been born in the same Irish county as Jackson's parents. The Pakenhams were of the aristocracy though the son had literally fought his way up from a private in the ranks to a major-generalship. He was then only thirty-seven years old, but had proved himself of unusual ability. He was a brother-in-law of the Duke of Wellington. He came to the New Orleans campaign fresh from the brilliant victory he had gained at Salamanca. Furthermore this western expedition was to be no round-trip affair. He brought with him his commission as governor of Louisiana. On Christmas Day, 1814, he arrived at the British front on Lake Borgne and took charge. Jackson knew then whence the attack would start, and he had a good notion where it would actually be made.

Jackson knew that he must miss nothing. He kept alert and in motion. Every British movement had its own significance. And when one thing was settled another would arise to trouble him sorely. For ten days he had been expecting the arrival of 2,500 Kentuckians under Colonel Thomas. Where were they? What had happened? On January 4 they arrived in good spirits, but only one man in three had a rifle. Jackson's ingenuity rose to the emergency. From somewhere in New Orleans he obtained 400 rusty rifles. But too many were still unarmed.

Jackson frowned, then smiled. "All right," he said, "that's the best we can do. Part of you shoot and part of you load."

A lanky Kentuckian grinned back at him. "And when we ain't shootin' or loadin' we'll throw rocks."

Jackson turned away contentedly. There was a fighting man after his own heart.

The General had but a brief snatch of sleep on the night of the seventh. At one o'clock he said to his aides, "We have slept enough. Tomorrow we settle things." During the remainder of the darkness he visited his army, regiment by regiment, position by position. At daybreak he stood on the parapet of earthworks, peering through the fog and haze to where his alert ears could distinguish the faint sounds of soldiers gathering. That, January 8, was to be the day. As he watched, a rocket rose and soared and burst. The attack would not be long coming.

Then the fog settled down, spreading a curtain against all view of the enemy. There was a while of that blindness, perhaps three fourths of an hour, and then a stiff breeze rose suddenly and blew the fog away. It was a thrilling sight that was revealed. There, less than half a mile away, came the British, marching steadily, in perfect formation. The rifles of the Americans could be deadly at 100 yards, much less so at 200 and almost useless at 300. Jackson's orders were explicit and relayed to all the companies. Each soldier should time his firing to the range of his rifle. He told them further where to aim, right above the breastplate of the oncoming soldier.

The British, marching briskly, got quickly within range of the American rifles. It was time to go into action. The soldiers under Carroll and Coffee took aim and fired. They stepped back to load and the second line stepped forward to fire. This alternation went on. The British ranks, terribly thinned, closed ranks and came on. Colonel Dale, commanding a Scottish Highland regiment, was killed, then General Keane, then General Gibbs, then General Pakenham. The battle was over before nine o'clock, though to make sure the American batteries kept firing for a while. Those British were seasoned veterans, but almost to a man they testified that they had never experienced such rifle fire as was poured into them by the Tennesseans and Kentuckians. Many of the British got back to fight with Wellington at Waterloo.

Jackson was never to give the Kentuckians much credit for

the part they played in the battle. History, however, has been more generous, and oddly enough the General, to his death, preferred "Hunters of Kentucky" to all other songs. For that matter the citizens of New Orleans, in considerable part, were not disposed to give General Jackson credit. But history has fully confirmed the identity between the General and the victory.

The imagination is entitled to a bit of play here. Suppose that means of quick communication had existed then, and that the news of the treaty of Ghent had been forwarded to the War Department in time to reach the army at New Orleans. What shifts in history would that have made? What American traditions would never have existed? What pages in our national history would have been vitally different, if not omitted altogether? Who would have been the seventh President of the United States?

But the battle was won, the war was won, the Louisiana Purchase made safe for all time. The strength of the nation, up to then anchored in the Atlantic seaboard, shifted westward and southward.

Mrs. Jackson, by arrangement, went down to New Orleans to be with her husband there and to return with him to Nashville. And it was well that she had made the journey. Jackson was to need her steadying influence during those exciting and trying days. The martial laws he imposed on the city were galling to many of the citizens, and a great many troublesome situations developed. His strength and determination needed the reassurance that his wife's presence could and always did give. Before they left the city early in April, New Orleans had in most part been won over.

Their departure for Nashville had about it a touch of grandeur, of Creole magnificence. Michel Bringier, a planter from up the river, had served under the General at the battle. His new house on the east side of the river from Donaldsonville was finished and ready to be christened. Bringier asked the

General and Mrs. Jackson to accompany him up the river and stop over for that purpose. The invitation was a major compliment. Then too it was on the way back to Nashville. It would not delay the trip more than a day. So the Jacksons accepted the invitation. Upon their arrival at White Hall, the old residence, the Bringiers ordered all clocks stopped. Time did not matter when Rachel and Andrew Jackson were guests. The next day, the General, with a broad flourish, christened the place "The Hermitage." The Bringiers were delighted, and the home bears the name to this day. After that the Jacksons went on up the river to Natchez, a place of golden memories for them. They remained there for a day, and then struck overland by the Natchez Trace for home.

Word of the victory had reached Nashville as quickly as a pioneer message could be brought. Early one night—the exact date is not known—a horseman clattered into the town with the news. He ate his supper at the Tavern while his horse was fed. Between bites he told the pop-eyed locals the story he was bearing. Then the messenger was back on his horse, carrying his news on deeper into the inland, on to Washington. We do not know the name of the rider, but Miss Carrie Freret, formerly archivist at the Cabildo, was confident that it was Wade Hampton. We do know that one of the Wade Hamptons was available, and all of that name had horsemanship in their blood. While the rider remains unsung, his was one of the nation's notable rides.

The Jacksons arrived in Nashville on the fifteenth of May. A hysterical welcome greeted them. Gone for the time were the old hostilities. A conquering hero had come home. Somehow word of the approach ran ahead of the arrival, and a great delegation met them on the Natchez Trace, halfway to Franklin, and rode back as an escort of honor. A great many thousand felicitous words were spoken. For months Old Hickory's enemies were inarticulate. In fact for a year little was said or done to annoy the Jacksons. After a day's visit in Nashville they went on out to their own Hermitage and settled down to life. But the General came back into Nashville often, there to commune with his comrades, of whom a new batch was getting into the city almost every day.

The Nashville country had been well represented in the war. General James Winchester from out at Cragfont was in command of the troops on the ill-fated northern campaign. Colonel William Hall, also of Sumner County, added a full regiment to Jackson's army; Colonel Thomas H. Benton, of Williamson County, still another. Captain John Donelson, brother of Rachel, commanded a company. These men were gradually getting back to their homes, generally stopping for a day in Nashville to celebrate. Coffee's and Carroll's men were arriving in daily groups to add their din to the town's excitement. But the fever slowly settled down, and at their log-cabin Hermitage Rachel and Andrew Jackson took up plantation life again and awaited the future's unfolding.

The nation gradually adjusted itself to the results of the victory at New Orleans. There ensued for the United States a long generation of peace, broken only in occasional troubled spots. General Jackson directed the affairs of his plantation, participated in local issues and freely gave to the country the service it wished of him. He led an expedition against the Florida Indians and quelled some vestigial trouble started by the English. He was a candidate for President in 1824, but was defeated by John Quincy Adams of Massachusetts. Jackson blamed Henry Clay for his defeat, and began making ready for the campaign of 1828.

This time he defeated Adams, but it was a grief-stricken man who on January 19, 1829, left the Hermitage bound for the White House. Rachel had died at Christmastime, 1828. That cast a deep shadow on the rest of Andrew Jackson's life. His wife's death left him a desolate man. Slander had been cruel during the campaign, which his wife outlived but a few weeks. It was always his belief that she died of the stress caused by the cruel and ruthless things that had been said about her, and him. He was to need her desperately during the two terms he served.

THE WAR WITH MEXICO

There was a great deal of talk about Texas during the terms of his Presidency. Even before that the keener-visioned foresaw trouble with Mexico over the territory known as Texas. That trouble struck with tragic and dramatic force at the Alamo, in the last year of the General's term.

The development, the beginning and the conduct of the war with Mexico were of compelling interest to Nashville. Of all the nation's cities Nashville seems to have had closest contact with that war. The name Sam Houston comes up first when it is mentioned, though his main service was before it formally began. He was a magnificent physical specimen, most commanding in appearance. He was more than six feet tall, large, powerful, daring. His body could and did turn aside the slings and arrows of pestilence and disease, though wounds received in the war with the Alabama Indians were to trouble him more or less during his life, but never to retire him from the work he was doing. He affected a finery and color in his clothes that left his backwoods observers puzzled but a bit charmed. He was without fear and he generally dominated any situation in which he was cast. He was alien to all forms of inertia, and his eyes were always turned toward adventure.

He was born in the Timber Ridge community of Rockbridge County, Virginia, a section ranking high in the heroic records of the time. He reached Nashville by way of east Tennessee in time to fight against the Creeks in Alabama. His bravery and good judgment attracted the attention of General Andrew Jackson, and this was the beginning of a friendship that lasted through life. He had gained considerable popularity in Nashville and in 1823 was elected to congress. He served four years and then was elected governor. In 1829 he was re-elected, but some difficulty developed, and he resigned the governorship and removed to the western country. For several years he lived with the Cherokee Indians, but gradually his searching eyes came to rest on Texas.

Texas was the object of the thoughts of a great many Tennesseans of the time. In 1823 Mexico indicated the need for settlers in the great Texas plains. That year Stephen Austin was given the right to establish a colony of 300 people near Bexar. As if that was the signal, the Americans began moving in. Within ten years 20,000 moved across the boundaries into Texas, many of them from Tennessee.

Then the welcome cooled, and Mexico passed regulations barring further colonists. To that the Americans paid little attention. Naturally trouble, minor at first but becoming serious, began to develop. The new Texans and the Mexicans did not make agreeable neighbors. They had too little in common, their ways of life were too far apart.

Finally General Santa Anna, President of Mexico, marched northward to punish the intruders. He found the army of Texas gathered in the Alamo, an ancient mission building on the outskirts of San Antonio. He sent a peremptory demand for surrender. Colonel William B. Travis replied with a cannon ball, fired at the Mexican column. Santa Anna arranged the 2,500 soldiers under him very carefully for the assault. Early on the morning of March 8, 1836, he stormed the Alamo. There were 188 men there, some of them sick, all exhausted and hungry. After repeated waves of attack the Mexicans broke through the walls, and then systematically moved room by room through the structure, killing all of the Americans. In the end not one was left to record the magnificence of the martyrdom suffered there.

It was stupid for General Santa Anna to think that with one bloody blow like that he could settle the issue once and for all. It was a monumental underestimating of his foe. The whole matter might have been resolved amicably and economically before that massacre. After that it was too late, though a decade was to pass before the conflict rose to its crisis. Next, the Mexicans ambushed and destroyed a small force under Colonel Fannin. The colonel was taken alive and executed.

Now the time was ripe for the appearance of Sam Houston. The Texans rallied under his leadership and, on April 21, 1836, fought the battle of San Jacinto. Houston's army was small but he completely outmaneuvered and defeated a large army under Santa Anna. Texas immediately declared itself a free and independent republic, a declaration which Mexico promptly repudiated.

The Texas Declaration of Independence was written by another former resident of Nashville, George Campbell Childress. He had practiced law in the Nashville courts, and after that had edited a Nashville newspaper. Childress had another vital connection with Nashville. His wife was Amanda Jennings, daughter of Dr. Obadiah Jennings, minister of Nashville's First Presbyterian Church.

General Sam Houston was promptly elected President of the new republic of Texas. His election did not fail to increase the unhappiness of the Mexicans. For them matters had moved beyond the point of arbitration. The land of Texas was too choice for that. The Texans, on the other hand, were most eager for admission to the United States. But in many of the states there was serious opposition to this. The question of admission became the central issue of the presidential election of 1844.

James Knox Polk, of Nashville, running with the unequivocal blessing of Old Hickory, the final political blessing he was to give, was the Democratic candidate. Henry Clay of Kentucky was the Whig candidate. It was unlikely that he would have been elected in any case, but he proceeded to make that certain by a letter which he wrote to a friend:

I consider the annexation of Texas at this time, without the consent of Mexico, as a measure involving us certainly in war with Mexico, and probably with other foreign powers. It would be dangerous to the integrity of the Union, and not called for by any general expression of public opinion.

Clay was correct in his forecast of war, but he misjudged public opinion. Again he went down in defeat. Polk's election was regarded as a mandate for immediate annexation. So, in 1845, Texas was formally taken into the Union as the twenty-eighth state. But a war had to be fought to ratify that action. The war began with the battle of Palo Alto, fought on May 6, 1846. The news traveled fast and reached Nashville quickly.

The year 1845 was an eventful one in Nashville. In the middle of the year Andrew Jackson died. Two weeks after the death of Old Hickory occurred the impressive ceremonial of placing the cornerstone of the new Capitol, a rite performed with a martial gesture. The town buzzed with rumors of war, the rumors settling down to verity as the year matured.

The general opinion of Nashville was all but unanimous in favor of the annexation of Texas. With the number of Tennesseans actually involved it could not have been otherwise. A mass meeting was held at the courthouse as early as May 18, 1844, and there the demand for immediate annexation was issued. But soberer minds delayed this action awhile. At another mass meeting, held on July 6, Dr. John Shelby offered a resolution which affirmed sympathy for the people of Texas, and the wish for Texas to be admitted, but insisted that the matter should not be discussed in terms involving the integrity of the nation. That cooled the war eaters slightly, but not much. After Polk's election even the Nashville *Whig* fell into line, saying editorially, "Let Mexico be summarily and soundly thrashed." That made it just about unanimous.

When the news of the declaration of war, following hard on

the news of the battle, reached Nashville, the word *war* began to fall from every tongue. Governor Aaron Brown called on the state to furnish 2,800 volunteers, and promptly got 30,000. Since then Tennessee has been known as the Volunteer State. Two Nashville companies were accepted for service immediately, the Nashville Blues, under the command of Captain Benjamin Franklin Cheatham (later a general in the Civil War), and the Harrison Guards (reminiscent of the campaign of 1840) commanded by Captain Robert Coleman Foster. A week later the Texas Volunteers were parading on the square, eager to go. Then the Hickory Cavalry sprang to arms. For weeks after that the streets were bedlam with the sounds of bugle, the calling out of orders and the never-ceasing impact of heavily shod feet marching on cobblestone pavements.

On June 5, 1846, the First Tennessee Regiment, commanded by Colonel W. B. Campbell, started for Mexico. On his staff were Major Sam Anderson, Major Richard Alexander and Major Robert Farquahrson. Lieutenant Adolphus Heiman was adjutant. Heiman was then Nashville's most distinguished architect, and several buildings planned by him still remain. He became prominent in one of the Confederate armies, too, and met his death in one of the Mississippi campaigns.

The First Tennessee left Nashville with a grand flourish. A stirring parade was held on the city's main streets, coming to its climax on the grounds of the Nashville Female Academy, at Church and McLemore Streets. The young ladies, 500 of them, stood and watched with bright eyes as the soldiers marched by, marching perhaps with more spirit than precision.

When Colonel Campbell was passing, Miss Irene Taylor, niece of Zachary Taylor, came proudly out from a cluster of girls and held up her hand. Colonel Campbell drew his horse to a stop, and she handed him a banner which the Academy's senior class, working in rotation, had finished the night before. In bright letters, boldly standing out on the banner's rippling folds, was an inscription, composed from the spartan souls of the young ladies, *Weeping in solitude for the fallen brave is better than the presence of men too timid to strike for their country*. Colonel Campbell gravely accepted the banner. The men of the regiment justified the trust, and when the war was over they brought the banner back and gave it, torn, worn and bullet-riddled, to the young ladies who had entrusted it to their keeping. At the Academy that banner was an honored exhibit till something happened to it during the vandalism incident to the Civil War.

The war with Mexico brought much hardship. Disease was prevalent, there was often a scarcity of food and the systems of transportation were almost tragic in their inadequacy. Colonel Robert Coleman Foster has left a graphic account of the difficulties he and his comrades encountered.

The soldiers were carried by steamboat from Nashville to New Orleans. The boats generally were unbearably crowded, and almost half the volunteers were sick during the passage, some so seriously that their participation in the war ceased at New Orleans.

They made the trip down the rivers in six days, only to find at New Orleans that no provision had been made for boats to carry them across the Mexican Gulf. On June 17 Colonel Foster wrote his father, Senator Ephraim Foster, in Nashville, "The weather is so extremely hot and our quarters so close that I fear that if we are not soon removed general sickness will prevail." But the ship *Charlotte*, the brig *Orleans* and the barque *Chaffin* were made ready and the troops left on the eighteenth.

In many of its parts the war with Mexico wasn't an affair of much glory. There was no lack of courage, and there was some fine leadership, but health conditions were tragic. Jealousy raised its ugly head too early and too often. There was a sharp contest between the Tennessee and Mississippi troops as to which participated with more glory in the siege of Monterey. Colonel Campbell of the First Tennessee and Colonel Jefferson Davis of a Mississippi regiment each claimed the advantage for his own troops. The accumulated testimony seemed to indicate that the Mississippians were at first ordered to lead the charge, but at the last moment, for some reason, the Tennesseans were placed in front with the Mississippians following closely.

Then the Tennesseans were given considerable concern by accusations made against their own General Gideon Pillow. Pillow, for a brief time, had been a law partner of President Polk at Columbia, Tennessee. That was almost twenty years before, but the warm friendship had continued. The latter part of 1842 and all of 1843 Pillow had devoted to promoting Polk for the Democratic nomination. Polk was nominated and elected, and at the beginning of hostilities named Pillow as brigadier general of state troops. Pillow was an educated and courageous man, but lacked the qualities necessary to direct discreetly and with continuity a large body of troops. He objected to General Scott's handling of the army in words that regrettably found their way into print. The matter was finally brought to the attention of the President, who found Pillow undeserving of censure.

There was a sharp conflict between Pillow and Colonel Robert Coleman Foster. One of Foster's soldiers shot a pigeon contrary to orders against firing guns. Pillow had the man bound hand and foot and tied to a wagon. Foster, hearing of it, rode to the spot and cut the man loose. Pillow then placed Foster under arrest. That was not exactly the beginning of a feud, but it gave one the excuse to develop. Pillow's attack on Vera Cruz was made with valor and some skill, but his zeal in reporting it brought on some dissension.

Lieutenant Simon Bolivar Buckner was his opponent in a very long-drawn-out affair. Buckner was born in Kentucky, at Munfordville on Green River. He was appointed to West Point in 1840. He was graduated with high standing and was immediately chosen an instructor in history, geography and ethics. He served a year and then withdrew to take part in the struggle with Mexico. His defense of General Scott against

General Pillow's attack began a feud which was to last for a long time. When the war was over Buckner lived in the outskirts of Nashville for more than a year.

General Pillow was a candidate for the United States Senate, and in defense of his war record repeated his old accusations against General Scott. Buckner, who had defended Scott a decade before, wrote three articles that appeared in the Nashville *Republican Banner*, claiming that he did it from a sense of duty to the army, the truth and his old chieftain. The articles were signed "Citizen," but it was generally known that Buckner wrote them. They were masterpieces of irony, ridicule and sarcasm. Randall McGavock wrote in his diary, "It is thought by some that Pillow will fight him, but I doubt if he will notice him except through newspaper editorials." Pillow was defeated by Andrew Johnson in the election. But the final act of this drama found its way back into battle. It was played at Fort Donelson, seventy miles below Nashville, on February 15 and 16, 1862.

The Tennessee troops reached Mexico City on January 17, 1848. Peace was formally declared on February 2, and about the first of March a small vanguard of returning soldiers reached Nashville on the steamboats *Val Leer* and *Countess*. Their reception befitted their victorious homecoming. One day, a fortnight later, the veterans and citizens were hurriedly assembled at the front of the courthouse. There an address of welcome was delivered by Dr. Collins D. Elliott, president of the Nashville Female Academy. The newspapers reported it one of the city's pinnacle points in eloquence. Later the banner presented the departing troops by President Elliott's young ladies was returned. The troops kept on coming back until all of the soldiers from Nashville had reached home except eighty whose lives were a part of the payment for victory.

So ended the war with Mexico. In that war there was no leader who could be compared favorably with General George Washington, or who could match the fierce dominance of General Andrew Jackson. It was waged against a foe with whom our acquaintance and understanding were very slight. The distances were great, and that phase of warfare which today we call logistics brought on problems almost insuperable. But, for all of that, we won the war, and the conditions were such that President Elliott could be pardoned for referring to it in a moment of great enthusiasm as "our own war."

The terms of the treaty yielded to the United States the territory of California, New Mexico, Arizona and all of the land north and west of the Rio Grande. Tennesseans had gallantly justified their reputation on the battlefields. And when there was no battle to fight they had jousted with one another. If fighting was involved, Tennesseans could be counted on to "volunteer." Now they were back home for an interval of peace.

But even then Mars was working hard on a massive production to be acted in great part in tragic magnificence on the stage of Nashville.

THE SPLENDID BUT SAD SIXTIES

Geography called many of the decade's tunes. The location of Nashville made it of major importance in the war which began in the spring of 1861. It was one of the main gateways to the South, and there was little chance that an army marching into the Middle South could evade Nashville. It guarded a river of great military importance, and in a less immediate way it guarded another river of even greater importance. It was the center of an area of rich and varied resources. James Robertson had not overstated the place's fine qualities. It would be most tempting to the North for many reasons: its communications with other great centers, the supplies it could yield an invading army and, certainly not least, the known fact that some of the city's leaders could not bring themselves to accept the cause of the South. Nashville was a proud city and those differences were later to add to its agony.

Nashville had all the fitnesses for peace. It had wealth, and it was wise in the ways of spending it. It was keenly conscious of the rest of the world. It loved to travel. It was committed to the arts and to the churches. The word education seemed to have a special meaning in Nashville. Yet when the war began it reached Nashville almost soonest of all, and it remained there almost longest.

The decade following 1850 was in many ways the most brilliant of Nashville's first century. The years of the depression of the late thirties had lost their leanness, and in the due maturing of the economic cycle the fifties were fat with plenty. There were in Nashville far-visioned men who sensed the terrible sequel to their current grandeur, but their unformed prophecies in no wise dimmed the brightness of the time. It was a fine era, filled with fine living. It was almost as if Destiny, perceiving the end of a civilization, had decreed that it should go out in a blaze of glory. Somewhere on some unearthly hill the Three Sisters sang their mystic song, wore their tapestry, smiled inscrutably and waited. The sun rode the heavens with a fierce sort of brilliance. Soon it would sink and the shadows of Nashville's Götterdämmerung throw themselves across the land. The twilight of the Nashville gods. But not yet awhile. One last fling before the glory of the Old South lost itself save in story and song and in the bright traditions bequeathed to posterity.

The directory of Nashville carried some potent names in those days. Some of them survived the trial by fire and heartbreak; a few didn't. Dr. Felix Robertson's first-born was still practicing medicine from an office on Cherry Street near Broad. He was getting old but he still cured his patients and hunted foxes between cures. He was generally regarded as Nashville's number one citizen.

Francis Brinley Fogg was practicing law from an office on Cherry Street near Deaderick. His son, Henry Middleton Rutledge Fogg, the only remaining child of the three born to him and Mary Middleton Rutledge Fogg, was his law partner. The wisdom and kindliness of the father were proverbial in the city, and yet he rarely smiled in those fateful days. Perhaps some hint of impinging tragedy weighed heavily on him. If so, it was prophetic indeed. On January 19, 1862, Henry Fogg was to fall at Fishing Creek, within a few minutes of the death of General Felix Zollicoffer, whose aide he was. The body of the son was brought back from the Kentucky battlefield to the Fogg home, on Church Street, where the Watkins Institute is now. There, clad in his uniform of gray, this young man, two of whose great-grandfathers had signed the Declaration of Independence, lay in state. The father, Connecticut-born and of Northern sympathies, walked the floor. His face was unmoved, but tragedy was in his heart. His last child had been slain by his own people. The gods of Nashville were at twilight then.

The Foggs are worth further word. Mrs. Fogg, descended from Edward Rutledge and Arthur Middleton, names carried on that undying document, was one of the most remarkable women of all Nashville. She was a deeply religious woman, a literary woman and most oddly a scientific woman. She was deeply devoted to the South, yet deeply in love with her husband, who was Northern in belief and statement.

McGavock has been a name of distinction in Nashville since the beginning of the place. Various families of McGavocks came from Rockbridge County, Virginia; others from Max Meadows (an abbreviation of McGavock's Meadows) in Wythe County. The earliest map of Nashville was drawn by David McGavock when the settlement was six years old. The McGavocks were a canny group and prospered in all their enterprises. They expressed their good taste in the fine houses they built. One of them, Randall, built his house at Franklin and named it Carnton for the old McGavock home in County Antrim, Ireland. But the twilight of the Nashville gods fell upon the land, and five Confederate generals lay dead on the Carnton porch.

Lysander McGavock built Midway, halfway between Nashville and Franklin. It was at its best in the fifties. In the sixties its floors were soaked with the blood of Southern soldiers, and among the wounded moved Mrs. McGavock, bringing food and water and good cheer. Another McGavock built Two Rivers, a short distance north of the town of Donelson. The house was planned by William Strickland, at that time directing the building of the state's Capitol. Jacob McGavock built on Cherry Street, only two hundred feet from the site later used for the Maxwell House. Jacob McGavock had joined two great names by marrying the daughter of Felix Grundy.

The Maneys lived on McLemore Street, on a part of the site now used for Christ Church. Their home was a place of cultural distinction in Nashville. Their son, Henry Maney, was one of Nashville's most promising literary figures. He died at the age of thirty-two, leaving to his credit *Memories over the Water*, a gentle and vivid account of his European travels, several volumes of poetry, and a record of two years as editor of the Nashville *Gazette*.

In 1850 Belmont was completed and occupied by Joseph and Adelicia Acklen. There for a decade life was carried on in the grand manner. Whenever a visitor of importance came to Nashville, the Acklens entertained with all the splendor of a royal levee. In the autumn of 1858 William Walker, whose gray eyes were already entangled with Destiny, stopped for a visit with his friends on his way from Washington back to Nicaragua. The dinner given him by the Acklens was described by Randall McGavock in his journal as "the finest ever served in the city." Such praise from Randall, who well knew fine dinners, is convincing.

Many other names stood out at this time: the Ewings, the

Cockrells, the Porters, the Fosters, the Overtons, the Leas. The sun of the Old South was bright then whose light a little later dimmed to dead gray shadows. William Walker lay dead in an unmarked grave at Truxillo, and soldiers in blue stood sentry on the top of the Belmont water tower. And how many of those who dined that night with William Walker were dead too: Henry Fogg, Baillie Peyton, Randall McGavock, Henry Maney, Francis McNairy. How thick then were the shadows.

Philip Lindsley reached the city Christmas 1824, and there has been no interruption in the line of his posterity since that time. He came from the presidency of the College of New Jersey to assume the presidency of the University of Nashville. In 1850 he resigned. He had envisioned a university of great size, but it turned out to be one merely of great quality. His son, John Berrien Lindsley, took up matters where his father laid them down. The father was a man of unusual scholarship, the son one of unusual versatility. In 1854 he married Sarah McGavock, daughter of Jacob. Their grandchildren and great-grandchildren are still vital factors in the life of the city.

There were great names in Nashville then: Cheatham, Litton, Berry, Douglas, Bass, Adams, Nichols, Howell—names able to leave a glory that Nashville's Götterdämmerung could not dim out.

The year 1860 was a fine crop year in the Cumberland country and Nashville prospered. The word progress was on all lips, and the thought of it in all minds. It was the beginning of the end of the stagecoach days. Railroads converged on Nashville from four directions. A suspension bridge, opened in 1860, gave easy access to the city from the north. The world's news ticked into the city over lately strung telegraph wires. Night was metamorphosed into day by the Nashville Gaslight Company, which bought coal from a mine owned by the Honorable John Bell, and by a form of pure magic turned it into gas. The steam fire department, operated by a paid staff, was put into action in 1860.

The Medical Department of the University of Nashville was one of the country's best. The Western Military Institute, located in Kentucky during its earlier periods, flourished on the stimulated pageantry of war and the prophetic fumes of battle. Five daily papers, eight religious publications, a medical journal and a magazine devoted to temperance were being published in the city when the decade opened. In the field of the arts Washington Cooper, George Dury, C. C. Giers and Adolphus Heiman had considerable prestige.

The population of Nashville in 1850 was 16,988. There were 175 named streets, totaling in length about sixty miles. There was a high demand for luxury in the city. As an instance, about 3,500 tons of ice were used annually. The ice came mainly from Lake Kingston, in Illinois, where it was harvested in large blocks, brought to Nashville by steamboat and stored in sawdust for summer use. There was a satisfactory amount of industry in the city then, though most of its wealth came from the soil. The manufacture of drugs was flourishing, as was that of plows. It was an important center in the making of bridles, saddles and other parts of harness. There was excellent business at the lumberyards.

I mention one business, later to flourish, because of its bearing on this story. It was the United States Army and Navy Leg, manufactured by James Morton. This description is taken from an advertisement: "Made of willow wood, with india rubber springs, and an ankle joint formed by a ball of polished glass, and all enameled on the outer surface with a flesh colored preparation." Mr. Morton's capacity was 200 legs a year, all of course made to order. His industry hints grimly of the darkness that had fallen on the city.

All of the ills which can spring from human ingenuity seemed to break on Nashville early in 1862. And certainly not the least was the division within the city. It was of course committed to the South, but some of its strong men were Northern in sentiment and sympathy—as instances, Francis Fogg, Russell Houston, William T. Berry, Return Jonathan Meigs. In this division there was heartbreak. Then, in the early days of the conflict, Nashville passed into alien hands. From late February 1862 till the end of the war Nashville suffered the most grievously of all the Southern cities.

At the beginning there was little doubt that the South would win. It became a day of resolutions, high-sounding, patriotic resolutions. The drone of someone reading resolutions sounded everywhere, affirming, denying, endorsing, opposing. In January 1861, three months before the war began, a meeting held at the courthouse adopted and published the resolution, "That the election of Abraham Lincoln to the presidency, though offensive to the people of Tennessee, is not sufficient cause for the dissolution of the nation."

Three months passed and the sinister thunder sounded at Fort Sumter. Events trod upon one another's heels after that. President Lincoln called on Tennessee to furnish two regiments of soldiers. The government of Tennessee could not bring its citizens to bear arms against flesh and blood so dear. There ensued resolutions refusing compliance with the President's call, but also denying secession as the state's rightful program. On April 20 another resolution declared that "all controversy should be merged in the imperative necessity of resisting an armed invasion of southern soil."

It had grown too late to talk of peace or neutrality. The spring winds that drifted into Nashville bore the contagion of conflict. On the day that resolution was signed, the enlistment of troops began in Nashville. The Cheatham Rifles, the Rock City Guards, the Home Guards, the Shelby Dragoons, the Hermitage Light Infantry, the Tennessee Rangers, the Hickory Guards, the Tennessee Patriots were organized in quick succession. Leslie Ellis, John H. Anderson, John Archibald, Saint Clair Morgan, Randall McGavock, Boyd Cheatham and

George Maney assembled their companies, most of which were later merged in the forces gathering at Fort Donelson. Great clouds of limestone dust lifted from the streets of Nashville as its young men marched and wheeled, training for a field of glory that too often turned out to be something very different. On April 25 Tennessee declared itself independent of the United States. On June 8 that action was endorsed by popular vote in Nashville: for—3,029, against—250. The country had become the divided states of America.

The women, on whom the impact of war has always fallen hardest, went promptly into action. The Soldiers Relief Society of Tennessee was organized, Mrs. Felicia Grundy Porter, President. Its announced mission was to minister to the needs of distressed soldiers, in the camps or on the battlefields. In September the Ladies Hospital and Clothing Association was formed, Mrs. Francis B. Fogg, President. The service which these ladies gave has never been adequately told.

On September 14 the second stage of the war set in. General Albert Sidney Johnston, in command of the Western Department, arrived in Nashville and set up headquarters in Edgefield, that part of the city lying north of the river. He addressed a mass meeting at the capitol, and greatly pleased his hearers by the salutation, "Fellow Soldiers, I call you that because you will be soldiers before long." On November 25 he called for a provisional army of 30,000 men. On December 2 Governor Isham Harris levied the war's first Tennessee draft.

The first news that reached Nashville was of victory. Generals Polk, Cheatham and Pillow had defeated Federal troops commanded by a general named Grant at Belmont on the Mississippi. There was no note of triumph in the second message. One of General Johnston's first measures had been to send an army, headed by General Felix Zollicoffer, into eastern Kentucky to prevent invasion from that quarter. Zollicoffer was a brilliant newspaper editor, prominent in Nashville's civic and social affairs. His fitness for military leadership is not quite so clear. On January 19, 1862, at Fishing Creek in Wayne County, Kentucky, he was defeated by the Federals under General George Thomas.

The disaster didn't stop at mere defeat. General Zollicoffer was killed, and in the same half hour fell Henry Fogg and Baillie Peyton of the general's staff. The remains of Fogg and Peyton arrived at Nashville by river January 25; General Zollicoffer's February 1. Nashville caught a vivid glimpse then of the troubles ahead. Baillie Peyton was one of the section's choicest sons. His grandfather had come through the woods with James Robertson in 1779 on their founding journey. His grandmother had come by the rivers with John Donelson. Henry Fogg was a great-grandson of two signers of the Declaration of Independence. There is tragic irony in the fact that the fathers of both the young men were loyal to the Union throughout the war.

That was but the beginning. On February 12 the Confederate authorities requested for use as hospitals the buildings of the University of Nashville. Fort Henry on the Tennessee River had been captured, and casualties would be coming in. The Federal land troops marched from Fort Henry across the narrow neck of land separating the rivers and attacked Fort Donelson on the Cumberland from the rear. At the same time the Federal gunboats came up the Cumberland and attacked from the front. The fort was not only caught in this grip but was the victim of internal division.

Technically General Floyd was in command, but he was under charge by the North of having removed materials of war to Southern territory while serving as Secretary of War under President Buchanan. His dominating idea seems to have been to escape capture by the enemy. The other generals in command were Simon Bolivar Buckner and Gideon Pillow. Their mutual differences in and after the war with Mexico had a large part to play in the disaster on the Cumberland.

There was an alarming amount of sickness among General

Albert Sidney Johnston's troops stationed at Bowling Green, sixty-five miles north of Nashville, and large numbers were sent from there to the university hospital. By the night of the fourteenth almost 700 soldiers, sick or wounded, had been received from Bowling Green, Fort Henry and Fort Donelson and cared for as well as limited space and equipment permitted. Doctors Hoyte, Lindsley, Winston, Peake, Wheeler, Landes, Thomas and Garthan cooked for and treated the men twenty-four hours a day.

On the fifteenth word came that the Confederates had won a great victory at Fort Donelson. There was great rejoicing throughout the city. In the evening a large convocation assembled at the Capitol and listened to impassioned addresses delivered as a proper celebration of the triumph. They but whistled, passing the graveyard. The echoes of the final peroration had no more quieted when the streets began resounding to the march of armed men. It was General Albert Sidney Johnston's army retreating south from Bowling Green, marching sullenly, angrily through a dismal rainfall. All that night they marched, and all the next day, interminable columns of wet and humiliated soldiers. On the night of the fifteenth their campfires burned for miles along Mill Creek.

At noon on Sunday the sixteenth came the terrifying news of the surrender of Fort Donelson. Governor Harris himself on horseback galloped through the principal streets calling out the news of the surrender. From that time through the rest of Sunday and all of Monday the wildest excitement prevailed. The turnpikes and highways from midafternoon Sunday were crowded with outbound vehicles, many going not knowing where. Anything with wheels, filled with women and children, fought its way out of Nashville, the capture of the city then being assured. All the southbound railroad trains were crowded. One, leaving at five, Sunday, carried most of the boarding students of the Nashville Female Academy. It was the end of a flourishing institution, likely the largest boarding school for girls in the world. An effort was made to revive it at the close of the war, but discontinued schools were difficult to revive at the end of the war. The governor and the legislature adjourned hurriedly to Memphis, General Johnston having so counseled.

It was still raining on the seventeenth. The rivers were rising and there were prospects of a flood. The retreating Confederates were still passing through, though in smaller groups. Retreat is always a dismal matter for a soldier, but it becomes poignant when his path is sprinkled with tears from the clouds. A crowd of civilians moved on the headquarters of General Johnston, angrily demanding to know whether the generals intended to fight. At first there was no reply, and the mob's anger grew. "We will make these high and mighty ones tell us whether they intend to surrender our wives and children to the enemy." Generals Hardee and Floyd finally persuaded the mob to disperse.

There was much looting, particularly by the civilians. John Berrien Lindsley recorded in his diary, "I saw stout men by the score walking off with bacon and hams, and women tottering under the same."

General Johnston placed General Floyd in charge of the post at Nashville. He faced confusion even worse than at Fort Donelson. "I saw an old woman," wrote General Basil Duke, "apparently in an advanced state of decrepitude staggering under a load of meat that a quartermaster's mule could hardly carry."

At midnight on the nineteenth the Confederate gunboats at the Broadway landing were destroyed. The city lay at the mercy of the oncoming Union troops. Early on the morning of the twentieth the military authorities burned the suspension bridge which for a decade had been the special pride of the citizens. By daylight of the same morning the railroad bridge and the ordinance works were on fire. As many of the quartermaster's stores as could be handled were carried to secret places in various parts of the city. For instance, all clothing was moved to the cellar of Adrian Van Sinderen Lindsley's home.

On the afternoon of the twenty-fourth the advance guard of the Union forces arrived in Nashville. An hour later Mayor R. B. Cheatham and John M. Lea visited John Berrien Lindsley to request his carriage to convey the commissioners, appointed by the city, to the Federal headquarters for a conference with General Buell and his staff. Those who rode in the carriage were the mayor, John M. Lea, Russell Houston and Robert Coleman Foster. The commissioners performed the perfunctory gesture of surrendering the city. They were assured by General Buell that property and all allowable liberty of the citizens would be respected.

That was a melancholy day in Nashville. That evening the shadows gathered over a heartbroken city. It was as if Valhalla was on fire. The next morning the Union fleet steamed into Nashville. The spectacle of its arrival caused William Driver, whose sympathies from the first had been with the North, to speak a phrase that has gone into the permanent lexicons, "Old Glory." Thenceforth, until the bugles sounded *cease firing*, Nashville pretended to be something which it never was and never could be, a Northern city.

The Federal investment was rapid and complete. The soldiers sprinkled the city and suburbs with their encampments. Before nightfall all of the Confederate sick and wounded had been cleared out of the buildings of the University of Nashville, and into it were brought more than 300 Northern soldiers. The Federal troops, after the immemorial practice of conquering armies, paid little respect to private property. It was often cold, and the easiest wood for the campfires came from the trees and fences, even the finest ones, that graced the elegant old estates. The grounds of Belle Meade were despoiled; so were those of the Andrew Ewing home, the Collins F. Elliott home, the Berry home, all of historic quality. As the war wound on, Nashville grew more desolate.

On March 12, 1862, Andrew Johnson, the newly appointed military governor of Tennessee, arrived and assumed office. In a public address he appealed to the people to accept the sovereignty of the United States Government. There was little response from the people. Then the governor went into action. He issued a demand for the officers of the municipality to take the oath of allegiance. Two days later he received from them a formal refusal. He then ordered their arrest for treason and appointed a new staff of city officers, naturally all vocal in their protestations of loyalty to the Union. On April 26 it was decreed that the school superintendent, the members of the board of education and all teachers in the public schools must solemnly swear to protect, support, and defend the United States against all enemies, domestic or foreign. This in considerable degree caused the discontinuance of teaching in the public schools.

Governor Johnson seemed to believe in the efficacy of the oath taken under compulsion. And in some instances it seemed to work. Former Governor Neil Brown was arrested for treason and given the oath, and thereafter he espoused with vigor the cause of the United States. His Union sentiments were not shared by other members of his family. His brother John, captured at Fort Donelson and a prisoner at Fort Warren in Boston harbor, was greatly outraged by the news. Colonel Brown refused to see Mayor John Hugh Smith of Nashville when that official visited Fort Warren.

Almost all of the preachers of the town refused to sign the oath. On July 17 Governor Johnson summoned them to his office and demanded it of them. They refused and seven of them were sent to a cell in the state prison. Berrien Lindsley visited them there and refreshingly found humor in the situation. Some of the preachers, before the war, had been vociferous in their ecclesiastical hostility. Lindsley wrote in his diary, "They now live in a continual love feast."

The city council, having been hand-picked for similar purposes, passed resolutions thanking the officers and soldiers of the United States for "the unexampled courtesy and kindness extended our fellow citizens." The felicitous phrase does not seem quite appropriate. There is the melancholy example of young Francis McNairy, killed in battle, who lay unburied in his home for days, General Rosecrans refusing the pleas of his mother to be granted the use of the First Presbyterian Church for his funeral.

One of Governor Johnson's early acts was to issue orders that whenever the person or property of a loyal citizen was molested, five or more of the most prominent citizens of the community, sympathizers of the South, should be arrested and imprisoned, and from their property ample remuneration made.

The occupation of Nashville was followed by all but complete isolation of the town's Southerners. No newspaper friendly to the Southern cause was printed after the surrender at Donelson. Rarely did the people get undistorted news from their compatriots outside. Within ten days after the occupation the Nashville *Times*, flying the Union flag, was on the streets. Soon the *Evening Bulletin* appeared. Then, in series, the *Daily Union*, the *Press* and the *Dispatch*. All news, of course, was favorable to the North.

The religious press was not spared. The equipment of the Methodist Publishing Company was confiscated within a week after the occupation. It was used thereafter for the printing of army blanks and official bulletins. Within the month articles of confiscation were entered against the *Tennessee Baptist*.

In August the systematic fortification of the city was begun. A large part of the labor was done by slaves, provided under duress by the owners who were required also to supply them with tools and subsistence.

On September 1 all saloons were ordered closed. This commendable endeavor was only tentative, it seems. From 1863 till the close of the war drunkenness was common on the streets.

The blockade of the city by river and railroad placed

famine prices upon the commodities of life. These prices were listed as early as September 14, 1862: sugar, forty cents a pound; butter, one dollar; potatoes, four dollars a bushel; firewood, twelve dollars a cord. By Christmas the wood was selling at thirty dollars. The order was broadcast that citizens should report to headquarters any guests within an hour of arrival.

Work in the city gradually slowed to a standstill. Why plant seeds and reap harvests if the Yankees waited to seize them? Soon a great many were just waiting, hands folded. Matters would not likely grow worse. Refreshing indeed are the pictures one may glean from Berrien Lindsley's diary. The wear and tear and vandalism of war never dulled his spirit of inquiry. He experimented with two new kinds of strawberries: McReady's Seedling and the Triumph of Ghent. He protected the library and laboratories of the University of Nashville, a prodigious achievement. He built a canoe with a glass panel for the study of water life. He referred to Union soldiers as "branded with the mark of Cain," yet he invited dozens of them to dinner. He was always lending surreptitious help to Southern soldiers and sympathizers, yet he took the oath, apparently motivated in considerable degree by his desire to strengthen the claim which he was even then beginning to formulate for damage done the library of the university.

The demand for all citizens to take the oath was a cruel phase of the war. In three days more than 1,800 swore allegiance to the United States. The cruelty of this compulsion may be understood when it is remembered that for the most part those taking the oath affirmed loyalty to a cause against which their sons and brothers and dear friends were daily offering their lives, loyalty to something in which they did not and could not believe. That, on the one side. On the other, the stark reality of war which is seldom gracious or generous. There was always the threat of the confiscation of property, of imprisonment. And in the background the grim determination of the military governor to reduce the people, by one means or another, to a state of hopelessness and helplessness. That is a ghastly way, but it is the way of war.

William Harding, the master of Belle Meade, refused to take the oath, and he went as prisoner of war to Fort Mackinaw, on the Canadian border. Washington Barrow refused, and to Mackinaw he went; similarly Joe Guild. Mark Robertson Cockrill, perhaps the best farmer in Tennessee, was articulate in his expressions of Southern sympathy. His partisanship cost him dear. The Federals took from his place on the Charlotte Pike "twenty thousand bushels of corn, twenty-six horses, sixty head of Durham cattle, 220 sheep, 200 tons of hay, 2,000 bushels of oats, 2,000 pounds of bacon." Furthermore, General Negley assessed a loan against him, permanent of course, of $1,000.

The nature of such pressure was to break down restraint. Men and women of Nashville whose blood and faith were Southern stood in line to swear allegiance to the United States. And the telegraph wires kept clicking into Nashville (as long as such was permissible) the dismal news that only some of her sons would be coming home. They had escaped the oath. Streets and houses can always be repaired, but Adolphus Heiman would plan none of those buildings; Randall McGavock would not again ride his favorite saddle horse, Tenth Legion, along those streets when once again they were made safe; no more would the kindly spirit and patrician face of Henry Fogg lend to the best of Nashville life. It was a heavy hand that was laid upon Nashville.

The months moved on. The streets became more broken, at times bordering on impassability. Great vacant places appeared where there had been trees. Clothes became frayed and shiny, and not often were shoes seen in a state of entire wholeness. There was progressively less food and it was harder to get.

But the occupying troops arranged for their own light moments. General Grant made a hurried visit to the city on December 19, 1863. In honor of his presence Duffield and

Flynn gave a special performance at their theater. The star was Edwin Adams, though the play is not recorded. But more and greater drama was to follow. On November 1, Mr. Adams played Hamlet. On February 1, 1864, John Wilkes Booth appeared in *Richard III*, and in March Miss Bella Golden drew more than 2,000 in two performances: *Pocahontas* and *A Husband at Sight*.

The wear and tear of war continued cumulatively. The gutters of most streets were stopped, forming great puddles in wet seasons. Matters became so bad that pedestrians could not cross Broadway between Vine and Summer streets. The *Daily News* mentioned editorially that a dead mule, lying unmolested on Broadway near Cherry, "does not improve the locality." More than half of Nashville's trees were destroyed, leaving the place stark and bald by the end of the war. Something over 200 houses were destroyed to make way for fortifications. Buzzards drifted ominously low over the city. "Nashville can provide the Pied Piper with an army of rats that that worthy never dreamed of," sighed the *Republican Banner*.

Women of ill character had plagued the town since the beginning of the war. In the summer of 1863, 150 of them were loaded on a steamboat which disappeared down the river, destination unknown. Smallpox raged in Nashville, and at one time more than 1,100 had the disease. Disease was almost everywhere, and whisky about the only available drug. This from the *Daily Press*, May 3, 1864: "More ardent spirits are consumed in Nashville than in Boston. The city is filled with thugs, robbers, highwaymen, and assassins. Murder stalks throughout the city almost every night."

Frequently the soldiers broke loose from all restraints. In November 1863 a circus came to town, and some cavalrymen made a wanton attack on it. In the resulting fracas two soldiers and one circus performer were killed. President Lincoln ordered August 4, 1864, set aside for fasting and prayer. That day more than sixty were brought before the recorder's court on the charge of drunkenness.

The war moved on, settling down to the practice of trading five Union men for three Confederates. The Union had the weight of manpower and in the end that policy won. By the fall of 1864 even the hopeful had about abandoned hope. The South had been drained of soldiers and food and strength. But not of drama. There was to be another act, a gallant and grandiose act, flaming across a Wagnerian sky; one last fling before the South settled down into its desolation and heartbreak.

Driblets of news began to trickle in during the early autumn. The Army of Tennessee, plagued by confusion and shifts in leadership, had run into bad luck at Atlanta. But then, so the news ran, the army was moving westward. Where could it be going? Where indeed but to Nashville? General John B. Hood, Kentucky-born, reared in California and Texas, was at the head of the army. He had in part the qualifications of a great leader, but not altogether. He needed steadying and restraint. When he was in the East under General Lee he was steadied and restrained, and at times rose to greatness. But he didn't have Lee on the march back to Tennessee, and only a giant could have survived the physical disasters that had afflicted him, an arm destroyed at Gettysburg and a leg at Chickamauga. But, strapped to his saddle, he rode at the head of the army westward through Alabama. At Nashville there was a long spell of waiting and wondering, and then word seeped in that the army was crossing the Tennessee at Florence, Alabama. That could mean but one thing, Nashville. And they were hopeful again. Have patience and in a little while Bedford Forrest would come leading his men along the Hillsboro Pike, riding into Nashville. Then, again, they could breathe the air of freedom.

But the hopeful ones did not take Destiny into their envisioning. The drama began to take shape at Spring Hill, thirty miles south of Nashville. The thing that happened there has not been satisfactorily explained to this day. It was at Spring Hill that the Confederates, without rhyme or reason or military common sense, let the Yankees, hurrying up from Pulaski, get by them. Angry and sullen and haunted by a premonition of impending danger, the Army of Tennessee followed their enemies along the Columbia Pike toward Franklin. General Hood rode with his men, his gaunt and seamed face burned to a brick-red with outrage and humiliation. His staff—Cleburne, Gist, Strahl, Adams, Brown, Cheatham and Carter—knew from the look on the commander's face that the army would not be tempered with discretion that day.

And it wasn't. The pike wound over the crest of Winstead's Hill, two miles south of Franklin. From the crest of the hill they saw lying quietly before them, in the great sweeping bend of the Harpeth River, the lovely little town of Franklin and plainly in view the fortifications of the waiting Yankees. General Cleburne advised Hood not to make the attack. So did all the others. They could go up the little Harpeth a piece and cross it, and thus bypass Franklin and the bluecoats waiting there.

General Hood did not reply at first but sat there on his horse, playing his field glasses along those mounds of fresh red earth. He put the glasses back into their case. Then he said hoarsely, "Form your men for battle." There was no further appeal the dissenting generals could make. At the northern base of Winstead's Hill, they formed the soldiers for the charge.

In a very real way the battle of Franklin was the most terrible of the war. It was fought in the shortest time of all the major battles. It lasted only ten or fifteen minutes more than an hour, though there was desultory firing for a while longer. No other battle of the war was so compressed in space, the main conflict occupying very little more than a hundred acres. Some who witnessed it claimed that the most moving spectacle of the entire four years was the Army of Tennessee starting out at the foot of Winstead's Hill and moving across those pasture fields in perfect order, their tattered battle flags flying bravely and bright with the last rays of a dying November sun. As long as daylight lasted, almost all of the entire charge was visible to friend and foe alike. Only at the lowest part of the sag were the Confederates out of sight of the Federals massed along the center.

The only comparable action of the war was Pickett's charge at Gettysburg. And yet Hood's loss was more than four times that of Pickett. In one hour at Franklin five Confederate generals were killed: Cleburne, Adams, Gist, Strahl and Brown. General Carter was mortally wounded and died four days later. Six more generals were wounded or captured.

The battle settled nothing directly. Indirectly it settled much. The Federal army under Schofield had had its fill of fighting and left for Nashville that night. Within three days Hood had thrown his gaunt and grim army into a great but thin half circle about Nashville's eastern and southern borders. The tie game was about ready to be played off.

Drama rose to its pinnacle at the battle of Franklin. Young Tod Carter lived on the Columbia Pike, at the city's limits. He had joined the army when the war was less than a month old and gone off to the war. He had never had an opportunity to come home, and for two years he had had no word from his family. His hungry eyes searched for the house and found it as he came over the hill. His home was the center of the fiercest fighting, his father and sister taking refuge in the cellar. At last, as Tod Carter reached his own yard, a bullet found him. His sister came out and carried him in. War can make strange homecomings. Less than a half mile away on the great porch at the McGavocks' the five generals lay dead.

For more than two years the Yankees had been fortifying Nashville. Three men were there to resist every man that Hood could throw against them. Hood coiled his forces about the southern margins of the town, stretching far around to the east. General George Thomas was in command of all Federal troops in Nashville. He definitely had the advantage, but he was in no hurry to use it. The authorities in Washington grew almost hysterical with impatience. General Grant sent a telegram ordering an immediate attack. But General Thomas' nickname, the Rock, had been honestly gained. He would begin his move when matters were most favorable, and not before. He rightly assumed that he was in the best position to judge. He waited out a blizzard that struck the city on the eleventh. He spent two more days placing his soldiers precisely where he wanted them.

On the morning of the fifteenth his men swarmed against that long, thin, gray line. There was never any hint of victory for the Confederates. All that day the battle went on. The first move of the Yankees was to drive General Hood's advance guard off Montgomery's Hill, almost three miles south of the city. Then they occupied the remainder of the day biting off little fragments of victory that accumulated into significance. All that night—and it was bitter cold—Hood worked feverishly and by desperate effort shortened his line by at least two miles. All the next day till late in the afternoon the hills and fields south of Nashville flamed with the fury of major battle.

At four o'clock, on Shy's Hill just west of the Granny White Pike, the gray line snapped and broke. In a great welter of agonizing retreat the Confederates climbed the Brentwood Hills and scrambled down their southern slopes toward the Franklin Pike. All day long Stephen Lee's Mississippians, based on Overton's Hill, with little ammunition but with great purpose, had kept the pike open. It was the only exit left for Hood's men. The Union forces came boiling down the Granny White and Hillsboro pikes in hot pursuit, but Bedford Forrest's cavalry kept snapping at their heels with such delaying savagery that the Confederates got away.

Well, that was the end of the war in Nashville. It wrote

very clearly into the records the beginning of the end every-where. The city council appropriated $1,000 with which to purchase a fine horse and saddle for General Thomas. At the same time Mayor John Hugh Smith was presenting a highly ornamented sword to the provost marshal for "services ren-dered in crushing this causeless and wicked rebellion."

On April 3 came the news of the fall of Richmond. A hundred cannon were fired in salute on Capitol Hill, and the enthusiastic performance of a brass band supplemented the hysteria. Once the bricks started falling it was not long till the building collapsed. Lee surrendered on the ninth, and the result was pandemonium on the streets of Nashville.

But the tumult and the shouting were raised by the riffraff; strong men whose hearts and minds were with the Union didn't join the mob that day. Their hearts were too heavy, their vision too clear. The war was over but there was no celebration among the fine old families whose names were Nashville's foundation stones. Out of the grim compulsion of war they had taken the oath, and now that oath haunted them against the homecoming of their sons. But those sons, clad in their soiled and ragged gray uniforms, would understand. There were too many sons who wouldn't be coming back. It was neither the place nor the time to celebrate. Leave that to the vulgar.

On the fourteenth of April President Lincoln was shot and killed by the actor who had played Richard III in Nashville just over a year before. The day that the President's death was announced was the first day in over two years on which there were no arrests for drunkenness.

When the war was over, the best of Nashville began to assert itself. There was little waiting with folded hands. Early in May the citizens began to turn their energies toward peace. In and near the city were collected stores and garrison equip-ment worth about $50,000,000. Get them away; they had no part in the oncoming of peace. The Federal authorities co-operated and the sale of those materials was begun. Toward the end of May work was started to level the breastworks on Capitol Hill. All over the city men with shovels and picks began smoothing out the evil vestiges of war. A constant rattle of hatchets and hammers sounded as men repaired fences and buildings. Peace had come.

But not that easily. The long drab days of Reconstruction were just ahead. To prey upon the weak and defenseless is one of the first urges of the brute. So the brutes converged upon the South, some upon Nashville. But converged is hardly the appropriate word. Of this melancholy period we have developed a considerable body of fiction holding that the carpetbaggers were all from the North. Not at all. The dark fact is that the South furnished its share. One who reads the first message of Governor Brownlow, the reconstructionist who took office in 1865, can find a plain forecast of those unhappy days:

As for the original conspirators who without provocation treacherously set the rebellion on foot, bad men who pressed it forward with all the malignity of fiends and cruelty of savages; who through rapine, arson, butchery, and perjury filled the land with mourning, they are entitled to neither mercy nor forbearance.

And that, in effect, was an invitation to evil Southerners as well as those across the line.

As a practitioner of the art of the Happy Ending I must not close this section on such a note. Here is an item of happy and historical verity. Wartime Nashville was the stage on which the Montague-Capulet theme was played time after time. There is a record of thirteen Northern officers—one suspects there were more—who at the close of the war married Nashville girls. Not one of those bridegrooms carried his bride back to his Northern home. They had conquered Nashville, but Nashville had the last word and conquered them. They stayed in Nashville, and mostly for the rest of their lives. They did not find things easy for a while, but gradually these men, without exception, grew into various phases of leadership in the city. One of them became postmaster of the city, one of them a trustee of Vanderbilt University, the name of one of them is on the cornerstone of the Nashville Public Library, one of them pioneered in the development of the phosphate industry in Maury County. But even more than that, all of them served well in the processes of reconciliation. Those weddings somehow make a happy ending to an unhappy theme.

That was almost a century ago. Time slowly but surely has wrought miracles of healing. There is no martial quality in those cannon that frown so impotently on Capitol Hill. The posterity of those ravished trees have grown into a stately maturity. The fine old houses with surprising quickness lost their worn and distressed look, and the new ones bear the flavor and artistic brilliance of their predecessors. The Old South, in many ways a scene of great beauty, has gone, but its memory lingers, reminiscent of a day that was, for all of its marginal ugliness, gentle and gracious.

The War of the Revolution was the direct motive for the founding of Nashville. Its early and dominating settlers were Revolutionary soldiers. The Spirit of 'Seventy-Six is still most discernible here. The unique role played by Nashville in the War of 1812 still casts its spell on the people, though they are more likely to think of the personalities involved. It would have been impossible for the community to forget Andrew Jackson if the war had never happened. It made Andrew Jackson more than merely unforgettable. It also gave Nashville the honor of being the home of the seventh President of the United States. The War with Mexico, in a fashion, was Tennessee's own war, with its focus resting squarely on Nashville.

Tennesseans shaped Texas for statehood. They gave vital help to the Texans in the achievement of that statehood. It

73

was the prospect of the war to guarantee statehood that awarded Nashville the honor of being the home of the eleventh President of the United States.

Tennessee had no major part in starting the war of the sixties. In fact, Tennessee was the last state to secede. But once the war was started it found its way inevitably to Tennessee, and the pressure of the war was never relieved till its end. Of all the states involved the casualty rate was highest in Tennessee. Of all the cities connected with the war Nashville suffered most. It was in the hands of its enemies longest. The war never moved away from Nashville. Tragedy rested heavily on the people, though it was at times relieved by drama, by romance, even by humor. But such relief was always short-lived. Grimness settled back down on the captured city. Deep in the minds of the people there was always hope.

More than thirty years passed before there was another war. The next one, fought in 1898, was short and not to be compared with others in significance. Even so, it was the end of the nation's isolation. The direct motive of the war with Spain was to free Cuba from the domination of the Spanish, though there was the added motive of revenge after the battle-ship *Maine* was blown up in Havana harbor on February 15, 1898. One outcome of the war was the acquisition of the Philippines as territory of the United States, for which a token price of $20,000,000 was paid to Spain. The loss by death to the forces of the United States was about 5,000, of whom 90 per cent died from disease. One item connects Nashville with this war in a small way. The gunboat *Nashville* fired the war's first shot, and the cannon from which it was fired was taken from the boat and by special act of Congress given to the state. It is now in the War Memorial Museum in Nashville.

The young men of Nashville fought in World Wars One and Two as did young men of other cities. There was no slackening of courage or of resourcefulness. The young men of Nashville served well, and frequently were commissioned as officers and excelled in leadership. If fortune smiled they came back home, and for the main part lived or are living the lives of good citizens.

But those were standardized wars, and lacked the drama, indeed the drama within the drama, of the older wars. In the wars of 1776, of 1812, of 1845 and 1861 Nashville's personality was set apart from its sister cities. In them existed a subtle and moving relationship between the nature of the town and the nature of the wars, a sort of personal kinship to the campaigns and battles, a sort of combat-between-cousins status, or of struggle between plumed knights and fire-spitting dragons.

But now we have had enough of war and its struggles, of talk about war, of trying to beat someone to the draw. There has been some gain in the wars we have fought, but gain paid for exorbitantly. Another war might find the gain diminished, the price raised.

3

NEIGHBORLY RELATIONS

NASHVILLE is the metropolis of south-central Kentucky. It is not more than fifty miles distant from Kentucky along a considerable length of boundary line. Almost from its beginning it has been attractive to Kentuckians in a special way.

Kentuckians are a history-minded people. They love to reflect on the past and talk about it. They find in Nashville a depth of history that draws them. It is an outstanding religious center, and to that appeal Kentuckians are responsive. It abounds in colleges and in such attractions as are collateral phases of colleges. Kentucky, which established the first college west of the mountains, finds that most appealing. It is a medical and surgical center of more than sectional prestige, and a great many Kentucky people come to Nashville to be diagnosed, hospitalized, treated and operated on. Kentuckians buy tires and cement and shoes and sacks and various chemicals and automobile windows made in Nashville. And so a great many Kentuckians come down to help produce them, and a great many more to buy them.

Many Kentuckians hold insurance policies originating in Nashville, policies that are paid, when emergency arises, by checks bearing a Nashville imprint. A great many Kentuckians read their morning and afternoon news in papers published in Nashville. The lower tiers of Kentucky counties from Glasgow to Cadiz are valued patrons of Nashville's stores and shows and art, of Nashville's colleges and hospitals. A college in Bowling Green has provided several regular members of the Nashville symphony orchestra. Bus loads come from Bowling Green and Hopkinsville for concerts and performances. The Kentuckians drive down to visit the Hermitage, the Parthenon and the Capitol, and to shop in the stores.

This is no late development. There is sound basis for this neighborliness both geographically and historically. A great deal of sisterly likeness exists between the two states. Kentucky was settled four years earlier and reached statehood five years earlier. Tennessee is 1,800 miles larger in area and is larger in population by 350,000 persons. Their first settlers were identical in ancestry and general traits. Their topography follows a similar outline: the mountains, the knobs, the rivers. Kentucky's Bluegrass is in the east central part of the state, Tennessee's Bluegrass in its west central. Their placement shifts from the regularity of the major features. In the bluegrass of Kentucky horses are bred, trained and raced; in the bluegrass of Tennessee they are bred, trained and ridden. In both states the rivers are dammed and houses are built on the shores of the resulting lakes, whose waters are fished in, swum in, boated on and then permitted to escape into a million motors and a billion incandescent bulbs. Kentucky permitted the pilgrims under James Robertson to use one of its routes on their way to settle Nashville. A little later Tennesseans reciprocated with the Natchez Trace for the use of southward-bound Kentuckians.

Let us be more specific. In pioneer times Bardstown in Kentucky had a close linkage with Nashville. Bardstown was, for a brief time, the cultural center of Kentucky. Its people were of excellent quality, and from 1788 to 1792 Salem Academy, at Bardstown, had the best reputation of any school in the state. To Salem, at Bardstown, came boys who as men loomed large in the state's career. To name a few: Archibald Cameron, Joseph Hamilton Davies, Ben Hardin, John Rowan, Felix Grundy. The principal of the academy was Dr. James Priestley, whose first appearance of record was as a scholar at

Timber Ridge Academy in the northernmost part of Rockbridge County, Virginia. Later Timber Ridge Academy was moved into Lexington and its name changed to Liberty Hall, still later to Washington College, finally to Washington and Lee. James Priestley was appointed instructor in several of the more impressive courses. Then he came to Bardstown. For some reason he left Salem Academy in 1792 or 1793. The academy never reopened, and today even its site is almost lost. In a little while Transylvania College began to draw Kentucky's cultural center to Lexington. Priestley taught for a little while in the ill-fated Cokesbury College at Baltimore, and then in an academy at Danville, Kentucky.

In 1809 he came to Nashville as president of Cumberland College. His election followed his endorsement by two former students of his at Bardstown. Cumberland College in Nashville was the outgrowth of Davidson Academy, chartered in 1785, and rechartered in 1806 as Cumberland College. When the vacancy came Felix Grundy remembered the excellence of Dr. Priestley's instruction at Bardstown and nominated him for the post. In his brief time in Nashville, Grundy had become an important citizen and gained the enduring friendship of Andrew Jackson. Grundy jestingly explained his own coming to Tennessee by saying that Kentucky had grown too small for him and Henry Clay both. He had married Ann Rodgers of Springfield, Kentucky. It was she who started, in the First Presbyterian Church, the first Sunday-school class ever organized in Nashville. Today in Nashville there are many descendants of the Grundys.

Robert Coleman Foster moved in 1792 to Nashville from his home in Bardstown. Foster was the founder of one of Nashville's great families. His son, Ephraim Foster, served as United States senator and was prominent in state and national Whig councils. The continuity of the Foster family is suggested by the fact that since the original arrival there has been no time when there wasn't a Robert Coleman Foster in the city.

Foster's endorsement of Dr. Priestley, added to that of Felix Grundy, was most convincing.

John Rowan, whose home was in Bardstown, had studied at Salem Academy. It was he who later built Federal Hill ("My Old Kentucky Home"). He sent one of his sons to Cumberland College to study under Dr. Priestley.

There is on record in the courthouse at Nashville an acknowledgment of the receipt of $206 for tuition paid to the administrators of Priestley's estate by Joseph Underwood of Kentucky. We do not know definitely who this Joseph Underwood was. The time suits that of the celebrated senator from Kentucky, and he was closely connected with Grundy and Foster.

Another Kentuckian who attended Cumberland College was James Rumsey Skiles, son of Jacob Skiles of Bowling Green, and descendant of the great inventor for whom he was christened. He attended in 1816. Later he married Eliza Bell, niece of Judge John McNairy and of Dr. Boyd McNairy.

Michael Campbell served in the Revolution under the immediate command of General Washington. About 1785 he settled in Bardstown. He served in the Kentucky legislature, but for some reason moved to Nashville in 1808. Here he prospered and engaged in many good works. He died in 1830.

The descendants of William Whitsitt have been specially favorable to both Kentucky and Tennessee. He was born in Ireland in 1731. Ten years later the family moved to Albemarle County, Virginia. He fought in the wars, and in time married Ellen Menees of Amherst County, Virginia. The family moved again, this time to Nashville in 1790. Six years later the Whitsitts moved to Kentucky, settling two miles north of Russellville. A son James, a Baptist preacher, remained in Nashville. He established the famous Mill Creek Baptist Church, and devoted a long and useful life to preaching in the early settlements of Kentucky and Tennessee. Margaret Whitsitt, daughter of William, married George Blakey, and they moved into Kentucky at the same time. In 1851 their son George, Junior, ran with Cassius Clay on the Abolition ticket for lieutenant governor and governor respectively. George and Margaret Blakey lived long and useful lives. He died at ninety-three and she at ninety-two. From them descended the Breathitts, of whom one became a governer, one attorney general and one lieutenant governor. Also of the Breathitt posterity are the Halls of Auburn, the Duncans of Russellville, and the O'Steens and Blakeys of Hopkinsville and Louisville. From the Blakeys have descended the Helms of Bowling Green and New York. The Whitsitts are still prominent in Nashville.

In 1798 Joseph Elliston, while yet a mere lad, moved from Elliston's Station in northern Kentucky to Nashville. In his early manhood he opened a silversmith's shop, which actually was Nashville's first jewelry store. He became one of the early and sturdy pillars of the Methodist Church, and took a leading part in the establishment of the McKendree church. Later he was one of the three commissioners appointed to supervise the construction of the Capitol. Elliston's home, which he named Burlington after the Elliston homestead in Kentucky, was planned and erected by William Strickland, the architect who had designed the Capitol. Burlington was one of the show places of Nashville until it was demolished several years ago to make room for the Father Ryan High School.

Peter Bass came from Maryland to Bloomfield, Kentucky, and there married Anna Stone, whose father had built one of the first brick houses in Kentucky, still standing. Later, the Basses moved to Nashville and provided ancestry for a major family. One of the Bass sons married a daughter of Felix Grundy. A granddaughter of this marriage was Mrs. Whiteford Cole, whose husband was president of the Louisville & Nashville Railroad. He was a grandson of Willis W. and Johanna Cole, who moved from Kentucky to Giles County, Tennessee, about 1820.

Judge Return Jonathan Meigs of the United States Supreme

Court was born in Winchester, Kentucky, in 1801. His Tennessee residence was in Nashville until the beginning of the Civil War.

John Catron, another Justice of the Supreme Court, was reared in Kentucky and moved to Nashville in 1812. He married Hannah Childress, daughter of Judge John Childress and kinswoman of Mrs. James K. Polk. A brother of Mrs. Catron, George Campbell Childress, moved to Texas and there wrote the famous Texas Declaration of Independence.

James C. McReynolds moved from Elkton, Kentucky, to Nashville in 1886. He gained eminence as a lawyer and was appointed Justice of the United States Supreme Court.

Kentucky has sent three of its sons to become governors of Tennessee. A. S. Marks was born in Daviess County, Kentucky, and spent his first nineteen years there. He moved to Winchester, Tennessee, in 1855. He was elected governor in 1878 and during his service became very popular in Nashville. Benton McMillan of Monroe County, Kentucky, and Austin Peay of Boyle and Christian counties were both elected to Tennessee's governorship. But it should be held in mind that Tennessee supplied Isaac Shelby as Kentucky's first governor.

The Rodes family, of note in Louisville, Danville and Bowling Green, Kentucky, and in Nashville and Giles County, Tennessee, all stem from Charles Rodes of Cornwall, England, who arrived in Virginia in 1695. The family has been of eminence both in law and finance. The Cheeks and the Neals, who founded the Maxwell House Coffee Company, were from Monroe and Cumberland counties in Kentucky. Kentucky's greatest editor, Henry Watterson, was from Nashville, and his wife, Rebecca Ewing, was a daughter of one of Nashville's great families. Thomas L. Bransford was born in Virginia in 1804. In 1814 the family moved to Glasgow, Kentucky, and in 1856 to Nashville. It has been an influential name in Nashville ever since.

A heroic figure connected with pioneer Tennessee was

Isaac Bledsoe, who lived near Gallatin. On December 1, 1785, his daughter Margaret married Joseph Desha, later governor of Kentucky. Their descendant Picketts and Breckinridges have added distinction to the story of Kentucky.

John Preston Watts Brown, of Frankfort, entered the University of Nashville in 1828. There has been a John Preston Watts Brown in Nashville ever since. The fourth of the J. P. W. series was president of the Nashville division of the Tennessee Electric Power Company at the time of his death.

Robert Mills of Elkton, Kentucky, enrolled in the University of Nashville in 1826. After a year in the university he moved on with the advance guard of Tennesseans who were Texas-bound. He accumulated land, slaves and general property on such a scale that during the latter years of his life he was commonly called the "Duke of Brazoria," and on that theme a master's thesis has recently been written at the University of Texas.

One of the most colorful of all of the citizens of Nashville was William Walker, famed in the records as the "Gray-Eyed Man of Destiny." He was a very scholarly youth and his classical tendencies were encouraged by his mother, who had been a Miss Norvell of Glasgow, Kentucky. At fourteen he was graduated with great distinction from the University of Nashville. Then he spent a year in the University of Pennsylvania and two more in European universities. He engaged in several activities but found none to his liking. At last he conducted an expedition against Nicaragua, conquered the country and made himself president. Matters went well with him for a while, but in the end he was taken by Honduran troops and executed in 1860. William Walker's sister Alice married Lawrence Richardson of Louisville.

Another connection of the same period between Nashville and Louisville was the marriage in 1856 of James Ross Todd of Louisville to Mary McGavock of Nashville. She was a daughter of Jacob McGavock and a granddaughter of Felix Grundy.

Kentucky has long been a proving ground for Nashville pulpits. Nashville has had six preachers from one Baptist church in Bowling Green. From Frankfort to Nashville have come three ministers of the Presbyterian Church, and three of the Christian Church. The present minister of the oldest Presbyterian church in Nashville came to it from Middlesboro, Kentucky, and the present secretary of the Southern Baptist Convention from Bowling Green, Kentucky. The present minister of Nashville's largest Christian church came from Lexington.

The first preacher in Nashville was Dr. Thomas B. Craighead, who arrived here in 1783 from Frankfort, Kentucky, and who was principal of Davidson Academy for more than twenty years. The First Presbyterian Church was organized in 1814, Dr. Gideon Blackburn, pastor. Later he served as president of Center College, at Danville, Kentucky. The First Baptist Church of Nashville was the development of a series of sermons preached in 1820 by the Reverend Jeremiah Vardeman of Kentucky.

The Reverend Philip Fall visited Nashville first in 1820. Three years later he became minister of the First Baptist Church. But in a few years he shifted to the newly formed Christian Church. After a little while he went to Kentucky as the president of a Christian college there.

Nashville's most popular preacher of all time was Dr. John T. Edgar, pastor of the First Presbyterian Church from 1833 to 1859. He was born in Delaware in 1792. When he was three years old the family moved to Frankfort, Kentucky. He studied theology in the College of New Jersey and was graduated in 1816. President Andrew Jackson became very fond of Dr. Edgar, and the minister both baptized the General and preached his funeral sermon.

The original Catholics arrived in Nashville directly from

Bardstown. Father Stephen Badin visited Nashville several times about 1800. Bishop Flaget of Bardstown was the first Catholic bishop to officiate in Tennessee; that was in May 1821. Father Richard Miles, who was consecrated in the Cathedral at Bardstown in 1838, was the first Catholic Bishop of Nashville.

The ministers of the Methodist Church have come from Kentucky only in exceptional cases, nor have many gone from Tennessee to Kentucky. Methodists tend to use home-grown preachers more than the Baptists or the Presbyterians. However, the present general secretary of the Division of Higher Education of the Methodist Church is Dr. John O. Gross, formerly of Barbourville, Kentucky. The business manager of the same division is Dr. James S. Blair, also from Kentucky, and Dr. Jamison Jones, another Kentuckian, is editor of *Motive*, the organ of the division.

There has not been much exchange among the Episcopalians of the two states, although Dr. Prentice Pugh of Uniontown, Kentucky, has served as rector of the Church of the Advent at Nashville for thirty-eight years.

There is a similar record among the physicians. When James K. Polk was in his late teens he was taken from his home in Tennessee for an operation by the renowned Dr. Ephraim McDowell of Danville, Kentucky. The doctor's charm no less than his skill endeared him permanently to his patient. Later Dr. McDowell came to Nashville to operate on Mrs. Thomas Overton. The surgery was successful in every way. When Dr. McDowell was ready to return to Danville, Overton inquired as to the fee. The question embarrassed the surgeon. Doubtless he was recalling that he had made a long tiring trip and had forfeited a good bit of practice at home. He stammered and said, "Two hundred dollars."

"I'll never pay it," said Overton firmly.

"Perhaps it is too much. You make it what you think is a fair fee."

"You have saved my wife's life. She is a very valuable woman. Make it five hundred or nothing."

Dr. Adam Goodlett came from Lexington, Kentucky, in 1805, and was from then till his death one of the section's leading practitioners. Dr. William T. Briggs transferred from a practice in Bowling Green to Nashville in 1851. There he joined the original staff of the medical college of the University of Nashville. His son, C. S. Briggs, born in Bowling Green, was graduated from the same college and taught courses in anatomy.

Dr. T. A. Atchison was graduated from the Transylvania Medical College. He practiced in Bowling Green for several years, then moved to Nashville to practice and teach courses in Special and General Therapeutics. Dr. William P. Jones practiced medicine in Kentucky, his native state, for some years before coming to Nashville in 1849. He was superintendent of the state hospital for the insane for eight years, and postmaster of Nashville for eight more. After that he taught in the medical department of the University of Tennessee.

Dr. John D. Kelly, after a brief practice in Kentucky, came to Nashville and practiced for twenty-eight years. He was appointed collector of internal revenue for the district of northern Kentucky in 1866, and died in 1870. Dr. Paul Eve was graduated in medicine at the University of Pennsylvania. After a varied experience in this country and Europe he was appointed Professor of Surgery in the University of Louisville. In 1851 he joined the staff of the new school of medicine in the University of Nashville. Dr. W. K. Bowling, a descendant of John Rolfe and Pocahontas, practiced medicine in Logan County, Kentucky, from 1836 to 1850. Then he moved to Nashville to practice medicine, to teach in the medical college and to edit a medical journal.

Dr. Charles K. Winston practiced medicine in Green County, Kentucky, until 1851 when he accepted membership on the staff of the medical college, of which he subsequently became president. Tennessee, and particularly Nashville, have been and remain a great provider of the medical and surgical talent that Kentucky requires, and an impressive number of the leaders in that field have come down from Kentucky to Nashville to perform a reciprocal service.

We have already related some of the earliest educational connections between Kentucky and Nashville. Transylvania College in Lexington was in high favor among the young men of Nashville very early in the last century. A number of them attended there; some of the Basses did, some of the Ewings, some of the Watkinses. There exists in a Nashville library a thesis written in Transylvania in 1826 by Stockly Donelson of Nashville. Oddly enough it deals with the development of blooded horses. To add to its quaintness it was written in Latin. Under Dr. Horace Holley, Transylvania prospered greatly. It was for at least two years during the Holley administration the largest college in America. In 1823 President Holley was invited to Nashville to consider the presidency of the university. During the visit he was a guest at the Hermitage, and as a mark of genuine hospitality Andrew Jackson had his personal portrait painter Ralph Earl paint a likeness of the distinguished guest. That picture of him hangs now in the rooms of the Tennessee Historical Society. The presidency of the university was offered Dr. Holley, but he chose to remain at Transylvania.

Collins D. Elliott, who was graduated from Augusta College in Kentucky in 1826, served as president of the Nashville Female Academy for over thirty years. One of the Vanderbilt Training Schools was established at Elkton, Kentucky, and conducted there until the project was discontinued. On the present staff of George Peabody College for Teachers there are fourteen native Kentuckians. As an indication of the general spread of Kentuckians in Nashville twenty-four members of the Downtown Kiwanis Club were born and reared in Kentucky.

Kentucky is Nashville's most friendly neighbor.

4

SEND FOR A DOCTOR

THE FOUNDERS and early settlers of Nashville brought with them their own means and ways of curing the ailments that plagued them. There were of course no doctors and no drugstores, but the forests were filled with roots which when properly steeped and taken or rubbed on left the stricken one vastly improved.

Bear grease offered specialized aid to a sharp knife in the treatment of corns and bunions which were a pioneer pestilence. Rattlesnake grease eased rheumatic pains. A wild-onion poultice was a great limberer-up of a stiff neck. Water collected in an old stump was an efficient remover of warts. "Life everlasting," sometimes called rabbit tobacco by the pioneers, could be boiled into a tea generally recognized as a prime toner-up of the run-down. Sassafras tea, brewed from the root of the red sassafras in March and April, thinned the blood from its winter thickness and caused it to flow with more speed and purpose. And so on.

The pioneers met their emergencies with a resourcefulness sometimes incredible. This is the authentic account of a remarkable performance of surgery before there was ever a doctor here. On January 11, 1781, David Hood went out from the stockade toward the sulphur spring to look for a deer. Over where the ball park now is the Indians found him, scalped him thoroughly and left him for dead. An hour or so later, missing him at the stockade, the men went out to look for him. They found him unconscious and, they thought, just about dead. They carried him back to James Robertson's cabin. And there the Father of Nashville did a tremendously audacious thing, but it worked. He took a small shoemaker's awl and a light hammer as his instruments. He held Hood's mutilated head on his lap and by the light of a grease lamp he perforated very thickly the whole scalped area, the awl penetrating lightly into the bone. An exudation issued from the holes and quickly hardened into a protective covering. David Hood was a tough and resistant fellow who got well in a surprisingly brief time and took proper revenge upon the Indians. The treatment was based on fragments that Robertson had heard told by French doctors back in North Carolina. And so was surgery initiated in Nashville, a place now greatly committed to surgery.

As has been said, no physican came with the settlers. The first one to establish a home in the settlement was Dr. James White, an early man of mystery. The year of his arrival is not clear. It was odd for a man so remarkable to open practice in a wilderness, which Nashville then was. He was a graduate of the University of Edinburgh, at the time the world's most notable center of medical learning. While there he had several courses under Dr. William Cullen, then probably the world's most famous instructor in medicine. Later, Dr. White studied at Saint Omer, the great seat of medical learning in France. He was a very literate man in medicine, in law and in theology. He brought with him a great deal of money, though no one ever knew its source. He was when sober clearly a man of learning, and of power and discipline of mind. But he didn't quite fit into Nashville.

In 1797 he sold his land and house and office and, with his son, moved on to Maury County. He lived there awhile, then moved on to Mobile, and then to Louisiana. He sent the son, Edward Douglas White, back to Nashville for study at Cumberland College. The young man was graduated with credit in 1814, and later became governor of the state of Louisiana. His son, Edward Douglas White, Junior, rose to the Chief Justice-ship of the United States Supreme Court. The family was one of distinction in Louisiana, but almost all we know of Dr. James White is derived from an address by Dr. Felix Robert-son, published in 1854 in the *Nashville Journal of Medicine and Surgery*.

The next physician to reach Nashville was Dr. John Sap-pington. There are only a few details available as to his actual practice. It is known that he placed Sappington's pills on the local market, and that they became popularly regarded as a sort of cure-all and were used extensively. Dr. Sappington told the public exactly what the pills contained—mystery with a covering of sugar. At an appointed time in the morning the doctor stepped outside the door of his office and rang a bell to announce that it was time for his patients to take a pill. He stayed in the settlement three years, and then he, too, moved on to Louisiana.

His brother, Dr. Mark Sappington, reached Nashville a little later than John. One of his sons, Dr. Roger Sappington, practiced in Nashville until his death in 1824. The career of another son, Dr. Frank Sappington, was cut short by a tragic duel with Dr. Francis May fought somewhere in the vicinity of Broadway and Spruce streets. Dr. May's bullet entered young Sappington's forehead and he died immediately. A third son, Dr. John Sappington, practiced at Franklin, Tennessee, for several years. He then moved with the tides of migration to Missouri, where he developed considerable prestige in his pro-fession. This Dr. Sappington was an ancestor of the actress, Ginger Rogers.

Dr. May, who had come to Nashville from the Virginia Valley, was so troubled by the unfortunate results of the duel that he soon moved to Knoxville. After his death his widow married Judge John Overton and from 1824 on helped shape the history of Nashville from Traveler's Rest.

Nashville's first drugstore was opened by Dr. James Hennen

in 1794. He diagnosed minor troubles and sold cures for everything, such as ipecac, asafoetida, myrrh, powdered pomegranate root, laudanum, calomel and a highly publicized emulsion made from willow sawdust.

Dr. William Dickson began practice in Nashville but was soon elected to Congress and retired from medicine. Dr. Thomas Claiborne from Knoxville and Dr. Joseph Hays from Abingdon, Virginia, formed a partnership in Nashville in 1800. Dr. Claiborne moved to Natchez in 1810. In 1804 another drugstore was added to the town, opened by Dr. Watkins and Dr. Catlett, both of whom were practicing in the section. Dr. Watkins soon sold out to his partner and returned to Virginia. Dr. Catlett became an outspoken member of the anti-Jackson faction, and served as second to Charles Dickinson in the duel fought between him and Andrew Jackson in 1806.

Nashville's most influential physician of the first half of the nineteenth century was Dr. Felix Robertson, born the night his father practiced surgery on David Hood. Little is known of Felix Robertson's childhood. It seems likely that he attended Davidson Academy because of his father's part in the creation of the Academy. Besides, it was the only school in the community offering training that would prepare him for the Medical College of the University of Pennsylvania. He had an early leaning toward medicine, and he began the study of it in the office of Dr. Thomas Claiborne, brother of Louisiana's first governor. After that apprenticeship he rode on horseback to Philadelphia where he studied under the great Dr. Benjamin Rush. His sister Lavinia, the youngest of the Robertson children, rode with him and entered a school for young women. He was graduated in 1805 and began his practice in Nashville in 1806. He was the first Nashville physician to become a specialist. His practice, naturally general at first, gradually narrowed into the treatment of children's diseases.

He was a charter member of the Medical Society of Tennessee, organized in 1830. He was president from 1834 to 1840, and again in 1853. He was mayor of Nashville in 1827, and for two years was president of the Bank of Tennessee. He was trustee of Cumberland College and its successor, the University of Nashville, for fifty-four years. The finest boat on the Cumberland River was launched in 1854 and named the *Doctor Robertson*. He never prescribed whisky for a patient, and a motto on the wall of his office read: "Never use Medicine except when absolutely necessary." He was a favorite among the members of the medical society of Nashville. At a memorial service held the month after his death one physician said, "Dr. Robertson has doctored more doctors than any doctor in Nashville." He took no part in the Civil War. He was opposed to secession, but he rebelled against the sight of Northern troops on the streets of Nashville. During the last three years of his life he accepted only emergency cases and was rarely seen outside his home. He died three months after Lee's surrender. He had lived a rich life and it was time for him to go.

Dr. Boyd McNairy was born in North Carolina in 1785. He arrived in Nashville at the age of five. His older brother John had come in a party two years earlier, one member of it being a young red-haired pioneer named Andrew Jackson. Boyd McNairy entered Davidson Academy in 1797, and remained there under the tutelage of Dr. Thomas B. Craighead until he was ready for study at the University of Pennsylvania. He was graduated from the academy in 1803 and entered the university the same year. At Philadelphia he met a girl named Ann Marie Hodkinson, who was there attending school. She was the daughter of Peter Hodkinson, one of the celebrated shipbuilders of the time. Young Dr. McNairy brought her back to Nashville as his bride. She loved music and the young physician ordered a piano sent from Philadelphia to Nashville. It was at that time real trouble to get a piano from Philadelphia to Nashville, but the instrument arrived in good order. McNairy was gifted in his profession and he quickly developed a good general practice. Being a McNairy he had a flair for politics, and being a devout Federalist he revolted against the strange doctrines that Andrew Jackson was proclaiming in the western settlement.

Yet it was Dr. Boyd McNairy who, when Jackson was shot by Jesse Benton on the market square in the summer of 1813, asked for the wounded General to be brought to his home on Summer Street. The wounded man was in such fragile condition that it was necessary to rig up a stretcher, worked by pulleys attached to hooks in the ceiling. Ten days later they carried General Jackson back to the Hermitage and the feud was resumed. Those hooks remained in that ceiling until the building was demolished in the eighties, grim but eloquent reminders that when humanity called in those virile days personal enmity could be set aside, at least temporarily.

Only once in his career did Doctor McNairy depart from the role of general practitioner. That was in 1840 when he was appointed general superintendent for the Insane Hospital. Besides the practice of medicine and Whig politics he raised flowers, played the violin and for twenty-eight years served as trustee of the University of Nashville. From some old newspaper comments it is learned that his fiddle repertoire was not limited to jig pieces. At times his wife provided the accompaniment to his playing, and in one item it was stated that he sometimes carried his fiddle when calling on his patients—a very early form of therapy, one assumes. In politics he was a strong partisan of Henry Clay, for whom he named his youngest son. When Henry Clay attended the Whig convention in Nashville in 1840, Dr. McNairy and his family moved out of their house and turned it entirely over to Clay during his stay in the city. Two years later he provided John J. Crittenden with the same hospitality. Dr. McNairy died on November 21, 1856. Perhaps it was better so since he escaped the agony of the Civil War.

Dr. John Shelby, a nephew of Isaac Shelby, the Revolutionary patriot who became the first governor of Kentucky, was born in Gallatin in 1786. In common with the more ambitious and able of the section's medical students of that early day he chose the University of Pennsylvania, from which he was graduated with special honors. In 1813 he joined the army under General Andrew Jackson and served as a surgeon in the Creek War. He was wounded and lost permanently the use of one eye. He served as postmaster of the city from 1849 till 1853. He amassed considerable wealth, mainly through early deals in land. The first college of medicine founded in the section was sponsored by him and bore his name.

Not much is known in detail about the Shelby Medical College. It was chartered in 1857 as the medical college of an institution projected by the Methodist Church and to be christened Central University. There had been some thought given to the establishment of a college of medicine as early as 1826. It was indeed a long and tiresome trip to Philadelphia, and Transylvania was far enough away to emphasize the need. The town had been doctor-minded just as it had been preacher-minded since its beginning. In 1858 the Shelby Medical College, located on Broadway near the present site of the First Baptist Church, opened and continued for three sessions. The physicians besides Dr. Shelby who were most closely connected with the school's beginning were Dr. Thomas L. Maddin, Dr. John H. Callendar and Dr. John P. Ford. Dr. Shelby died in 1859. The college outlived him by two years. Its closing was due to three things: the minds of the people were so concerned with the imminence of war that their efforts in behalf of the college weakened; the parent institution, Central University, never existed except for some plans on paper and as a matter of hope; also, the Shelby College was never in a position to compete favorably with the school of medicine of the University of Nashville which had grown powerful in its half-dozen years.

The story of the University of Nashville's medical college is an important one. In 1829, Philip Lindsley, president of the university, said of the city: "It is the only place in Tennessee where a school of medicine would even be thought of." As a matter of fact Nashville thought of a school of medicine a great many times before it had one. In 1843 the talk of such a college compressed into a real effort to establish one. A plan was put on paper, and the faculty tentatively named. Then the zeal faded and the project died.

Perhaps Nashville's most versatile and indefatigable citizen of all time was Dr. John Berrien Lindsley, son of the president. He was interested in almost everything and at some time had specialized in most. He shared his father's passion for a school of medicine. When Berrien Lindsley desired anything greatly he went into action. He was the catalytic agent who brought into a working unity the best thinking of Dr. W. K. Bowling, Dr. A. H. Buchanan, Dr. Charles Winston, Dr. John M. Watson, all of Nashville, and of Dr. Charles Caldwell, who came down from Louisville to give aid to the movement.

In 1850 the efforts, long accumulating, seemed about to break through the civic inertia that so long had baffled the promoters of the movement. On September 28 of that year the above-named physicians met and issued an appeal to the University of Nashville to accept and sponsor within limits a school of medicine. They pledged to relieve the university of the heavy expense of the undertaking. When tuition and fees from the medical students failed to meet the expenses of the college, the professors were pledged to pay the deficit out of pro-rata assessments. The petition was given impressive publicity, and for the first time the townspeople joined in the movement.

The university accepted the sponsorship of the college under the conditions stated, and the college was opened in 1851. There were thirty-three members of the first graduating class in 1852, thirty-six in 1853. The rise was constant until 1861 when 161 were graduated. The physicians already named, with the addition of Dr. Robert Massengale Porter, composed the first staff. Dr. Paul Eve was added a few months after the session began. The specialized ability of the teachers gave the medical college excellent prestige almost from its beginning, and the enrollment surprised even the most optimistic. By the beginning of the Civil War 3,289 had enrolled in the school, and 909 had been graduated. These were of inestimable service to the Southern armies.

The first staff of the college was of remarkable quality, both personal and professional. John Berrien Lindsley was, in his versatility, the Benjamin Franklin of Nashville. He was graduated at the University of Nashville in the class of 1838, a close friend and classmate of William Walker, the "Gray-Eyed Man of Destiny." Several letters exist, written to Lindsley by Walker while he was President of Nicaragua. In one of them Walker requests Dr. Lindsley to send him a man competent to serve as an expert agriculturist for the country. Walker too had been trained in medicine, though he had never practiced. Lindsley was a graduate in medicine of the University of Pennsylvania. He was an ordained preacher in the Presbyterian Church. He had throughout his life a burning interest in the various fields of the natural sciences. He became the first president of the Nashville Board of Public Education, the first secretary of the Tennessee State Board of Health and one of the nation's pioneers in prison reform.

Dr. Robert Massengale Porter was of comparable versatility, at least in training. The Porters have been a ranking family in Nashville ever since the first Porter arrived in 1793. He came to this country from Ireland, landing in Philadelphia. From there the trip into the southwest was made on horseback. When he reached the settlement a young woman sat behind him on his horse. She was his young bride. He had made the acquaintance of Susan Massengale in east Tennessee during a spell of sickness which he suffered en route. Massengale is still one of the better names in the section from which she came.

The Porters founded a linen business here which grew in

size and prosperity. They built a fine house which is today a show place. They had part in all of the community's better activities. They reared a nephew whom Andrew Jackson regarded highly even when the nephew was still a lad. It was Jackson who counseled him to study law, which he did. Jackson then advised going to Louisiana and growing up with the state. Young Alexander Porter followed that advice too. He settled at Franklin in the Teche country, developed a fine practice and built a mansion, Oaklawn, one of the state's notable estates. He became judge and then United States Senator.

Robert Massengale Porter, son of the Porters, cousin to Alexander, was graduated with high honors at the University of Nashville in 1836. He immediately entered the Harvard Law School, where he studied under Story and Greenleaf. He was graduated again with high honors in 1838. He practiced a year with his cousin in Louisiana, then withdrew permanently from the law. In June 1840 he entered the theological department at Princeton. His professors were Charles Hodge, Samuel Miller and Archibald Alexander. In 1843 he was graduated with no lessening of honors. But he never preached a sermon. In September of that year he entered the medical department of the University of Pennsylvania. He was graduated with the usual honors in 1845. He then spent a year in Paris, taking graduate courses in anatomy. He used still another year in visiting hospitals in Germany, England, Ireland and Scotland. He knew then the work he was to do. In January 1848 he began the practice of medicine in his native city. And so he found his way to the staff of the new medical college. But only five years of service were allowed him. On May 27, 1856, he performed a demonstration on a cadaver, newly acquired by the college. He developed a peculiar infection within twenty-four hours, which grew rapidly worse. On July 1 he died.

Dr. Paul Eve's reputation was international before he reached the Nashville staff. He was graduated in 1826 from a college in Athens, Georgia. From there he entered the medical department of the University of Pennsylvania, being graduated in 1828. Then he decided to go abroad for further study. In Paris he had his first opportunity to practice "military surgery." That was in the three-days revolution of 1830. In 1831 he offered his services to Poland in her struggle to escape Russian domination. It was, he claimed, his opportunity to make a token repayment for the service Poland had rendered in our Revolution. He promptly demonstrated an ability so outstanding that he was soon promoted from a surgeonship in one of the Warsaw hospitals to Surgeon of Ambulances in General Turno's army. The Polish government thought so well of him as a man and as a surgeon in time of need that he was awarded the Golden Cross of Honor.

He returned to America and in 1832 began a brief practice in Augusta, Georgia. In the summer of that year he was elected Professor of Surgery in the Medical College of Georgia, a position he held for seventeen years. In 1849 he accepted the professorship of surgery in the medical department of the University of Louisville. Three years later he accepted a similar position in the newly formed department of the University of Nashville. When the Civil War began he offered his skill and services to the Confederate Army. He served first as surgeon general of Tennessee, and then as chief surgeon of General Joseph E. Johnston's army. He ended the war as director of a hospital in Richmond, Virginia. Late in that year he returned to his old position in the University of Nashville. Twelve years later he died while treating a patient in his office.

Some very prominent people in this area have been descendants of Pocahontas and John Rolfe. One of them was W. K. Bowling, born in Virginia in 1808. He took his first course of medical lectures at the Medical College of Ohio, being graduated in 1836. He began his practice in Logan County, Kentucky, near Adairville. His office was in a cave just outside the village. In 1851 he assisted in founding the medical department of the University of Nashville, and was immediately appointed Professor of the Practice and Institutes of Medicine. He founded the *Nashville Journal of Medicine and Surgery* and edited it for twenty years.

The other members of the college's original staff, indeed those of the first decade, were less colorful, but of no less capacity as instructors. The College of Medicine remains one of the city's best traditions. It was a brilliant institution in its day, but its day closed too soon.

It was a casualty of the war. The university never provided its medical college with funds, but it did give it a background, a home, an anchoring place. The university had a hard time of it even before the war. It was always in need of money. But when the war had drained away the substance of the South there were few young men who could afford even the low tuition charged. Aside from that, it was several years before the young men could be spared for the college. They were needed imperatively at home. There was much to rebuild in the South.

But the medical college was never entirely without students. Some attended part of each day, some part of each session, but they managed to keep on coming. The college was held together until 1874 when something happened that gave Nashville a school of medicine in perpetuity. Vanderbilt University was then getting under way. Its start was impressive by reason of a great deal of money given by Cornelius Vanderbilt, and by a great deal of zeal and wisdom on the part of Bishop Holland McTyeire and Dr. A. L. P. Green of the Methodist Church, and by the unusual administrative ability of the newly elected president, Landon C. Garland. Their vision of the university included as one appropriate and vital department a school of medicine. The first idea was to bring back into life the Shelby Medical College, but that had been out of existence too long to provide more than a nucleus. The University of Nashville had a college of medicine, impoverished and feeble then, but of notable achievement. There were many conferences and adjustments, and then the two universities assumed jointly the responsibility of offering in one college full training for physicians and surgeons.

On the staff of the new college were most of those who had taught medicine in the University of Nashville, a few from the old Shelby Medical College and some members chosen from the practitioners of the city. One special and unique provision enabled the graduate to choose whether his diploma would be issued by Vanderbilt or by the University of Nashville. That arrangement worked well for twenty years. Then it was judged better for each institution to take responsibility for its own work, and so each one went its separate way. The University of Nashville continued for a while, but then was merged with the College of Medicine of the University of Tennessee. The Vanderbilt School of Medicine, while not one of the largest, is certainly one of the best in the country. It has no plans to be much larger. It accepts fifty freshmen a year out of more than ten times that many applicants. Vanderbilt fondly hopes that all of the fifty will become good physicians, and great specialists, and a pleasing number have answered that wish in its entirety. There have been graduated at Vanderbilt 5,184 physicians.

MEHARRY

Nashville's other medical college is Meharry, established in 1876 to train physicians, dentists and nurses for service among the colored people of the South. It was at first one department of Central Tennessee College, located on the southern margin of the city at First Avenue and Chestnut Street. It gradually rose to a position of eminence, at least locally, in that service. In 1931 it moved to its present well-equipped campus, adjoining that of Fisk University. In its career it has graduated 3,689 physicians, 1,531 dentists and 1,904 nurses. Now one out of every four Negro physicians in the nation is a Meharry graduate.

Nashville is a hospital town, and, expand as all of its fourteen hospitals may and do, the applications for admission always outrun its capacity. The investment in hospitals has risen to about $52,000,000, and the annual increase is impressive. There are about 6,500 available beds. There are thirty-two nursing and convalescent homes with approximately 485 beds. A sick person formerly spent the period of his sickness at home. There the nurse, if he had one, resided, and there the doctor called and carried on his professional duties. Generally, the physician today is unacquainted with the home. The patient may come to his office for treatment and counsel, or if the trouble is more serious the doctor will treat him in the hospital where everything is specially arranged for that purpose. The Nashville hospitals are as well-equipped as any in the nation. If some major technique in promoting health is developed anywhere in the world, it will be in use in the hospitals of Nashville in a period impressively brief.

Nashville is a physicians' town. There are 450 of them, or one for every 850 residents. They live their professional lives in hospitals, precision-adjusted in all of their various phases, and in perfectly arranged offices, each subject to its own routine of complications. But there is a secretary or receptionist present of competency to uncomplicate all the issues that arise. The physicians examine, consult, diagnose, and the surgeons among them operate. The verdicts, pronouncements and knives are keen, and the bedside manner is a compound of Hippocrates, Solomon and Enrico Caruso.

Nashville doctors have exercised unusual leadership, as manifested by the selection of six of them as presidents of the American Medical Association: Paul Eve, W. K. Bowling, W. T. Briggs, John A. Witherspoon, W. G. Haggard and H. H. Shoulders. The 450 physicians of Nashville are a major force in the welfare of the city. They offer the least possible co-operation with the morticians, and the most with the census takers.

5

SCENTS FROM THE KITCHEN

NASHVILLE has some very good restaurants, but in all of its career it has had only one that became a password and countersign among diners, only one whose prestige broke across state borders. That was the dining room of the Maxwell House from 1869 to about 1900. In that period it had as much fame as any restaurant in the South, almost as much as any in the country. The shining quality of Maxwell House food remains a stable topic when the conversation turns to dining. Some of the old menu sheets are still available, and the eyes of a true Nashvillian grow warm when he sees one.

Nashville's scarcity of famous dining rooms is a bit odd since its favorite preoccupation is dining. But in a sense this isn't odd at all. The people of Nashville are so well fed at home that they feel no particular dependence on commercial dining rooms. They patronize restaurants when they are shopping, or too busy to go home for lunch, or when for any reason they wish to vary the routine a bit. The town has always been committed to good food and plenty of it. Such food may be found in abundance in Nashville homes.

Some curious premonitions are stirring in the minds of those who regard, almost with fright, any shifting in the good old order. The Latin Americans are most subtly making approaches with their chilis and barbecues, their tamales and frijoles; the Italians with their raviolis and their pizzas; the Germans with their hamburgers and potent sausages; the French with their bouillons and exotic sea foods and sauces. We are under great culinary pressure from these countries and our young are yielding somewhat disturbingly, but in the end they will come back to the foods of their fathers—and mothers. Fried chicken will once more be queen of the table, and syllabub the proper ceremonial at meal's end.

Of course the diners of Nashville are steak-minded. Steak is our national meat. And for very good reasons. Its proteins are most strengthening. A gentleman in Nashville who was becoming a bit overaware of his weight consulted his physician. Should he discontinue his daily rations of steak? By no means. If all the fat was trimmed off, steak would be an excellent reducer. That verdict had reached steak lovers on the opposite side of town before nightfall. Then steak is quite well standardized all over the nation. Good steak may be had almost anywhere, and there are no mysteries involved in its preparation. A great deal of steak is consumed in Nashville with a great deal of appreciation.

Even so, it isn't eulogized with anything like the fervor that Tennessee ham is—that is, true Tennessee ham, Tennessee ham at its best. At its worst it can be most regrettable. But the true lover of Tennessee ham is endowed with a sort of sublimated sixth sense. A Tennessee ham may look all right, but something tells him, that one he should not buy; this one he should. He is not often deceived. The ham that swings so alluringly from a country-store porch may be a beauty and still a villain. The amateur will buy it. The true ham devotee will take the one next to it and make no mistake.

This town is devoted to ham and has been for more than a century. The firm of Martin and McAllister on Broad Street advertised in the *Republican Banner* in February 1847:

> We have for sale one hundred thousand pounds
> of superior and well prepared Tennessee hams.

One wonders where the firm of Martin and McAllister got so many hams. That is a heavy supply for one store. But Martin and McAllister doubtless were not fooled as to their market. Very likely Nashville did an extra bit of feasting then. A Tennessee ham, to deserve the sincere use of the adjective *superior*, has been cured and cared for with great understanding and patience. Such hams, at least in the old days and at the better places, were cured with pomp and ceremony. They were shaped and carved as a sculptor carves. After that they were treated with salt. Though different methods were employed in that treatment there was artistry involved. Some with searching and pliant fingers rubbed the salt into the ham, then covered it with salt for a few days, then cleaned the ham and rubbed it again. Some mixed a little sugar with the salt. The majority merely brought the ham to its most receptive state, and then buried it in the salt. The different schools of procedure in salting have always had one agreement: unless the salt penetrates the bone the curers labor in vain. There perhaps is no *best* method for all hams. All methods, in instances, seem to turn out well. There are sincere ham lovers, particularly in east Tennessee, who prefer their hams unsmoked. The writer has eaten reasonably good ham cured with liquid smoke. The popular demand insists on a thorough smoking with hickory wood, though there are some sections that prefer apple wood, and a few use sassafras. Nashville casts its vote firmly for hickory.

But back to the salt. The hams are left buried in the salt usually three to four weeks, longer if they are very large or the weather unseasonably cold. Then the salt is removed and the ham washed dry. When thoroughly dry the ham is ready for the smokehouse. The thick, acrid, pungent hickory fumes envelop the ham for two weeks—three or even four if the smoke is intermittent. The smoke serves three purposes. It gives the ham a handsomer look; it permeates the meat with a pleasing flavor and fragrance that deepen as time passes; it throws about the ham a protective covering of something chemically related to creosote. The skipper flies arrive hopefully and then depart baffled. Not many middle Tennesseans would buy or want a ham unflavored and unburnished by hickory smoke.

Only scanty records are available dealing with the curing of pork by the pioneers. The earliest one this writer has seen, a mere fragment, was written in 1796, the year that Tennessee was granted statehood: "I begun smoking our porkmeat Monday." At first the settlers lived on fresh meat, of course, mainly wild. But that must have grown tedious and unappetizing. The settlers who established the section might have brought, by way of their fathers and grandfathers from North Ireland, some of the basic processes of curing pork. Very likely they would have learned something from the Indians. The Pennsylvania Dutch, with whom they were neighbors for a while on their westward movement, might have been specially helpful. The Westphalians long before that were well acquainted with the curing of pork. Likely the ancestors of the Pennsylvania Dutch would have shared in the skill of the Westphalians.

It is almost certain that the Scotch-Irish ancestors of the Cumberland settlers picked up some valuable hints from the Dutch. This quotation is from the diary of Mary Coburn DeWeese, written on October 2, 1787: " 'Tis but a few days since my friends in Philadelphia thought I would not be able to reach Kentucky. But believe me when I say that I am now sitting on the bank of the Susquehanna, and now can take my ham and biscuits with the best of them."

The young lady reached Kentucky all right, and now her great-great-grandson, Dr. Herman Lee Donovan, recently retired as president of the University of Kentucky, can take his ham and biscuits with the best of them. So can her great-great-granddaughters, Mrs. Roy Avery and Mrs. Claude Callicott, both of Nashville.

By 1810 a few smokehouses had appeared on Nashville's most progressive premises. The best-known smokehouse in the

South is the one at Andrew Jackson's Hermitage. It was built in 1832. Almost without doubt there was one before it. Where else could the ham that so excited Lafayette in 1825 have come from? The enormous size of that tulip log, hollowed out for salting purposes, proves, if any doubt persists, that ham occupied a place of distinction on that magnificent table in the dining room. Very probably no meat has been cured in that smokehouse for seventy years, and yet such is the unweakening power of hickory smoke that the tang of it is still plain to anyone who leans a bit into the door.

The strategy of curing hams is largely shaped by the weather. Summer and autumn are for fattening hogs (mainly on corn in Kentucky and Tennessee), but when December comes the man with hogs to kill watches eagerly for the wind to veer to the north, and the sky to become hard and grim. Generally he has a dependable prescience in such matters and will know the night before whether the morrow will be a good hog-killing day. He doesn't sleep much, for there is a great deal of preparation to make. The morning dawns cold and nipping. A log fire roars in the killing lot. Large stones piled on the fire rapidly reach the superheated stage. Enough of the heated stones are dunked into a barrel two thirds filled with water to raise it to the scalding point. That is the older method. Now the water is likely to be heated by means less primitive.

A hog freshly killed and bled is lowered into the scalding water for exactly the correct number of minutes. Then the hog is suspended from a rack, head downward, and the hair scraped off cleanly. Next the hog is "dressed," its inward organs removed and cared for. After that it is hung back on the rack, and left to remain there during the night for cooling-out purposes. It is then placed on a table and cut into its conventional parts: hams, shoulders, bacon, etc. The hams are carefully trimmed and shaped and left for twenty-four hours to cool further. They are carefully guarded, though, against freezing, which is likely to damage a ham beyond repair. Then come the salting and smoking sequences. And after that the ham is handed over to the gracious offices of time.

The consensus of Nashville ham eaters holds that the meat reaches the peak of delectability at two years, which really means two summers. A few insist on further maturity. One host recently served, with a royal flourish, a ham ten years old. A good ham will fry well at one year, but it will bake better at two, and a few in Nashville insist that it should be four. The ham is at its best when it slices well without crumbling. Its slices should show richly red with delicate veinings of white. These are made by a finely distilled and distributed sort of fat, without which the flavor is incomplete.

The two principal ways of cooking a ham are frying and baking. Ham for frying should be sliced not too thin—four and not more than five slices to the inch, say the experts. Put the slices in lukewarm water and let them remain there for fifteen minutes, longer if the ham is quite salty. Ham for frying should be ringed well with fat. Sprinkle a thin sifting of brown sugar on the ham. When the skillet is hot start the frying. Rub the slice about on the skillet to spread the frying fat. Cook slowly and turn often, and be very careful not to overcook. When the meat is tender pour on hot coffee for the gravy. Some use water, and a few insist on milk, but milk does not integrate as well in ham gravy as in chicken gravy. The most exacting judges demand coffee.

The preliminary gesture in the preparation of a baked ham is to scrub it with mild soapsuds or with vinegar, using a stiff brush to remove all mold, and a sharp knife on such hard-shell as may have developed. The mold on a ham is sometimes used to illustrate how ignorant a Northerner can be. Every true Southern speaker is likely to use this at any crossroads where he makes a speech: "I once sent a ham to a friend in the North. We didn't hear from him. So after a while we wrote to him asking about the ham, fearing that it had got lost in transit. Then we got a very apologetic letter from him. He hated to tell us, but the ham was spoiled. It was covered with mold when it arrived. There wasn't anything they could do but put it in the garbage." The applause is all that any crossroads speaker could ask for.

Of course the mold is all right. In fact it is a good sign. One of the best ham curers in our section always rubs some mold from an old ham onto one of the newly cured ones to get it properly started. But get the mold off before cooking. Place the ham in tepid water for an hour or so. Then lift it into a large boiler half filled with water. Bring to a boil and immediately reduce the heat. Let simmer an hour for every three or three and a half pounds of ham, turning as often as is convenient. Be careful not to let the water get to a hard boil at any point after the beginning.

When the ham has reached a state of tenderness take the boiler from the stove and let the ham cool in its own liquid. Lift it onto a table and remove the skin. Cover with a skim of brown sugar. A few use sorghum molasses instead. Insert a whole clove on the skinned and scored surface at intervals of an inch. Bake the ham in an oven, using a slow heat until the color is a rich brown, basting it a few times. The brown sugar and the cloves are not intended to add any new flavors, merely to promote and expand those already basic in the ham, and to bring them together into a more pleasing synthesis. The true devotee of a country ham will have nothing to do with alien flavors. Suicide is as immediate in his intentions as placing mustard or catsup or any other kind of dressing on his ham. There are some foods that can be helped by the exotic compounds, but not the Tennessee ham.

The proper carving of a ham is considered one of the gracious arts south of "the rivers," as Mason and Dixon's line is locally referred to. Such a ham should be sliced very evenly and very thin. Alas, the art of slicing is waning a bit, but not yet in tragic degree! The real masters of the art of slicing stand, and no guest worthy of being there ever shifts his eyes from the performance. The artistry is acknowledged by reverent though slight noddings of the head, and sibilant though restrained intakings of breath.

In Nashville's collective mind the proper accompaniments to good ham are the very best of hot biscuits—beaten biscuits, not bought in a store. Sandwiches made of beaten biscuits and thin slices of old ham are generally served at teas and receptions given by society. In the local idiom they are referred to as "ham biscuits." Without them the party would be considered stale and unprofitable. One other thing that fits perfectly on such a table is a large, amber-colored, boat-shaped glass dish filled to capacity with sweet pickled watermelon-rind squares. There are other things of course, but these are what really matter. They give the proper tone to such gatherings.

The old smokehouses are disappearing. The sources of supply of good ham are slowly but surely diminishing. The old smokehouses fall away or go into disuse, and none are being built. Considerable inquiry has not discovered a farm smokehouse built in the last twenty years. A few large ones have been built as commercial ventures, but none of the homey ones of which the owners were so proud in the old days. It is a good and gracious thing to be able to serve ham, well cured and well cooked, to one's friends, but it has become a sort of costly hospitality. The production of a country ham demands a frightening lot of work. Furthermore, the high prices currently offered are so tempting to the farmer who has two or three hams hanging in his attic that he often lets them go. If his family really wants ham he can get two ready-to-eat packing-house hams for the same money that one he has cured will bring. So, in a sense, the taste for country ham is weakening among the very people who developed it.

But some interesting sources of supply have been developed to take care of those who demand the best of ham. An instance is the firm of J. W. Brown, on the Memphis highway, thirty miles from Nashville. In 1899 White Bluff was an un-impressive country village, a status which in some of its phases it has not outgrown. The senior Brown ran a general store, not far from the railroad station. One day the Memphis train was held there for a half hour while a minor wreck ahead of it was repaired. A passenger strolled across to the store to kill time. For some reason he bought the store's only ham and took it home with him. He liked that ham so well that he wrote Brown a note of appreciation. The note stirred something in the Brown mind. That something has been growing for a long time. This year the Browns, sons of that one, expect to cure more than 5,000 hams of fine Tennessee quality, and their customers range from Boston westward to the Hawaiian Islands.

Alloway Brothers in Nashville do not cure hams, but by long and careful observation the members of the firm have spotted the farmers on whose products they can best depend. Mr. Oldham—no punning, we assure you—is in charge of the ham department at Alloway's. These are his words:

"We sell about 1,500 hams a year. In that time we turn down orders for more than four times that many. We have found that we lose by every poor ham we sell. The Tennessee ham has been very good to us. We will do everything we can to protect its reputation."

Warner's, in Nashville, has been handling hams of good quality for more than ninety years. Its sales have diminished steadily, but only because they can't get enough hams measuring up to their standards. The best-looking hams in the section are cured by Ralph Winters of Clarksville, Tennessee. He is an artist in trimming the hams, and he can time the smoking to the best-possible color effects. Milton Roe, sixty miles to the north at Bowling Green, sends a considerable number of excellent hams to Nashville every year. There are perhaps half a dozen high-grade ham specialists in Nashville, but lately they are wearing a baffled look. Where are they going to find the proper hams for their customers?

"There isn't much chance of me being around for fifty years longer," said an old farmer from the county recently, "but if I am there's one thing I won't expect to see, and that's a smokehouse. By then people will be too trifling to have them. A smokehouse means work, and it's getting so we don't like to do any. It's a lot less trouble to go to a grocery store and buy a ham that has had the brine squirted into it."

The smokehouse may be in danger, but the Tennessee ham is too well entrenched in the affections of too many people to be permitted to disappear. The future smokehouse will likely be a large, modern one, with an impressive array of electrical equipment. But it is hoped that somewhere within it there will be an ample supply of hickory wood. Perhaps the Browns, the Winterses and the Roes will have developed easier ways of covering a Tennessee ham with its traditional glory, even of reducing the labor without weakening the flavor. But the Browns and Roes and Winterses will find that there is a quantity beyond which the virtues of the ham will begin to dwindle, a bulk which will mean dilution. A Tennessee ham is the most personal of foods. It should not be allowed to become lost in a crowd.

Even aside from the gift of hams, the hog has been a noble contributor to Nashville's dining tables. Some of the best sausage in the nation is available here. But a sausage lover, no less than a ham lover, should proceed with care. Too much of our sausage isn't good at all. The safest way to learn a dependable brand to stick to is by experience. And that choice has to be reaffirmed every decade or so, since the sausage-making places change managers, and this may make a serious difference. Sausage wouldn't be sausage if it didn't have some sage in it, but not too much sage. Too much might mean carelessness, or it might mean faults worse than too much sage. Sausage needs a little red pepper, but this too must be used with restraint. Leave the hot stuffs for the Latin Americans. Sausage, for Nashville, should have no garlic at all. Salt and sage and pepper are all the flavorings that belong in the best pork sausage, and those measured with care.

In the ante-refrigeration days sausage could be kept well into the summer season by cooking it and storing it in crockery jars, covered with lard—and this was another bit of instruction gained from the Pennsylvania Dutch. We don't have to keep it in lard now. Some superior sausage is made in the outskirts of Nashville, fresh daily.

Spareribs and backbones are weekday favorites here, though lately the butchers and meat dealers have meddled disastrously with the proper proportions of meat and bone, and so have lessened the favor for these comestibles. It may be true, however, that what was lost in backbone was gained in sausage. Sweet potatoes go well with backbones and kraut with spareribs. Kraut has been in Nashville for a century and a half. Almost surely the ancestors of Nashville's pioneers learned to make it from the Pennsylvania Dutch.

Crackling bread has favor here, though its season is brief, and no one would think of eating it daily. It is too rich and heavy for that. It is made by stirring cracklings, a by-product of lard-making, into the corn bread batter.

Spiced round, a great Christmas delicacy, was developed here, and today is not made outside this section. It is red beef, pickled and pleasingly flavored, and artistically threaded with strips of pork fat. The color effect is good and the taste both pleases and surprises.

Nashville is the turnip-greens and hog-jowl center of the universe. These two were used in fitting combination in Nashville by 1810, and the townspeople's appetite for them has not waned. It is likely that at first they were boiled too long, wasting some of their better parts. Then a home-economics fad for semi-rawness came in and took some of our cooks captive. But we got over that. Now we are cooking the greens just about right. Turnip greens, well selected and cooked with carefully chosen hog jowl, served with corn bread and liberal portions of butter and ample glasses of buttermilk, will leave the average citizen of Nashville in a state of uplift. Nowhere are pole beans, cooked with ham hock, better done or held in higher esteem than right here. The beans preferably should be of the Kentucky Wonder variety. The ham hock will take longer to cook, so it is to be boiled awhile before the beans are dropped into the pot. But the beans, no less than the turnip greens, must be thoroughly cooked. One who prefers the other kind would do well to move across the rivers, and so escape the tempest in beans-and-greens pots stirred up by home economists who got their training north of the rivers.

This is a greens town, though at least half of the citizenry use the term *sallet* instead. A great deal of mustard greens is sold in the grocery stores. In late years there has been some market for spinach, and some kale, and an increasing amount of poke greens. This is never cultivated but grows wild in the fields and thickets and is brought in to the stores by the country people. It was very probably the Cherokee salad that so heartened the hungry colonists under John Donelson on the way to establish Nashville. It has to be cooked with great care so as to neutralize the touch of toxicity that exists in its raw state.

Since the time of its founding Nashville has been loyally committed to sassafras tea. This is brewed from the root of the red sassafras. Its season very well conforms with that of the turnip greens and poke, and it goes well with them. It was held in high value by the early settlers as a spring tonic. I remember hearing my grandmother say many times, "Sassafras tea thins the blood out of its winter thickness." When in season sassafras root is for sale by every store in town. It is pleasing to the taste, and its color is delightful. Lately an enterprising firm of moderns has developed and offered for sale an *instant* sassafras tea. Its future remains a bit obscure.

This is an Irish-potato town, as are most towns. There is a vast amount of French frying done in the restaurants, but in the homes the preferred method remains mashing, whipping, adding salt and butter and a little cream, and then baking in the oven until the top is a rich brown. Potatoes so prepared go well with fried chicken, and the fried-chicken gravy goes well with the potatoes. Potatoes of adolescent size are a great favorite when boiled with pole beans.

Nashville is a fried-chicken town. It can claim very little uniqueness in that since most towns, and specially most Southern towns, are fried-chicken towns. Fried chicken had become a staple long before the Civil War. Since then the consumption has increased a great deal faster than can be explained by the increase in population. Fried chicken used to be available not more than three months a year. It may now be had in abundance during the entire year. Chicken raising has multiplied within reasonable bounds in Tennessee, but the chicken-growing area of northeast Georgia, where the yield is simply incredible, is within easy trucking distance of Nashville. Also, since the business is carried on with care and science the old troubles are avoided and the meat is much finer and cleaner. Chicken today is the cheapest meat available.

It is four years from the time the pig is born until the ham is in prime state for eating; two and a half years from the time the calf is born until the porterhouse is ready. The chicken requires about six weeks. The frying chicken sells for about thirty-five cents a pound, dressed for cooking; the ham in comparable state of preparation for about two dollars. The ham which used to be regarded as standard for two meals a day is now a luxury, and regarded as such. Fried chicken while not quite routine will be served very likely two or three times a week. Chicken is fried as well in Nashville as anywhere in the nation. It is not a hurry-up performance, and the diner who expects snappy service had better adjust his appreciation to hot dogs. For the best Nashville results the chicken is fried in a large heavy skillet. A small amount of grease—bacon fat is a favorite here—is placed in the skillet, and when it is hot, the chicken, floured a bit, is put in. It is fried very slowly and turned very often, and the lid is placed on the skillet during the final period of cooking. Nashville is inordinately fond of the gravy which skill and devotion can coax from good chicken. The essences of the chicken commingle with the bacon fat or lard, flour and milk are stirred in, and the gravy let sizzle long enough to cook the flour. The best of hot biscuits can be used as a very proper common carrier for many things. For instance, blackberry jam; for further instance, fried-chicken gravy. Or the gravy may be used to give mashed potatoes a multiplied delight.

Without baked ham and fried chicken there naturally would have been no church meetings with "dinner on the ground," one of the most beloved of all Southern social phenomena, though now fading into the distance. After diligent search one may still find one out in the sub-suburbs. There are much singing and much preaching in the morning. Whether the preachers have learned the signs the hard way, or whether they are hungry too, it doesn't much matter. By half after eleven the sermons begin to draw to a close: "And finally, brethren . . ." or "In closing let me say . . ."

Some of the ladies have been out near the tables all the time, and by the time the preacher's *amen* has softened into silence all the other ladies are scampering toward them. Each lady knows the table assigned to her and heads for it. Ensues the business of spreading the cloths, of opening the baskets, of putting dishes into place, of spooning the food into the dishes when needed, and of placing those dishes with art and artfulness. The lady prepared that food in her own kitchen. She knows that it is good and she is proud of it. She does not wish its virtues to be obscure, but instead to appeal specially to all who cast an eye on it. And in the matter of eye-casting there will be experts present and in action. She brought the food to be eaten and appreciated. She will go down in defeat if it isn't.

Brother So-and-So says a long and fervent grace, the fervor more esteemed than the length.

And then begins the business of dining. The lady stands by her table and serves all comers, keeping an anxious eye on any dish not much in demand. With dedication and salesmanship she offers that dish to all who are in a manifest state of indecision. The supply of fried chicken goes into a rapid diminuendo. Those churches develop fried-chicken-eating congregations. Her husband stands at her side in an alert pose. She motions him to the ham, and he starts slicing, stopping every third or fourth slice to whet his slicing knife a few strokes. It was a whole ham to begin with, and the diners spot it quickly. The normal quota is two pieces of fried chicken and a slice of ham. A thirteen-year-old daughter stands with her parents and she gives out the pickles, green, crisp and translucent, with sweet and sour balanced delectably.

The lady turns a furtive eye on the adjoining table. It also is bountifully supplied with fried chicken, but instead of ham there is barbecued lamb. The lady measures the demand to discover whether her ham is as popular as the lamb on the next table. Plates of corn light bread are placed conveniently for the diners to help themselves. The daughter puts down the pickles and takes up a great dish of potato salad. This is a comparative newcomer in the Nashville country, brought in by the German emigrants in the 1870s, but it caught on fast. Potato salad is now a staple for basket meetings, picnics, back-yard dining and Sunday night suppers. Corn light bread is rarely found outside a hundred-mile radius with Nashville as its center, but it is a noble achievement.

The mistress of a table at a basket meeting would suffer from a feeling of incompleteness if there rested on her table no great bowl or platter of deviled eggs. The deviled part adds to the native flatness of the eggs a sweet, sour, spicy tang that tends to be habit-forming.

The people of the Nashville area are avowed partisans of the pickle. Pickle making begins in July when the cucumber crop is at its peak. It continues through the watermelon-rind season in August. It reaches its noblest efforts in September when it is seen that the green tomatoes on the vines will not attain a satisfactory ripeness. So they are gathered and made into sliced green tomato pickles which the experts—of whom there are many in Nashville—can turn into one of the most satisfying condiments ever placed on a table. But the green tomatoes not large enough for slicing are not wasted. They are chopped or ground, and compounded with chopped peppers, cauliflower, cabbage, vinegar, sugar, cinnamon, etc., and cooked into something that can add year-round piquancy to dining. The smell of it being prepared emerges from the kitchen, makes its way through the house, and out onto the street to inspire hope and cheer in the passers-by. One of Nashville's choice cooks, Mrs. Henry Goodpasture, can make pickles that are purely inspired from the succulent poke stalks brought in from the woods and fence rows.

Let us now give thought to the desserts. The first and middle parts of the meal have been good. Nothing must happen now to weaken that delight. Almost all of the nation's communities are pie centers. Nashville is one of the greatest. We made and served main-course meat pies before we went into the making of fruit pies, or the early forms of custard pies. Our first use of fruit in a pie was in the form of a primitive sort of cobbler. Gradually we improved the cobbler and it became a prime favorite. We made peach cobblers, damson cobblers, blackberry cobblers and gooseberry cobblers. The most delightful dessert this reporter holds in memory was a damson cobbler. Such can be made only by one skilled and devoted. The chess pie, if not first developed in Nashville as seems likely, reached here very early. It is of the custard posterity, and to have feasted on one properly made is a memorable event. Homes not blessed with the best of cooks can buy chess pies at a few of the stores. One department store with a special fondness for chess pies and aptness in making them has sold as many as 4,000 on a single Saturday.

This is of course an apple-pie town. One of the oldest and best restaurants closed not long ago on account of the age of the proprietors. The place had a great local reputation for its apple pies, and the owners were able to sell its recipe to a rival restaurant for a considerable sum. The average Nashville diner wants to eat apple pie for lunch five days a week, to feast on chess pie on Sunday, and to experiment with the other pies the remaining day. There is some favor for lemon custard pies. Mince pie fits well into certain meals, but its season is brief, and even then it is not likely to offer serious competition to apple and chess. November is the pumpkin-pie month, and it is in some demand at Christmas. The pumpkin pie is at its best when the pumpkin flavor is held under severe control. The hint of the pumpkin is much better than the certainty of it.

Nashville has been a cake town since wheat flour became available, which was some time about 1795. By the middle of the last century it was a cake town indeed. At a Monday-afternoon reception given by the Hardings at Belle Meade for Mrs. James K. Polk in March 1861, six kinds of cake was served: chocolate cake, ribbon cake, lady cake, devil cake, Italian cake and angel cake, great towering cakes befitting the magnificence of the estate and the dignity of the honor guest. At the head of this array sat in regal splendor a large crystal bowl, filled with something the surface of which was rigid with creamy folds and corrugations. It was syllabub, pure cream, delicately flavored and whipped with Madeira wine. Oddly and sadly enough we do not have syllabub any more, but it was a great delicacy then. Those people who spend a great deal of time fondly regarding the past and speculating on its institutions explain the loss of syllabub by affirming that it could be made only by one called, and that no calls have been issued for three quarters of a century.

When the reception was given for Mrs. Polk, Susannah was making syllabub at Belle Meade. Susannah was a "called" syllabub maker, as everyone, including Susannah herself, knew perfectly well. When she made syllabub fear fell upon her helpers. The egg beater rose and fell in majestic rhythm. At precisely the proper second the Madeira wine was poured in very slowly. Then the beater again was put on its circuit, though then it moved with a folding motion. Susannah stopped the beater with the stroke that wrought perfection. One less and the syllabub would have been thin and watery; one too many and it would have been tough and leathery. Nashville still has the cakes, but the syllabub rests with honor in the archives in which are stored man's lost blessings. There are no more Susannahs.

Boiled custard for more than a century has been a great favorite in Nashville. Almost every housewife prides herself on her custard-making art. But it is not a standardized performance. There are about as many ways of making boiled custard as there are housewives, and every one of them may turn out a good product.

There have been many great dinners served in Nashville. As a matter of fact a number of great dinners are served daily in Nashville with no benefit of publicity whatever. But some have gone into the place's history. Also there have been some great suppers and some great breakfasts. Miss Jane Thomas in her celebrated account of old Nashville's people and events tells of a Christmas breakfast of which the menu was: sausages, baked spareribs, quail, hominy, light bread, hot biscuits, coffee, chocolate and milk. She also mentions that the breakfasters proved their appreciation by their performance. Protein-laden breakfasts were popular in the old days, and perhaps sensible. A lot of work stretched out from breakfast.

One of the city's most colorful dinners was served at the home of Jacob McGavock on Cherry Street, though in a manner of speaking the dinner was untrue to Nashville. Also, too few of the details are available. McGavock's father-in-law, Felix Grundy, had just been elected to the United States Senate, and to celebrate with a flourish in the grand manner all the members of the legislature were invited. Doubtless a carefully selected group from Nashville's elite was included. The dinner, every item of it, was prepared in New Orleans and delivered by fast steamboat. We do not have the menu, and that is troubling, but there do exist personal descriptions of the affair. The house was a large one with double parlors on the first floor, and corresponding rooms on the second. The upstairs rooms, joined by wide folding doors, were used for the dinner. The doors were opened to their widest so as to get the maximum space. In each room the tables were set in the form of a cross, and the foot of the tables joined where they met in the doorway. At the junction place was a pyramid of jelly glasses at least three feet tall. The dinner was a brilliant affair, but it might be reasonably guessed that the guests returned home that night vaguely wishing that there had been a slice of Tennessee ham among the delicacies from New Orleans. Also the commentaries of some of the rural lawmakers as they wended their ways homeward might have been worth recording.

In November 1837, Dr. and Mrs. Felix Robertson served a dinner to thirty of their friends, of which this was the menu: "soup, very rich and highly seasoned, and with much rice; two very large boiled fishes, elegantly cooked and served with creamed Irish potatoes, bread and pickles; a large boiled ham at one end of the table, and a great roast of beef at the other; all kinds of winter vegetables and pickles (cucumbers, mangoes, sweet peaches, watermelon-rind squares, etc.). Desserts: apple pies, custard pies, cakes and jellies. Drinks: coffee, tea and milk."

In May 1857, the physicians of the nation held their annual national convention in Nashville. The final and crowning event of the convention was the banquet served to the doctors in the brand-new Capitol, and it was done in the grand manner. The arrangements made for seating remain obscure. It is doubtful whether any caterer today could place 3,000 diners in that building, but the ladies in charge did. The food was cooked in Nashville kitchens and kept hot when necessary over pits contrived on the Capitol grounds. We can have no doubt that those kitchens were at their best, but we can only guess at what was prepared in them. We can only guess also at the mode of transporting that food from those kitchens to the hill, and at the serving. Obviously everything was well handled.

But Nashville piled another Pelion of excitement on that Ossa dinner for the doctors. Gaslights blazed from the Capitol's chandeliers that night. It was Nashville's first use of gas for lighting. The word of it got about and the populace, almost as one man, congregated about the building, and a few of the bolder ones got inside. The feasting Knights of the Saddlepockets offered some interest, but the people had seen doctors eat before. The lights were what they had climbed the hill to see. And as far as the records go the audience offered the feasting doctors not the slightest interruption.

The first passenger train on the Louisville & Nashville Railroad reached Nashville on October 28, 1859. It was too significant an event to go unheralded. The city celebrated with a great basket dinner held out in Ramsey's Grove, in Edgefield. The food, except that barbecued at the Grove, was prepared in Nashville's kitchens. The press reported that 4,500 people went home sated with food worthy of kings, and greatly excited because "the railroad, filled with the spirit of the occasion, stationed an engine at a point on the track nearest the Grove and arranged with an engineer to blow the whistle during the event."

On July 16, 1889, the National Education Association opened its thirty-second annual convention in Nashville. There were more than 5,000 visitors, including all the names that really were names. There were trips to the Hermitage, to Belle

Meade and to other spots of distinction. The great day was Tuesday when a mammoth barbecue was given the out-of-towners, plus 1,000 citizens, out in Richland Park on the Charlotte Pike. Those assembled were welcomed long and earnestly by Governor Robert L. Taylor, himself no mean practitioner of the fine art of welcoming. But this was only the beginning. State Superintendent Frank M. Smith added further and ample welcome, and closed his address with the rendition of a poem written by Mrs. Odie Newhouse. The third address of welcome was by Mayor C. P. McCarver. Then Miss Finnegan read an original poem, "Tennessee's Welcome." Address of welcome number four was extended by Professor W. R. Garrett, who represented the teachers of Tennessee, and not with unbecoming brevity. There was then a musical interlude, a welcome in music played by the Total Abstinence Band. To the compounded greeting thus extended replies were made by Dr. A. R. Marable, of Worcester, Massachusetts, president of the National Education Association, by ex-President W. E. Shelton, by Secretary J. H. Canfield and *seven* others.

Consider, please, the situation: fourteen addresses, two original poems, some numbers of stirring music, a hungry audience and a royal Tennessee barbecue waiting in a grove hard by. A tragic picture, indeed. The best barbecue cooks of middle Tennessee had been commandeered for that day, and the tables groaned beneath the yield of their art. There were barbecued mutton and pork in ample supply for all. There were corn bread, ice-cold buttermilk, lemonade and nine kinds of pie. The newspaper had them listed. *Nine!*

The Ladies Hermitage Association always gives a breakfast to honor a visiting President. Eight Presidents have sat for breakfast at that magnificent dining table. It is always a breakfast because that was Andrew Jackson's favorite meal, and a faithful effort is made to serve the menu that he found most pleasing. In October 1907, President Theodore Roosevelt was in Nashville to attend a meeting with the other trustees of Peabody College. So he was invited to a breakfast out at the Hermitage, and while there he coined an immortal phrase. The master of ceremonies was Joel Cheek, a Kentuckian who had come down to Nashville to make his fortune. His product, Maxwell House Coffee, was rising rapidly in the national esteem. In the middle of the breakfast Mr. Cheek couldn't resist the temptation to plug his coffee a bit. He leaned over and asked the President how he liked the coffee. With characteristic quickness came the reply: "It's good to the last drop." The coffeeman had the wit to see the value of those words, so he set them to staring from all the country's billboards.

Nashville is now, and always has been, food-minded. But time has brought a new sort of democracy into her kitchens. The cook, when there is one, isn't in as supreme command as she used to be. The lady herself now goes to the food stores for the things she needs. She likes to look at the food on the grocery counters and shelves. She likes to give thought to the fruit and vegetables in the cooling bins. She likes to study the price tags, and to measure what she sees against the quality she has seen in other stores. She likes to meet clumps of other ladies in the aisles and hold forums on foods and cooking and child rearing. She is in most instances an avid student of cookery.

Nashville is one of the best cookbook markets in the nation, and there is at least a one-foot shelf of cookbooks in every kitchen. They range from that to a five-foot shelf for each of the ladies who really wish to survey the field. The town's housewives are not only vigorously competitive but vigorously co-operative as well. The lady does not hoard her choice recipes. She shares them with her fellow housewives. But sometimes there is a lady of the other sort. This story, presumed to be true, is of one who served a fine new pudding at her luncheon. It caused a great deal of favorable comment by the invited guests. Her friends expected a copy of the recipe, but they didn't get it. For a week they waited expectantly, but with no results. Then one of the most aggressive asked her for it.

"That's my secret," said the hostess, smiling sweetly.

But her smile faded when her outraged neighbor hired the cook right out of her kitchen.

Almost always a new dish causing favorable attention has rapid circulation in Nashville. "No sense in keeping a recipe secret," said one lady. "The thing to do is to outcook the others."

The grocery stores are moving nearer Nashville's kitchens, but not very fast. In most cases the ham is bought uncooked, and the rite of cooking performed in the kitchen by the lady herself. In no other way can she develop her greatest pride, and that of her family, in the dinner. The cake may have had its beginning in a bakery, but the chances are that it was baked in the kitchen. The ready-mixes, and they are reasonably good, are for those in a hurry. They do save some time, but the product is definitely not so good. The canned soups are good enough for the rush hours, but any good Nashville cook can give personality to a soup that never emerged from a can. Corned-beef hash is all very well for those rushing to meet a deadline, but a Nashville cook can make hash which serves nobler ends than merely to stock the stomach with the required starch and protein. Certainly there is a can opener in every kitchen, but it lasts well.

Perhaps bread has yielded to modernity faster than any other item. There is a lot of bread purchased from chain-store shelves, but the hoecakes, the corn pones, the hot biscuits, the corn light bread are still native to the kitchen.

Young Nashville, like Young Everywhere-Else, is likely to bring in a minority report favoring unlimited distribution of hamburgers, hot dogs, frankfurters, barbecues and the like, all drenched in torrid compounds. But when the fever of their youth has quieted they will return to the fried ham, hot biscuits and blackberry jam of their mothers.

The kitchen is still the most active room in a Nashville house, the room most relevant to making it a home.

6

THE SPIRES STAND HIGH

NASHVILLE has been a religious city since the Founders reached here on Christmas Day, 1779. That very day they listened to a sermon preached by a pioneer layman. It was a sermon of thanksgiving. They had come triumphantly through great tribulation, and were grateful for their safe arrival.

Nashville has been a center of the church since the arrival of Presbyterian Thomas B. Craighead, late in 1783. He was a remarkable man, a little liberal in his views for the time in which he lived, but a man of learning and goodness. He was born in Pennsylvania. In 1771 he entered the College of New Jersey, the president of which was the great classicist and theologian, John Witherspoon. Young Craighead was graduated with honors in the class of 1775. He located in North Carolina, with sundry preaching engagements in Lancaster County, South Carolina. It is more than merely possible that there he met Andrew Jackson, since the lad's mother at the time was living with her people, the Crawfords, in the neighborhood. His next station was the ministry of the pioneer Presbyterian church at Frankfort, Kentucky. It was there that he met and married Elizabeth Brown, daughter of the Reverend John Brown, one of the great preachers and schoolmasters of the Virginia valley. Dr. John Brown, also one of President Witherspoon's young men, was the ancestor of the Browns of established fame in and about Lexington, Virginia; Lexington, Frankfort and Louisville, Kentucky; and Nashville and Maury County, Tennessee.

Dr. Craighead came to the settlement of Nashville to preach to its Presbyterians. Two years later he became president of Davidson Academy, chartered by the legislature of North Carolina in 1785 in response to a plea by James Robertson, the Founder. The academy was never large but the work it did was impressive, and from such records as exist its curriculum was easily on the present college level. Dr. Craighead lived, preached, taught, died and is buried two hundred yards from the one-room stone building which served as academy and Presbyterian church.

Since Craighead's time the people of Nashville have been building churches and worshiping in them until now the place is well filled with them. Many of the nation's great pulpit voices have resounded in Nashville churches, and many of the nation's great guides and philosophers in religious work have labored in Nashville. Great visions have been glimpsed here; here great doctrines have been put into words. Ecclesiastical wars have been waged here in the name of God. But when their tempests sank into calm the same still small voice could be heard speaking.

The shadowed days and years through which the city has lived seem to have deepened its devotion. Churches lie thick on Nashville's map. Its commitment to their varied and manifold work is carried on with zeal and consecration. This is the fringe of the "Bible Belt," a phrase usually used ironically and irreverently. Nashville accepts it both proudly and humbly. It has had its part in giving sincere meaning to the phrase.

Nashville is the natural center of a great area whose first settlers were the Scotch-Irish. Their religious zeal, fierce at times, is reflected observably, though perhaps less audibly, in that of their posterity. The Scotch-Irishman was a strenuous competitor in any activity in which he engaged, and specially those of his church. He was, to begin with, a Presbyterian, and as such he laid the community's foundations. Sometimes he found his fellow Presbyterians so unyielding that he withdrew from them and became a Methodist, sometimes a Baptist, rather often a Cumberland Presbyterian, sometimes a Disciple. Generally, indeed, if he left the Presbyterians he went to another church, and in that group set a pattern of stubbornness.

Nashville has been, and in large part remains, Protestant. In that it is merely following its inheritance. The town was forty-one years old when the first Catholic group arrived. It was seventy years old when services were first held here by members of the Jewish faith. It should be said here that both of these religious beliefs have flourished.

In Nashville religion and education have gone very well together. In its long history there have been infrequent times when each was a trifle suspicious of the other but these differences faded out as understanding grew. There are here now six colleges affiliated with churches. These colleges are in the nature of both effect and cause. The churches needed the colleges for their protection and perpetuity. The colleges in turn have tended to multiply the churches and to intensify interest in them. It is in these colleges that young preachers are likely first to appear. From these colleges the pulpits draw their culture, their discipline in thought and pronouncement and their deeper understanding.

More Christian literature is published in Nashville than in any other center in the world. More than a decade before the war Dr. Alexander Little Page Green, of the Methodist faith, moved by the belief that the printed page has creative influence which lasts and spreads, set efforts in motion that resulted in the establishment of the Methodist Publishing Company. That only set a pattern and a challenge for the other churches. Now on every working day in the year an infinity of pages are printed in Nashville under the sponsorship of the churches. These published materials give coherence, guidance and challenge to the churches of a great area, in fact of the nation.

Almost all of the founders were Presbyterians. The exceptions, few to begin with, started growing before many years passed. After Dr. Craighead, the next Presbyterian minister was Dr. William Hume, who reached the settlement in 1801. He was born on August 15, 1770, near Dumfries in Scotland. He was a grand-nephew of David Hume, the philosopher, and a first cousin of Joseph Hume, the surgeon and politician. It is quite likely that he was an acquaintance of Robert Burns, who died in Dumfries four years before Hume sailed for America. Dumfries was a small town, and William Hume was greatly fond of poetry. Surely he had managed an acquaintance with the immortal poet. He attended the University of Edinburgh for three years but did not remain to be graduated. He became convinced that he was called to the ministry, and in 1800 he was ordained by the Secession Church. That year he offered himself for such missionary service as the Presbytery of Kirkaldy might direct. An assignment was not long coming. He was sent to a settlement in America's southwestern wilderness.

He set out at once. He landed in New York, traveled by stagecoach to Pittsburgh, thence by river to Cincinnati. He crossed the Ohio into Kentucky and spent a little while with Kentucky's great Presbyterian pioneer, Dr. David Rice. There was much of which the two could talk. Undoubtedly Rice was eager to hear echoes of the latest theological thunders in the Scottish heavens, or for that matter any comment on the words and deeds of Scotsmen. Hume surely yearned to learn of the ways of the new country to which Destiny had assigned him.

There was a matter both serious and humorous which he had to explain to Rice. A Scottish dignitary had entrusted him with a cheese to bring to the Kentuckian. But it was a cheese that Rice was never permitted to see. The customs officer at New York demanded the payment of duty. Hume had very little money and he needed all of it. He had brought the cheese in full faith of its welcome in the new country. The customs officer was kindly disposed. He would waive the tax if the missionary would claim that he brought it as food. The Scotsman's stubborn honesty would not resort to such a subterfuge. So the cheese remained with the collector.

Dr. Hume reached Nashville in the spring of 1801. It was henceforth to be his home. The Secession group seems to have disappeared by 1818. That year Hume united with the Presbyterian Church of the United States. There was a great deal of stress and poverty for him to face and he did it with humble but unswerving courage. He never spoke harshly to anyone, nor ill of anyone. There is no record of a complaint coming from him, and yet at times he was denied the very necessities. There can be no doubt that often he was filled with a great longing for the sights of Scotland, for the sound of its voices and of the Scottish pipes skirling in the glens. But he knew that he was not likely ever again to see Scotland. Dear as it was, it was too far away. Nashville had become his home and its people his people.

In 1808 he was elected instructor in mathematics and foreign languages in Cumberland College. So he added teaching to preaching. In 1816 he became principal of the Nashville Female Academy, then but a year old. He held that position until his death in 1833. He taught and administered, but continued to preach whenever and wherever the need existed. For all of his gentleness he became close friends with some of the section's most vigorous spirits. The London *Observer* in its issue of March 1825 commented sharply, indeed angrily, on the tendencies of General Andrew Jackson, only recently defeated for the Presidency. Within the year the *Observer* printed this reply from Dr. Hume:

Permit me to mention that I am sorry that you have formed a bad, and I think, erroneous opinion of General Jackson. You state that, "Perhaps it was for the peace of the world that the presidency of the United States was reserved for a less violent spirit." I am persuaded that even a slight personal acquaintance would induce you to alter your opinion. I am honored with his friendship. He is one of the most upright men in the United States. I know his moral and religious principles. They correspond to what you teach. I officiate as minister of the Presbyterian church which he, in connection with a few of his neighbors, lately built. He is not at all disposed to disturb the peace of the world.

General Jackson's feelings for Dr. Hume were similarly cordial. In a letter written to his wife while he was away from home the General said:

I am truly happy that our church is about finished, and that pious and good man, Dr. Hume is to dedicate it. If such a man's prayers cannot obtain a blessing upon the neighborhood I would despair of the efficacy of prayer from any other.

A minister meets with a great many circumstances which, while they do not shake his faith, leave him shaken. Dr. Hume performed the ceremony of Governor Sam Houston's ill-fated marriage, in 1829, to Miss Allen of Gallatin. The life of the marriage was distressingly brief. When it had come to its tragic end, and Houston had resigned the governorship and was leaving for the West, he sent for Dr. Hume. What he wanted was the blessing which was then the custom for the minister to give those about to depart on portentous undertakings. The preacher inquired if there were Biblical grounds for the separation. Houston replied that it was a matter he would discuss with no one.

"Then I am not authorized to administer my blessing," said Hume and immediately withdrew. Later in the day Governor Houston, accompanied by Dr. Obadiah Jennings, minister of the Presbyterian church in Nashville, visited Dr. Hume with the repeated request. Again there was the inquiry as to scriptural warrant. For the second time the doughty Houston refused any explanation. Dr. Hume might be gentle and mild, but he never yielded a matter of religious or personal principle. He never saw Sam Houston again.

In 1806 William Hume married Rebecca Andrews, who had lately come to Nashville from North Carolina. They had eleven children and their posterity is still important in the section. From that day till this few major enterprises in Nashville have failed to bear the Hume imprint. As to the nature of the man let Edwin Ewing testify in an address, delivered in 1885:

He was a man of learning, a man of sense and general worth. He was a most laborious and painstaking teacher, and altogether the gentlest and most amiable of human beings. Many a trick and villainy was practiced upon him by the turbulent and mischievous boys at Cumberland College. These he always bore with meekness and forbearance that often disarmed them and shamed them. Once Dr. Hume's only horse—Old Roan, we used to call it—disappeared. Some days later he met an impudent ruffian on the street mounted on Old Roan, but Dr. Hume said nothing to him. When asked why, he said that he was afraid he would wound the man. Dr. Hume did not leave any writings as did his kinsmen in Scotland, but he left his good marks upon those times.

When Dr. Hume took up teaching, some of the ministerial labors he had been performing were perforce left undone. It was then that Dr. Gideon Blackburn entered the Nashville scene. Hume continued to guide and counsel the new minister for the four years he served the Nashville congregation. The two men were of a common consecration. Otherwise they were very different. Hume was small physically and a modest man. Blackburn was large, powerful and of great militancy, and was always thinking up something new and novel. His voice was resonant and of enough volume to carry any reasonable distance. He preached long sermons, rarely under two hours, and there is record of one sermon that lasted almost four hours, and with no loss of attention.

He was born in Augusta County, Virginia, and when he was twenty he was licensed to preach at Abingdon. He was graduated at Hampden Sidney College. He struck out into the wilderness and in time came to Franklin, Tennessee. He liked the place and founded a church there and Harpeth Academy, which grew into considerable fame. Then he went on to Nashville to become the first minister of the church, dedicated in 1816. Later he served as president of Center College in Kentucky. But his fondness for the new and novel didn't stand him in good stead there. He supplemented the liberal-arts phase of the college with some courses in practical agriculture. But it didn't stay supplemented, and he moved on to establish Blackburn College in the new country of Illinois. His service in Nashville remains a fine pioneer tradition.

Dr. Alan Campbell was the church's minister from 1820 until 1828. Nor was Dr. Campbell afraid of something new. It was early in his ministry that Mrs. Felix Grundy, after a conference with her pastor, organized and taught the first Sunday school ever held in Nashville. The idea was so new that it aroused considerable comment in the town, not only comment but serious opposition as well. The Sunday school was held in a small frame building not far from the main church. Another church not far distant carried this sign on its front: "No desecration of the Holy Sabbath by teaching on the Sabbath in this church." But the pastor and most of the Presbyterians stood by Mrs. Grundy.

Within a decade the McKendree Methodist Church had organized a Sunday school. The Sunday school was slow in reaching a few of the churches, but by the Civil War it was a definite part of worship in Nashville.

Dr. Obadiah Jennings succeeded Dr. Campbell. His pastorate lasted till his death in 1832. He was born in New Jersey in 1778. He manifested leadership both in school and college. He studied law and for a while practiced with a fair amount of success. When he was thirty-five he decided to go into the Presbyterian ministry. Three years later he was licensed to preach. For eleven years he preached in churches in Pennsylvania and Ohio. Then he came to the church in Nashville.

Dr. Jennings was a man of kindly nature but rugged in debate. In 1830 to his own surprise he found himself drawn into a theological debate with the great Alexander Campbell. The debate was held on Christmas Day and was planned to last four hours. It lasted twelve. Noon came and no one left. A great deal of excellent food went uneaten that day. Under the power of the speakers hunger was forgotten.

A daughter of Dr. Jennings married George Campbell Childress who moved to Texas and was prominent in the struggle for freedom from Mexico. It was Childress who wrote the Texas Declaration of Independence. Dr. Jennings' son studied medicine and became one of the city's leading physicians and surgeons. He was for several years a member of the staff of the University of Nashville's College of Medicine. Dr. Jennings' funeral sermon was preached by Dr. William Hume, who a year later followed him to the grave.

Perhaps the greatest Presbyterian preacher of the city's history was Dr. John Todd Edgar, pastor from 1833 to 1860. He was born in Delaware in 1792. He was graduated from the College of New Jersey in 1816. In 1827 he became minister of the Presbyterian church in Frankfort, Kentucky, and remained there six years. While there he and the great Henry Clay became close friends. The substance and the eloquence of Dr. Edgar's sermons were appealing to Nashville generally, and almost every Sunday a large number of visitors supplemented his congregation. One Presbyterian asked in a humorous and friendly manner, "Don't the Methodists have services on Sunday? I noticed a lot of their members here today." Dr. Edgar and General Jackson were very friendly, and the preacher had much part in the General's conversion. He baptized him into the church and a few years later preached his funeral sermon. Dr. Edgar died suddenly on the evening of November 13, 1860, and so was spared the great strain of the following years. He was succeeded by Dr. Joseph Bardwell, who had been his assistant for a year.

After the occupation by the Federal forces, early in 1862, the church building was used for hospital purposes until the close of the war. Then Dr. Robert Bunting was called as pastor. He accepted and remained for three years. He had been chaplain of a Texas regiment during most of the war. He was a man of enormous energy, untiring in his visits to both sick and well, and greatly committed to breaking across congregational lines in his zeal to be of service.

This story has been told to illustrate Dr. Bunting's activity: A country preacher was in Nashville for the first time, and the thing he wanted most was to make Dr. Bunting's acquaintance. He made his way to the preacher's office. He was told that the pastor was calling on Brother Foster, who was sick. The visitor found his way to Brother Foster's house. Dr. Bunting had just left to see Brother Adams who, too, was sick. He was informed at the Adams house that Dr. Bunting had just left for the house of Brother Baxter, another sick man. But he wasn't at the Baxter home. He had just left for Brother Seay's.

"I wish I could meet him," said the visitor, "but I don't think I can ever catch up with him."

Brother Baxter spoke from the bed. "Hurry over to the Seays'. Sister Seay is the one who is sick, and Dr. Bunting always prays longer with a woman."

Dr. Bunting was called to a church in Galveston in 1868, and was succeeded by Dr. Thomas Verner Moore. He was a minister of great distinction, but he died after three years of service. Dr. Henry van Dyke preached during a pastoral intermission of several months. In 1873 Dr. Thomas Hoyt of New York was installed as pastor. He was a man of extensive literary culture, most energetic and zealous in his preaching. He was, so the record affirms, "specially popular with the plain people." In 1880 he served as General Moderator of the Presbyterian Church. He withdrew in 1883.

In March 1884 Dr. Jere Witherspoon began a ministry which lasted a fruitful decade. He was a kinsman of John Witherspoon, Signer of the Declaration of Independence. Dr. Witherspoon resigned in 1893.

A year later Dr. James I. Vance succeeded him. He was by birth an East Tennessean, a graduate of King College and Union Theological Seminary. He had preached in Wytheville, Alexandria and Norfolk, Virginia. His ministry was so popular and prosperous that the congregation was greatly distressed when he resigned to take a church in Newark, New Jersey.

Dr. William H. Anderson, a native of Gibson County, Tennessee, and a graduate of Southwestern Presbyterian, followed him at Nashville. Dr. Anderson had preached for a church in South Carolina, and for five years for the First Church at Dallas. He remained in Nashville almost ten years. In that time, by his own record, he preached 1,920 sermons, baptized 336, performed 453 marriage ceremonies and conducted 387 funerals. He was a versatile man. He could preach well, of course, and he could also sing well. He played the violin a little and the piano with some brilliance. He returned to the Dallas church in 1910, and immediately Dr. Vance returned to Nashville.

No minister could have fitted the needs of the church better than Dr. Vance. There was about him the traditional asceticism of the preacher. He was serious even to the point of grimness. He was a learned man, alert and sensitive to whatever need arose in the church. The golden era of the church was the Edgar ministry. The second in importance was the second pastorate of Dr. Vance.

In that period occurred the church's Centennial, held November 8 to 15, 1914. It was a week of rejoicing and feasting, of great preaching and solemn worship, of giving thanks for a century of divine favor. Dr. Vance died in 1939 and was succeeded by Dr. Thomas Barr, who had been his assistant. Dr. Barr was pastor for six years and then resigned to take charge of the newly founded Trinity Presbyterian Church. In this work he continues.

Dr. Walter Courtenay, at that time pastor of a church in Neenah, Wisconsin, was called to his place. During his early period a movement to remove the church to a site outside the city was undertaken. A majority voted to make the move. A determined minority refused to accept the decision and bought the historic property from the majority. And so the separation was made. The majority moved to Oak Hill, eight miles south of the city on the Franklin Pike, Dr. Courtenay continuing as pastor. Those remaining in the Old Church rechristened themselves the Downtown Presbyterian Church. Dr. W. D. Gray, of Middlesboro, Kentucky, was chosen pastor. The building is more than eleven decades old, but it stands with impressive dignity on a site chosen in 1814. There is about it a curious and pleasing reminiscence of Nashville's lifelong commitment to worship.

The Second Presbyterian Church was started as a Sunday school in 1842 by Samuel Hill, Samuel Seay, James Hamilton and Alfred G. Adams. By November 1843 it had grown into a church with a membership of thirty-two, most of them transfers from the First Church. A Mr. and Mrs. James donated a lot at College and Gay, and a church was built. The dedicatory sermon was preached in the early fall of 1846 by Dr. Philip Lindsley. Dr. R. A. Lapsley served as supply preacher for four years, and as regular pastor for five. In 1856 the Reverend John S. Hays from Ohio was installed. At first he was held in high favor, but during the war he was accused by his members of a lack of sympathy for the Southern cause. When examined, he parried their questions. They asked him to offer prayer at the next service for the members of the church in the Confederate Army. He refused to do so, and after several further conferences chose the alternative of resigning.

The Federal authorities then took the church over and used the building as a headquarters and post chapel. A small group of the membership, with Northern leanings, was permitted to hold services. Because of this connection with the occupying army the church was detached from the Nashville Presbytery. It was readmitted in 1871.

Dr. J. W. Hoyte was pastor for four years, and was succeeded by Reverend John S. Young. Dr. A. S. Allen, installed in 1902, was pastor for twenty-six years. He was followed by J. V. McGee, and he in turn by Fred Stroud. In 1939 it was decided to move from its second site, to a very churchlike place at Belmont and Graybar Lane. The Reverend Thomas Hoover served as minister for a year, and Dr. John Leath of South Carolina for three years. Dr. J. B. Bittinger has been pastor since 1946.

The church is one of the most beautiful of the Nashville area. One of the pleasing traditions of the Second Presbyterian is to hold a celebration on the first Sunday in June for all who have been married in the church. After the morning service a barbecue dinner is served on the lawn by the men and women of the congregation. The accumulation of brides and grooms are the honored guests.

The Moore Presbyterian Church was established November 1873, and a building erected on Broad Street near Fifteenth Avenue. It was created as a memorial to Dr. Verner Moore, pastor of the First Church from 1868 to 1871. By a felicitous coincidence the first pastor was Dr. Frank Moore, who remained until 1878. He was succeeded by Dr. J. H. McNeilly, whose service when a young preacher had been as a chaplain in General John B. Hood's Army of Tennessee. All through that dreadful night after the battle at Franklin he had gone among the wounded, Southern or Northern, stopping for a moment of prayer with each. He was succeeded by another Scotsman, Dr. Angus McDonald, who remained twelve years, and he by still another, Dr. Benjamin Wallace, who served six years. Then, a young minister, Armand Currie, served for a year, but later was to correct that transiency. The modern period of the church began in 1934 with the ministry of Dr. Murdock McLeod. His tenure was ended by his death six years later. Under his leadership the church was moved from Broadway to West End at Craighead. Dr. W. E. Phifer was pastor from 1940 to 1950. Then Dr. Armand Currie returned and remains the pastor at this time. The church is an impressive building, impressively located.

Twenty-eight members of the First Presbyterian Church, led by John Overton and Baxter Smith, formed the Glen Leven Church in 1890. John Thompson gave the land for the site and the building was erected on Douglas Avenue. The first pastor was Dr. J. H. McNeilly, who transferred from Moore Memorial. He remained thirteen years and was followed by Dr. W. C. Alexander, who stayed twenty-two years. Following him, in order, came Dr. J. B. Bittinger, Dr. Otis Graham and Dr. E. W. Albright.

Harpeth Presbyterian Church on the Hillsboro Pike is the oldest of the Presbyterian churches now remaining in the area. It was established in 1811. The Hermitage Presbyterian Church, across the Lebanon Pike from the Hermitage, was completed and opened in 1823. Andrew Jackson was the chief mover and contributor in establishing it. It was in effect a token of his esteem for his wife's religious devotion. These two ancient churches have lost little of their original zeal.

The Woodland Presbyterian Church, across from the East Nashville High School, resulted from the merging of two Sunday schools. In 1853 Mrs. Mary Davis organized a Sunday school in her home for the children of the community. The next year D. D. Dickey started an afternoon Sunday school in a warehouse on Ramsey Street. After still another year the interest created brought the two together in one large school. The interest continued to grow and in May 1858 resulted in the organization of the Woodland Presbyterian Church, though for thirty years it was called the Edgefield Presbyterian Church.

Perhaps no church in Nashville has come up through greater tribulation than Woodland. During most of the Civil War no services were held except under the sponsorship of army chaplains. However, the building escaped relatively intact. In 1873 a terrible plague of cholera struck the city, taking more than 1,000 lives. For two months no light showed in the church, and not often were its doors opened. The pastor, Dr. James H. McNeilly, used most of his hours in visiting the stricken, praying with the dying and burying the dead. The plague wrought its worst and departed almost as suddenly as it had appeared. On July 17 Thanksgiving services were held and Dr. McNeilly preached from the text, *O Lord, my God, I cried unto thee and thou hast healed me*. On March 22, 1916, a fire broke out in the neighborhood. The wind favored the fire, and by night 2,500 were homeless. The church was gone. Again, the congregation rallied, and two years later the new building was ready. The church is serving well its mission. The minister since 1953 has been Dr. Henry Mahler.

Hillsboro Presbyterian Church is descended directly from Nashville's first Cumberland Presbyterian Church by way of Grace Presbyterian Church at Broadway and Seventeenth Avenue, South. It attained a building erected at Hillsboro and Dixie Place in 1922. In 1959 it moved into a new building at Singing Hills on Hillsboro Road. Dr. Donald Jones is the minister, and there are 550 members.

There are today eighteen Presbyterian churches and missions in the Nashville area with a membership of 8,500. Presbyterians lack the building energy of the Baptists, the Methodists, and the followers of the Church of Christ. They do not covet with such evangelistic fervor the increase of their buildings and membership, but most of all there is a continuance of families in their congregations. If, for instance, an Overton was a member of a Presbyterian church in the early times, there is a strong likelihood that his great-great-grandchildren still are. The Presbyterian church may not move so much to one side or the other, but it does move straight ahead. They have about them a stability, a certainty. Their tenacity of purpose has at times cost them dearly, but in the end has strengthened them. They have determined, most of all, the nature of Nashville. The matters about which they can be so stubborn come close to the very essence of worship.

THE CUMBERLAND PRESBYTERIANS

They were not next in chronological line, but they grew directly from the original stock. Pragmatism was never a native philosophy for Presbyterians. Having deliberately taken a stand they brace themselves, and there they stand. Had they been more facile the pages of history would be barren of some exciting episodes. For instance, the emergence of the Cumberland Presbyterian Church, so christened because its beginning took place in the heart of the Cumberland country.

In general retrospect, the Presbyterian demand for an educated ministry set a noble pattern for all the churches. But there were not enough college-bred preachers to supply the demand, and the hunger of the pioneers for more preaching is one of the more affective yearnings of our religious history. As the settlers moved out from the original centers the demand became acute for new churches and for ministers to preach in them. Preachers who were able to meet the academic demands simply were not available. The unsupplied churches protested and asked for a relaxing of the standard. The governing Presbyterian body held fast to the principle. That was the beginning of the breach, though there accompanied it some withdrawal from the more rigid articles of Calvinism.

The formal organization of the Cumberland Presbyterian Church took place in Dickson County, Tennessee, on February 4, 1810. The meeting held for this purpose was at the home of Samuel McAdow, forty miles west of Nashville. Three men, besides Mr. McAdow, had a part in the forming of the new church: Finis Ewing, Samuel King and Ephraim McLane. They accepted as their basic doctrine the Westminster Confession of Faith, though with revisions of the concept of fatality. They added to the theology of Calvin, of Knox, of Witherspoon the evangelism of Whitefield and Wesley and Roger Williams.

In the beginning most of the sermons were delivered by itinerant preachers, but in 1813 Robert Donnell began preaching regularly in Nashville. His ministry met with considerable opposition from the Presbyterians. He persuaded the authorities to permit him to preach in the courthouse. But not for long. His opponents succeeded in having the permit revoked. Mayor Tait then offered the use of the city hall. Unfortunately the mayor survived only a few months, and again they were without a meeting place. For a year preaching services were held in the home of a Mr. Castleman out from Nashville a little. Those meetings were fruitful, and many joined the new denomination. The political situation veered and again the courthouse was made available. In 1828 a congregation was formally organized, and in 1831 the Reverend James Smith was chosen as regular pastor. Under his leadership a new meetinghouse was begun on North Summer Street, near the present site of the Central Church of Christ.

By then the fever of opposition had subsided, and several members of other churches volunteered to serve on a committee to solicit funds for the new church from other churches. Among these solicitors were Governor William Carroll, Samuel Seay, John Bell, John Harding and Felix Grundy. The largest subscription was made by Felix Grundy. Robert C. Hatton, J. C. Provine, Matthew Bone and Wiley Reed served as pastors before the Civil War. Pastor Reed went off to the war soon after it started, and the church was without a minister until in 1866 the Reverend A. J. Baird was called. A new and ampler building was erected and was dedicated in 1874.

The great expansion of the Cumberland Presbyterian membership began about this time, though actually the movement never extended far beyond the denomination's birthplace. Kentucky and Tennessee remained the main strongholds though congregations were established in Missouri, Arkansas, Mississippi and Alabama. Nashville was generally regarded as the geographical center, and in some sense the home. But the feeling of expansion, which for a time was very exciting, began to lose its optimism, and when little progress was made there arose discussions as to the desirability of merger with the Presbyterian Church in the U.S.A. After a long period of talk, and give and take, this was accomplished in 1906, though the vote and the performance were by no means unanimous.

The Cumberland Presbyterians created a college at Princeton, Kentucky, in 1825. For a few years Cumberland College prospered, but in 1843 adverse circumstances caused its removal to Lebanon, Tennessee. There it became known as Cumberland University and achieved considerable fame, particularly in its law school. From it came some of the leading lawyers of the South and Southwest. Cordell Hull was among the alumni. The Cumberland Presbyterians now maintain Bethel College at McKenzie, Tennessee. The church had the opportunity to disappear, but in many instances a touch of Presbyterian steadfastness prevented the complete merger. The "Cumberland Presbyterian" on the bulletin boards of many churches remained the same. There are now in metropolitan Nashville thirteen Cumberland churches, with about 3,000 members, and church property valued at $1,250,000.

THE METHODISTS

From their beginning the Methodists were zealous and mobile churchmen. A wilderness on a river or a mountain was no more to them than a challenge. And so they reached Nashville early, in fact not very far behind the Presbyterians. The first Methodist to arrive in the settlement was James Haw, "schooled in pioneer hardships and Scriptures." The year was 1783. The next year he preached his first sermon in Nashville to a congregation of seven. That year he was joined by Benjamin Ogden, and together they organized the section's first approximation of a circuit. In 1788 Ogden moved on to new territory and was replaced in Nashville by Peter Massie. In 1789 three more Methodist preachers arrived, Francis Poythress, Thomas Williamson and Joshua Hartley. These were not highly educated men, but there could be no doubt as to their devotion. What they lacked academically was more than compensated by their zeal and sincerity. They blazed trails through great expanses of lonely wilderness. They preached wherever they could find a few gathered. All the dangers and hardships that the wilderness could turn against them offered no suggestion to turn back. They were inured to hunger and in considerable degree to illness.

But it was the Reverend Green Hill who made the earliest permanent marks on Nashville Methodism. He was fiscal agent of the colony of North Carolina in 1776, but, moved by a feeling that had been stirring within him for several years, he offered himself as a preacher. On Sunday, June 27, 1796, he reached Nashville, and that day heard a sermon by Brother Duzan. In the afternoon he wrote a letter to his kinspeople in North Carolina in which he commented tersely on the situation at the morning service: "Some people went away, but the greater part attended." Three days later at the home of Richard Strothers he mapped out his preaching arrangements. Brother Hill liked the section and settled down to his circuits. He built a home in the Brentwood district, and there was visited by Bishop Francis Asbury. He is buried near by. William Lambeth was appointed to the Nashville circuit in 1801, and William McKendree became the presiding elder.

The first Methodist meetinghouse was erected in Nashville about 1791. It adjoined the market, had but one room and was crudely built of stone. The needs of the growing town demanded the site, and the building was demolished. For a season meetings were held in the jail, then moved to the residence of Mr. Garrett on the Franklin Road. In 1812 a small brick building was erected on Broad Street, on a part of the lot now occupied by the Hume Fogg High School. This building too was merely tentative, lasting till 1817. That year a more commodious meetinghouse was built on Church Street, where the Noel Garage now is. It was used for fifteen years. Then, under the devotion and general management of four preachers, a "spacious edifice" was erected on the present site of McKendree Church. The names of those preachers are still meaningful in Nashville: L. D. Overall, A. L. P. Green, P. B. Robinson and John B. McFerrin. The first sermon was preached by Dr. William McKendree in 1833, and for him the church was named.

From then on it was a beacon light in Southern Methodism. The building was used for forty-four years. Then it was torn down and a new and fine church constructed. Two years later that building was destroyed by fire. It was for the congregation a major disaster, but it had faced crises before. A new church was built immediately. It in turn burned down in 1910. Again the McKendree congregation rallied and built its fourth church, the one that stands today.

When it was seen that Spring Street was becoming literally a street of churches the name was fitly changed to Church Street. Before the old century died the shift to the suburbs had set in. The churches have tended to follow the drift of population, and one by one moved out to be nearer the homes of their members. Now only three remain, the three that were there first, McKendree, the historic First Presbyterian Church (now the Downtown Presbyterian Church) and Saint Mary's Cathedral.

Very early Nashville became a crossroads of Methodist travel, and the great figures of the denomination manifested a special fondness for the place. Bishop Asbury visited Nashville

143

several times on his remarkable Southern journeys. He loved to stop at the William Maxeys' on the Gallatin Road, and at the home of his colleague, Green Hill, out in the Brentwood section. The fire-eating Peter Cartwright was never a pastor in or about Nashville, but he visited and preached in the town often, and by the blunt forthrightness of his statements won the hostility of some and the friendship of others, particularly the friendship of General Andrew Jackson. The Methodists multiplied in the town, for their leadership generally was good and their zeal never flagging.

Something should be said here of Dr. Alexander Little Page Green. His sermons and his ministerial strategy were most fruitful. He established his residence in 1829 and remained till his death in July 1874. He was born in Sevier County, Tennessee, in 1806. His father was one of the King's Mountain patriots, a stern austere man whose ideals were George Washington and John Wesley. The Green home was a haven for passing Methodist preachers, among them Asbury and Coke. The lad listened to what the visiting preachers said with a fierce intentness, and Methodism took its place in his heart and mind. His only chance for an education was that offered by a poor log school, and yet in time he became a distinguished patron of higher education. When he was eighteen he was licensed to exhort, and at nineteen to preach. He was assigned to the Jackson circuit of Alabama. There were many Creek Indians in that vicinity, and he learned to speak their language with some fluency.

Methodism was in good condition in Nashville when Green arrived. Some of the substantial citizens had become communicants: the Prices, the Ellistons, the Garretts, the Littons, the Weakleys, the Vaughans, the Mannings, the Hobbses, the Hoopers.

Joseph Elliston was one of Nashville's leading figures for a full generation. He came from northern Kentucky and reached the settlement very early. He quickly established himself as a silversmith, and in that business he made for himself a comfortable fortune. His home was a favorite with all visiting Methodist preachers. Bishop McKendree spent most of the winter of 1829 in the Ellistons' home. They mentioned young A. L. P. Green to the bishop, who asked that he be sent for. When the young preacher entered the room the great preacher arose and said pontifically, "I sent a young preacher to the Hopkinsville circuit. He experienced trouble making friends. Being counseled, he borrowed tools and made little things for the people, bucket stands, hooks to hang things on, many things like that. For one woman who needed it he made a churn dash. It was good work he did, and he earned the friendship of the people. Give thought to him." Having delivered himself, the bishop turned away from Green and sat down to continue his conversation with his host.

The counsel fitted into Green's nature. What better could he do, for instance, than help those for whom physicians were not available? So he studied medicine at some length in the office of Dr. John Waters. He was, of course, never licensed to practice medicine, but thereafter he supplemented preaching with healing. He never went to college, but in time he came to make colleges. He became a trustee of Nashville Female Academy, and of the Tennessee School for the Blind. He gave very vital help in the founding of Vanderbilt University. Of his worth to Vanderbilt, Bishop Holland McTyeire offered eloquent testimony: "To the foresight, zeal, and pleading of A. L. P. Green we owe more than to any other man the institution now rising in Nashville's western suburbs."

Dr. Green became a stockholder in both of Nashville's railroads, and a director in the Nashville Gas and Heating Company. And it was he who more than any other man brought to Nashville the Methodist Publishing Company, now one of the nation's great sources of the printed word. Certainly no preacher in the history of Nashville ever did so many things so well. But always his main work was as a consecrated minister of the gospel.

The marks of the section's best Methodist preachers are on McKendree Church. For instance, Dr. John B. McFerrin was appointed to the church three times; so was J. W. Barbee. A. L. P. Green was appointed twice; so were D. C. Kelly, John W. Hanner and Samuel D. Baldwin. These had single assignments: Robert Anderson, Thomas Randle, Philip Neely, Edward Slater, Adam Briggs, William Dorris, W. D. F. Sawrie, William Warren, R. H. Hargrove, J. B. West, W. A. Candler, B. F. Haynes, S. A. Steele, E. B. Chappell, W. B. Taylor, J. S. French, T. C. Ragsdale, J. D. McAllister, Collins Denny, M. M. Waldrip, H. V. Trimble, C. C. McDaniel, Earl Hamblett, Grady Timmons, King Vivian and Thornton Fowler. Dr. King Vivian remained seventeen years, which under Methodist rule is an unusual tenure. The fact that McKendree is entirely surrounded by business, big business, has placed no damper on its activities. Something is in progress almost every evening and often during the day. For almost thirteen decades the blight of inertia has not touched McKendree.

West End Methodist Church began as a small Sunday school organized by Mortimer Hamilton in 1856 in a little house on Laurel Street. The Sunday school survived until the occupation in February 1862. It reopened after the war in a government building on Stonewall Street. It grew into a church in 1870, and under the guidance of Pastor R. A. Young erected a frame church at Broad and Belmont streets, at a cost of $3,000. Services were carried on in this for seventeen years. Then Pastor W. M. Leftwich convinced the congregation that a new and more suitable building was imperative. The old church was torn down and a new one erected at a cost of $55,000, and dedicated free of debt. It was considered one of Nashville's show places. Time passed and this building too began to show wear; also business houses began to crowd in upon it. So in 1927 it was decided to move farther out.

The site chosen was on West End, fronting the Vanderbilt campus. That proximity was a part of the decision, for during all the period of strain involved in the separation of Vanderbilt from the Methodist Church South, West End Church and the university had in their joint fealty experienced no disturbing tension. For ten years the services of West End Church were held in Neely Chapel on the Vanderbilt campus. In 1940 all parts of the new building were completed and West End moved into its own home. Its pastors have been Dr. George Stoves, Dr. Costen Harrell and Dr. James Henley, now completing his seventeenth year, and in 1960 elected bishop and appointed to the Florida district. One would hardly expect to find a greater variety than these three preachers offer. Yet their work forms a composite and notable period in the life of West End.

The Tulip Street Methodist Church, in Edgefield, was erected in 1859. War was threatening then. It was to break with disastrous force two years later. The Federals occupied the city in February 1862, and immediately most of the churches, by military order, were turned into hospitals, or else used by preachers who came with the army. Some were destroyed outright since in one way or another they obstructed the Federal plans. One Methodist church, Hobson's Chapel, was required as a storage house for meat for the army. No services were held during hostilities at Tulip Street, but the building went unharmed. The first Methodist Conference held after the war was at Tulip Street in October 1865. President Andrew Johnson restored the churches to their congregations, and immediately the Methodists began putting their churches in order and reassembling their congregations. Tulip Street was a special beneficiary of the Centennial held in 1897. At its close the chimes whose music had been a pleasing phase of the celebration were given to Tulip Street. And there they remain.

North Edgefield Methodist Church was established and built in 1868. Ten years later its name was changed to the Foster Street Methodist Church, and ten years after that to McFerrin Memorial.

The main name connected with the beginning of the Belmont Methodist Church is Battle Clark. He led in the movement to start the church and build it, and services during the building were held at his home. The church was completed early in 1910, and dedicated on July 10. It was located, as it is now, at Hillsboro and Acklen, which then was the corporate limit of the city. The Hillsboro Pike ended there, continuing as a road repaired very little from the ravages of the war. The first pastor was N. Burch Tucker. Later pastors have been W. M. Alexander, B. B. Pennington, Bachman Hodge, John T. Ferguson, John W. Ruston and Ferris Moore. Belmont has the largest membership of any Methodist church in the city, and is one of the best equipped of all.

There are seventy-seven Methodist churches in Nashville, with a membership of more than 36,000.

THE BAPTISTS

There was, it is often affirmed, a very early tacit agreement between the Baptists and Presbyterians that the latter would occupy the towns, leaving to the former all the country areas. No official record of this agreement has ever been found, and it is extremely doubtful if there was one, though some of the preachers of both churches may have talked the matter over.

In 1793 two Baptist churches were established and in action, and both were in the fringes of the settlement. Mill Creek Baptist Church, four miles east of Nashville, was perhaps the more important. It certainly lasted longer. Its pastor, the Reverend James Whitsitt, was an important figure in the community's pioneer period. The other was the Richland Creek

Baptist Church, on Richland Creek, six miles southwest of Nashville. Its pastor was the Reverend John de la Hunte (later colloquialized to Dillahunty). He continued in the assignment until his death in 1812. Both Pastor Dillahunty and his wife died on the same day and were buried in the same grave, almost within the shadow of the church. It was, of course, a log structure, built on the southern side of the creek, directly across from what is today the Belle Meade golf course. Big Harpeth Baptist Church was organized early in 1800, about eighteen miles south of Nashville, Garner McConnico, pastor.

The preachers of early and middle Nashville stocked the town well with their descendants. All three of the preachers mentioned above have descendants in the city now.

Naturally if the agreement referred to above as to division was ever made between the Baptists and the Presbyterians, it could not have been expected to hold for long. The city was very alluring and the country was growing so. There was room enough for everybody, and there were rapidly becoming members enough. As a matter of history the Presbyterians had organized two rural churches in the section before 1800, and both still survive: Old Beech Church at Shackle Island, Sumner County, which began its long career in 1794; and Shiloh, five miles north of Gallatin, slightly earlier.

Soon the Baptists were regarding the town with contemplative eyes. In 1822 the Mill Creek Church gave thought to the issue, and those members who found it more convenient and agreeable to attend services in town withdrew and erected a meetinghouse on Church Street about where Loew's Theater stands now. It was completed in time to celebrate Christmas there. The Reverend Richard Dabb was installed as minister. He died less than three years later and Dr. Philip Fall was chosen to take his place. Dr. Fall came from Frankfort, Kentucky, as did Dr. Thomas Craighead and Dr. John T. Edgar.

In Louisville Dr. Fall had met the celebrated Dr. Alexander Campbell and heard him preach. Obviously the sermon had impressed Dr. Fall. So when Dr. Campbell came to Nashville the Baptist preacher missed no opportunity to hear him. Alexander Campbell, a native Scot, was a graduate of the University of Glasgow. His first preaching was as a Presbyterian, but he found himself withdrawing from the doctrines of his mother church. For a brief time he was a Baptist, but he found that belief no more acceptable. With the assistance of two other preachers, Dr. Walter Scott and Dr. Barton W. Stone, he established a church known variously as the Church of the Disciples, the Christian Church, and the Church of Christ. Dr. Campbell was a man of great power and very persuasive. His preaching was very challenging and a great number listened to him.

The dissent which had been stirring in the heart of Dr. Fall spread to members of his congregation. Soon it came to a vote whether to remain steadfast or make the change, and all but five voted to join the new denomination. The five were Mrs. Elizabeth Smith, Lipscomb Norvell, Mrs. Cecilia Fairfax, Major Henry Cartmell and Mrs. Sarah Cartmell. Under Baptist rules the majority determined ownership, and the church building became the property of the dissenters. That was in 1828.

The five worshiped in homes until 1830 when they began using the courthouse. After a brief period there they shifted to the Masonic Hall, and chose the Reverend Peter Gayle as pastor. He remained three years. During his ministry the five multiplied modestly, and the desire for a new church building and for a minister of great power began stirring within them. They found the preacher at Norfolk, Virginia. He was the Reverend R. B. C. Howell, renowned for his learning, his preaching ability and his religious militancy. He accepted the call and began his ministerial work in Nashville in January 1835. He immediately started a periodical, *The Baptist*. It was the section's first Baptist publication.

Three months after his arrival a Sunday school was established, and within six months a new building was under construction. Grass hoping to grow under Dr. Howell's tread was in for disappointment. The new building was located on North Summer Street near Deaderick. The Baptists used it a half century and then sold it to the Lutherans. They in turn used it until 1940, when it was sold to make way for a chain store.

Dr. Howell justified the call of the church. He was a man of culture, of devotion and of enormous energy. His popularity was not limited to the Baptists. At the dedication of the new building in 1838 all of the city's Protestant choirs took part in the singing. And that, for the time, was an unusual display of liberality.

Dr. Howell resigned in 1850 to take charge of the Second Baptist Church in Richmond, Virginia. But he answered an insistent demand and returned to his old church in 1857. The first three years of his second period were indeed propitious.

But the war which broke over Nashville seemed to vent its wrath on the churches. Almost all of the town's preachers were Southern in sympathy, and when the oath of allegiance was demanded of them, all but one refused. Those who refused were sent to the state prison. In his journal Berrien Lindsley recorded a visit he had made them in prison. They who had fought one another with such doctrinal zest were engaged in a veritable love feast. Prison had torn away their predilection. The preachers didn't remain in prison longer than enough to save the official faces of those who had sent them there.

On New Year's Day 1863 the First Baptist Church was requisitioned by the Federal authorities to serve as a hospital. It was stripped bare of all its church furniture, and cots were lugged in. On the second Sunday of the year the congregation met in a loft over a store on College Street and continued to worship there for seven months. Late in August the church was returned to the Baptists. But their rejoicing died soon. In November the building was again demanded for hospital purposes. The manager of a theater offered his auditorium for

Sunday use, and at the same time Dr. Fall, who long before had withdrawn from the church, taking with him most of the members, offered the use of the Christian Church of which he was then pastor. Once again the Federals returned the building to its owners, but in less than twenty-four hours demanded it back. Notwithstanding all these interruptions the congregation worshiped regularly, sometimes in homes, sometimes in stores, sometimes out of doors.

Dr. Howell weakened under the strain, but lasted through the war and the tensions immediately following. He died in April 1868. He was followed in quick succession by Dr. Thomas Skinner, Dr. T. G. Jones and Dr. C. H. Strickland. The church grew until the old building became inadequate. It was sold to the Lutherans for $10,000, and a new one erected at Broad and Vine at a cost of $80,000. It was ready for use in 1886. Three years later Dr. Strickland resigned to take a place in Sioux City, Iowa. Dr. E. V. Baldy followed him, and after a brief tenure he was succeeded by Dr. W. R. L. Smith of Virginia. The pastoral line continued with Dr. J. M. Frost, Dr. J. B. Hawthorne, Dr. Lansing Burrows, Dr. R. M. Inlow, Dr. Allen Fort, Dr. W. F. Powell and Dr. H. F. Paschall. Dr. Powell's tenure of thirty-four years as minister of the same church is one of the nation's longest. The First Church has the largest membership of any Baptist church in the city. Its present annual budget is $350,000.

The Second Baptist Church was established in 1844 and a building erected on Cherry Street, near the campus of the University of Nashville. The Reverend T. W. Haynes was chosen pastor. Fifteen years later a second church building was erected, and the name was changed to the Cherry Street Baptist Church. In the summer of 1850 fifty-eight members withdrew from the First Church, with the full blessing of Dr. Howell, and organized a church to be located on Spring Street near Vine, and to be known as the Spring Street Baptist Church. The Reverend J. R. Graves was called as pastor. In 1860, however, the name was changed to the Central Baptist Church. In 1870 the Cherry Street Church disbanded its organization and deeded its building to the Central Baptist Church. The first pastor in the new location was W. G. Inman. He remained until 1876. Then followed in succession M. H. Lane, O. C. Pope, G. S. Williams, Reuben Ford and G. A. Lofton, who became pastor in May 1887. His tenure was long and the church prospered. The neighborhood became less favorable for the work of the church, and although its membership at times has all but disappeared it remains and services are held regularly.

In 1867 there was a considerable population of Baptists in Edgefield. They needed and wanted a church, but the required leadership did not seem available. To supply the need twenty members withdrew from the First Church and joined with their Edgefield brethren. There was a period of preaching by laymen, but in 1875 the Reverend W. H. Nelson was called and remained three years. He was followed by James Waters, W. H. Strickland, C. S. Gardner and J. O. Rust. The ministry of the last two was very effective and brought the church to a high point.

The Immanuel Baptist Church was born out of the devotion of M. B. Pilcher, captain in General John B. Hood's Army of Tennessee. Captain Pilcher was severely wounded at the battle of Franklin. Since he had been a longtime friend of the Harrisons who lived at the southern base of Winstead's Hill he was carried to their home. He was one of several wounded brought there, and they were visited daily by the army's chaplain, Dr. Charles T. Quintard, an Episcopalian. Dr. Quintard kept a journal. Of one of his visits he wrote, "I next called upon and prayed with Captain Matt Pilcher, an excellent soldier and gentleman, though a Baptist."

In 1873 Captain Pilcher organized a mission on Stonewall Street, near Broad. The mission was active and of much service in the community. In 1875 it was named Immanuel Baptist

Mission. In 1888 it became Immanuel Baptist Church. Several ministers, each with a brief tenure, served in its early period. It was Dr. I. J. Vanness, 1890 to 1896, who gave the church substance and permanency. He resigned to become secretary of the Baptist Sunday School Board, and was succeeded by A. J. Ramsey, who served two years. Dr. T. B. Ray remained eight years. Dr. A. T. Robertson, of the seminary in Louisville, was supply pastor for two years. Dr. Rufus W. Weaver followed for ten years. It was during his ministry that the building at Seventeenth and West End was erected and dedicated. Dr. Ryland Knight was pastor from 1918 until 1925, Dr. Powhatan James from 1926 to 1931, Dr. A. U. Boone from 1931 to 1933, Dr. C. S. Henderson from 1933 until 1941, and that year Dr. Merrill Moore came from the presidency of Tennessee College. He served seven years. Dr. Gaye McGlothlin became pastor in 1948. The church at Seventeenth and West End has been sold and converted into an office building, and a new church erected and occupied on Belle Meade Boulevard.

Belmont Heights Baptist Church was organized in 1920, but has grown to be the second largest Baptist church in Nashville. It was the result of the merger of two small struggling churches, Belmont Baptist Church, located on Twelfth Avenue, South, and Southside Baptist Church, on Belcourt near Hillsboro. The decision to unite was made at a conference held at Ward Belmont College on the first Sunday in May, 1920. In the summer of that year a tent was pitched on the present site of Sterling Court apartments. There the first services of the new church were held. On the second meeting day, during services, the tent was blown down by a sudden storm. All but two of the congregation got out in time, and the two suffered only minor bruises. The tent was pulled back up and the sermon resumed. Late in the summer a permanent site was chosen at the corner of Belmont and Compton streets. Dr. George L. Hale was called as pastor and remained three years. Dr. John D. Freeman succeeded him for a tenure of two years; then Dr.

W. M. Wood for three years. In the fall of 1928 Dr. Kelly White of Bessemer, Alabama, was inducted as pastor. That began a long and fruitful ministry. In February 1946 Dr. White resigned to accept a church at West Palm Beach, Florida. A few months after, Dr. J. L. Sullivan became pastor and remained until 1950, when he resigned to accept a church in Abilene, Texas. The next pastor was Dr. Harold Purdy who came from Bowling Green, Kentucky, and who remains with the church.

The original tent had yielded to a crude one-story structure, bearing very little resemblance to a church. On March 20, 1927, this new building was dedicated, with preaching daily, almost hourly, throughout the week. But it was soon realized that it was inadequate for a fast-growing congregation. On January 15, 1956, a new structure, much more satisfactory, and of a size to seat comfortably 1,900, was dedicated. Belmont Heights' membership is now somewhat more than 3,200, and its annual budget is more than a quarter of a million dollars.

Since the beginning of the century a remarkable multiplication of Baptists, not only in numbers but also in names, has taken place in the city. The current statistical report of the Chamber of Commerce lists the number of Baptist churches in metropolitan Nashville as 129 white, and 100 Negro. This is a bit puzzling until one recalls that the Baptists have an amazing capacity for division. A great many groups find satisfaction in the use of the name. There are in the Cumberland mountains now not fewer than ten different kinds of Baptists. There are not fewer than four in Nashville. The Southern Baptists usually have good buildings, are well organized and are generally strong throughout the city. The buildings of some of the others are unimpressive, and their organizations somewhat vague. Sometimes services are held in houses or unused storerooms, in circumstances that leave no question as to entire devotion.

The growth of some of the recently established Southern Baptist churches has been noteworthy—as instances, Inglewood

Baptist Church, on Gallatin Road, founded in 1924 through the efforts of Mrs. Robert Overall. In its thirty-six years Inglewood has grown from twenty-three to 2,300, with church property of over $900,000. Its minister is Dr. Harold Stephens. Woodmont Baptist Church, on Hillsboro Road, was established in 1941, mainly through the efforts of Roy Green, at that time owner of a grocery store. The church now has 1,375 members and owns property worth $725,000. Dr. Allen West has been minister since the church's beginning. Grace Baptist Church, established in 1908, has now a membership of 2,750 and owns property exceeding in value a half-million dollars, Dr. Wade Darby, pastor. Judson Memorial Baptist Church, on Eighth Avenue, South, has a membership of 1,700 and property of about $575,000. Lockland, in East Nashville, has grown to a membership of more than 1,400, with property worth about $350,000.

There have been difficult periods in the lives of Nashville Baptists. Their beginning was followed by severe stress that required years to overcome. Then there was a season of good leadership and prosperity. The birth pains of oncoming war began to rack them sorely, and from an unexpected quarter. The Baptist churches, North and South, were contributing generously to send missionaries to the foreign fields. The North, having the majority, and therefore control, began declaring ineligible for missionary service all from slave states. The quarrel spread, took root, and in May 1845, at a convention held at Augusta, Georgia, the Southern Baptists voted a separation from the Northern churches. And that was the beginning of the Southern Baptist Church. The separation was apparently an organic one, since no particular effort has been made for reunion.

The Southern Baptist Convention, at Birmingham in 1891, created the Sunday School Board, and located it at Nashville. A Virginia pastor, Dr. J. M. Frost, was chosen to serve as secretary, though without budget, or cash in hand, or portfolio except in terms of his own strong conviction. His wife had received a bequest of $5,000 from a kinsman. Her husband borrowed it, and the Sunday School Board of the Southern Baptist Church was under way. Now, almost seventy years later, the board has moved into territory not included in Dr. Frost's dreams. There are more than 7,000,000 enrolled in its Sunday schools. In the year 1957 it published and distributed 14,000,000 general tracts, 11,000,000 promotional tracts, 73,-000,000 copies of seventy-nine periodicals, 1,618,341 volumes of new books, and reprinted 186 titles to a total of 2,355,581 copies. It owns and directs fifty bookstores in twenty-three states, and owns and operates ten office and storage buildings in Nashville.

THE CHRISTIAN CHURCH

The first Christian Church in Nashville had its origin in Nashville's first Baptist Church. The nature of that division has been mentioned in the preceding section. Dr. Fall, around whom the controversy raged, remained as pastor of the Christian Church until 1831. Two young men who had been trained under him, A. Adams and Tolbert Fanning, shared the pastorate for the next ten years. Then Dr. W. H. Wharton, a young physician ordained by his church to preach, supplied the pulpit for several years. Dr. Jesse B. Ferguson became minister in 1847, and under the power of his ministry the church flourished. Presently it had outgrown the building on Church Street. In 1850 the congregation bought a large lot on North Cherry Street, the site now occupied by the old Life and Casualty building. In 1852 a large and fine church was erected on it. Soon the congregation rose above 800. The choir was generally regarded as the best in the city.

Success preceded tragedy. Unhappily there arose within the church some factional troubles, so sharp that a court process was required to allay them. Then, as a climax, in 1857 the church burned down. The old building on Church Street had been sold to the Presbyterians. It was repurchased and put in order for worship, and to it the congregation moved back. It was used until 1888. Dr. Fall was recalled from the presidency of Transylvania College, and again was pastor of his old church for nineteen years. He resigned on the closing day of 1876 and returned to Kentucky for the few years he had left. Another minister from Kentucky, Dr. Samuel A. Kelly, succeeded him. He lived less than two years and his place was taken by Dr. R. C. Cave, then president of South Kentucky College at Hopkinsville. Poor health cut short his ministry and he was followed by his brother, D. Lin Cave, who remained for seventeen years. The old building became inadequate both in size and condition for the demands of the congregation. It was sold and for almost a year services were held in Watkins Hall.

In September 1889 the new building on Vine Street was completed and placed in use. It was rechristened the Vine Street Christian Church. Dr. Cave withdrew in 1898 and was followed by Dr. W. E. Ellis, who remained five years. Several pastors followed him in quick succession. In December 1907, Dr. Philip Yancey Pendleton was chosen pastor. He was a son of William Pendleton, who succeeded Alexander Campbell as president of Bethany College. In 1912, Dr. Carey Morgan of Paris, Kentucky, came to the church. Dr. Morgan impressed himself on the religious and civic life of the city as few ministers have done. He was popular among all denominations. He was succeeded by Dr. Roger Nooe, also of Kentucky. He retired after twenty-six years of excellent service. His successor was Dr. Curtis Jones of Richmond, Virginia, who was followed in 1955 by Dr. Arthur Braden, another Kentuckian. In 1957 a new building was constructed at West End and Ensworth and services were transferred to it. This church, in a very direct sense, is the parent of all the Christian churches in the section. There are seven of them with a membership of about 4,000.

The Woodmont Christian Church is relatively new but of

great importance in Nashville. It was established July 18, 1943, on Hillsboro Road at Woodmont. The need for it was discussed first by a group of men—William F. Carpenter, Forrest Reed, Charles Hawkins and Wilbur Sensing. That kindled an interest which spread quickly, gathering others into vigorous co-operation, and soon the building was in process. The first sermon was preached by Dr. George Mayhew of Vanderbilt School of Religion. Dr. Frank Drowota, a native of England, but then living at Mayfield, Kentucky, was called to the ministry in which he remains. On the first day of existence there were fifty-one members. Now there are 920. The value of the church property is estimated at $700,000.

THE CHURCH OF CHRIST

Alexander Campbell never quite arrived at a name for the denomination which he envisioned and whose foundations he helped to shape. Sometimes he called it the Christian Church, sometimes the Church of the Disciples, and sometimes the Church of Christ. During the nineteenth century it was mainly called the Christian Church. In that period it never drew its membership to a sharp focus of common belief. There was considerable dissent from the tendency of the church to organize its affairs, budgets, missions and the like and put all of its labors into regulated programs. Objection developed to the use of musical instruments in worship. But still both the liberal and conservative elements held together, though somewhat loosely at times, until 1906, when the division was made formal. In that year the Church of Christ, new in systematic and consistent christening, but old in fast-emerging religious concepts, began its formal career. The leaders who had most influence in the division and during the early periods were: E. G. Sowell, David Lipscomb, R. M. Gano, T. B. Larrimore, J. A. Harding and J. C. McQuiddy, all men of great conviction, vitality and eloquence. It seems almost certain that the old church on College Street, now the Lindsley Avenue Church, was the first to be called regularly a Church of Christ. It is the policy of the church not to develop large unwieldy congregations, but rather small, intimate, personal ones. The Church of Christ maintains David Lipscomb College, one of Nashville's well-equipped and fast-growing colleges. There are now in metropolitan Nashville about 125 congregations of the Church of Christ. Some of them are small, but all are devoted and active. The total membership is about 50,000, and property is valued at about $8,000,000.

THE CHURCH OF THE NAZARENE

The first Church of the Nazarene in Nashville was dedicated in 1912. There are now thirty-five congregations with a membership of 3,700. Trevecca College is carried on with considerable credit under the sponsorship of the Nazarenes.

THE CATHOLICS

There were quite early in Nashville a few individual Catholics, but too few to organize a congregation. The first body of Catholics reached Nashville in 1821 from their stronghold at Bardstown, Kentucky. The first priests were the Right Reverend Bishop David, and the Reverend Father Abell. Mass was said for the first time May 11, 1821. There were then something more than fifty Catholics in town, mainly laborers who had come from the north to work on the bridge that was then being put across the Cumberland.

The first Catholic church was erected in 1830 on the present site of the Capitol grounds. Most of the land was given by a lawyer named Foster, a Presbyterian. This generosity had in it a certain added appropriateness since Foster had come from Bardstown himself and had prospered in Nashville.

The church at Nashville was at first a part of the Diocese of Bardstown, but in 1837 the Diocese of Nashville was created. The Reverend Richard Miles was consecrated Bishop of Nashville on September 16, 1838. It was he who initiated the building of a cathedral in the city. It was located on the southeast corner of Cedar and Summer streets, and dedicated November 1, 1847. The cost was $47,000. The architect was William Strickland, then directing the erection of the Capitol. At first the cathedral was called the Church of the Seven Dolors, but it was soon changed to Saint Mary's. In 1849 a pipe organ, reported to be the finest in the city, was installed. Bishop Miles died in 1860, and was succeeded by the Right Reverend James Whelan.

The oncoming of the Civil War was most disturbing to all the religious bodies of the city, with the result that most of the churches were forced into a period of neglect. In the early stage of the war the Catholics were favored to have one of their own faith as chief of the occupying forces, General Rosecrans, which perhaps enabled them to emerge from the conflict in the most intact condition of all the religious bodies. In 1863 Bishop Whelan died, and he was succeeded by Father Kelley, who administered the affairs of the church during the ensuing stormy years. He was succeeded in November 1866 by the Reverend Patrick Feehan, soon to be consecrated bishop.

The Church of the Assumption was erected in 1856 at Vine and Monroe. It was constructed in considerable part out of the materials taken from the first church built on Capitol Hill in 1830. The Church of the Assumption was built under the direction of J. H. Buddeke and G. H. Wessel.

Saint Columba Church was erected on Main Street in 1873. Saint Joseph's Church was completed in 1886 on Knowles Street, near Hyne.

Andrew Hyne, who had come to Nashville from Kentucky in the early part of the nineteenth century, was a man of major substance in Nashville. He married Nancy Erwin, daughter of Joseph Erwin and sister of Jane, the wife of Charles Dickinson, killed by Andrew Jackson in a duel, May 1806. The Hynes house served for a while as the church rectory. The site was selected because it was a convenient place of worship for railroad men. The Reverend Father Scannell was assigned the ministry of the parish. The neighborhood became increasingly unfavorable for a church and gradually it dwindled.

Saint Patrick's Catholic Church in South Nashville was dedicated February 1891, the Reverend Timothy Charles Abbott in charge.

One of the notable figures of Nashville Catholicism was Thomas Sebastian Byrne, Bishop from 1894 till 1923. One of his great achievements was the building of the Cathedral of the Incarnation, on West End Avenue, completed in 1914. Every part of the cathedral was modeled after some famous edifice in the Eternal City. Saint Thomas' Hospital was built during his ministry. Six months after the death of Bishop Byrne, the Most Reverend Alphonse Smith was installed as the sixth Bishop of Nashville. He died in 1935, and His Excellency, William L. Adrian, was appointed Bishop. During Bishop Adrian's early term the interior of the cathedral was completely renovated.

Saint Ann's Catholic Church, at the corner of Fifty-first and Charlotte, is the result of the work of two Sisters of Charity who in 1917 began to stress with energy and devotion the need of the people of the western part of the city for a place of worship and instruction in the catechism. On December 18, 1921, the chapel was solemnly blessed and High Mass was sung. Some time later the Reverend Joseph Leppert was appointed pastor. He was succeeded by the Reverend John L. Donovan, and he by the Reverend George J. Flanigan, and he in turn by the Reverend William Freihammer.

Father Leppert became the priest at Christ the King Church when it was opened July 25, 1937. Father Thomas Duffey became pastor in 1953.

Saint Henry's Catholic Church in the outskirts of Belle Meade was dedicated in 1957, Monsignor Joseph Seiner, pastor.

There are fifteen Catholic churches in Nashville, with a

membership of approximately 16,000, and with church property valued at $6,125,000.

THE EPISCOPALIANS

The Episcopal Church, as an organization, reached Nashville in 1829, though individual members were here well before that time. The Reverend James H. Otey, a Virginian, was mainly responsible for bringing his fellow churchmen together in formal organization. He reached Tennessee in 1825 and preached to small groups in Nashville, Franklin and Columbia. Under his direction vestrymen for a church to be formed in Nashville were tentatively chosen in June 1829. Through his influence Dr. J. S. Ravencroft, Bishop of North Carolina, was brought to Nashville for a series of sermons. He awakened such interest that the Masonic Hall was crowded by the audiences. One result of this interest was the purchase of a lot on the northeast corner of Church and High streets, and the erection of a building to be known as Christ Episcopal Church.

The first services in the new church were held in July 1831. Among the members were: Mr. and Mrs. James Diggons, Mr. and Mrs. Matthew Watson, Mr. and Mrs. James Stewart, E. D. Hicks, Mr. and Mrs. G. M. Fogg, John Waters, Thomas K. Price, Mr. and Mrs. Francis B. Fogg, Mrs. Ann Shelby Minnick, Dr. and Mrs. John Shelby, Mr. and Mrs. Henry Middleton Rutledge, Eli Talbot, Henry Baldwin, Jr., William J. Hunt, Alex Litton, Henry M. Edwards, Thomas Washington, J. G. Washington, George Wilson, Thomas Claiborne, P. H. Skipworth, Andrew Hynes.

Dr. Shelby is remembered for many things, among them the founding of the Shelby School of Medicine, indirectly the forerunner of the Vanderbilt School of Medicine. At that time he was likely Nashville's wealthiest man. The Rutledges came to Nashville in 1816 from Charleston, South Carolina. They were people of distinction. Henry's father, Edward, had signed the Declaration of Independence, as had his wife's father, Arthur Middleton. Francis B. Fogg served as warden for fifty-one years, twenty-five as senior warden.

The first rector was the Reverend George Weller, 1831 to 1837. He was succeeded by the Reverend J. T. Wheat, who remained eleven years. The Reverend Charles Tomes, son-in-law of Bishop Otey, was next in the rectorship, from 1848 until his death in 1857. The Reverend Leonidas Smith served from 1857 to 1862. The Reverend W. D. Harlow conducted services throughout the war, though they were held irregularly. He was followed in 1856 by the Reverend William J. Ellis, of Georgia, who remained four years and whose successor was the Reverend William Graham.

Church Street, which at that time was a veritable concentration of churches, was in instances being found a less desirable location. In 1887 Christ Church purchased a lot on the corner of Broad and McLemore streets—McLemore is now Ninth Avenue—and there erected first a chapel, then a complete church building. Dr. Graham resigned in 1889, and was succeeded the following February by the Reverend J. R. Winchester, of Georgia.

In 1849 Rector Tomes of Christ Church had sponsored the establishment of a mission in South Nashville, at the corner of High and LaFayette streets. The mission was placed under the direction of the Reverend John Ingraham, later to write the popular novel, *The Prince of the House of David*. Dr. Tomes laid out roughly the field of the mission's service as "that area bounded on the east and west by the Cumberland River and the Franklin Pike, and north and south by Broad Street and a line approximately two miles south of that." It was a demanding area, and Dr. Ingraham was reduced to a state of ill health by its requirements. He failed to improve and resigned. After an interval the Reverend M. S. Royce succeeded him. His tenure too was brief, but he and Dr. Ingraham had made the people of the area church-conscious.

Late in 1851 M. W. Wetmore offered to give a lot adequate for a house of worship. In May 1852 Bishop Otey laid the cornerstone. The building was designed in a pattern of pure English Gothic by Wills and Dudley of New York. It was built of limestone with a great deal of cedar used in the woodwork. The seating capacity was 275. It was named the Church of the Holy Trinity, and the Reverend James Rodgers called as first rector. There was until 1858 a quick succession of rectors and supply preachers. The Reverend George Harris served from 1858 till the Civil War.

In 1862 the church was requisitioned by the Union Army, first as a powder magazine, then as quarters for teamsters. During this time the altar was used to butcher meat on, and the building generally abused. Later, damages in the amount of $1,600 were paid by the Federal authorities.

In 1869 the Reverend Moses Royce was chosen rector. His ministry was intelligent and consecrated—and tragic. In 1873 the plague of cholera appeared in Nashville. Its dread hand fell heavily in the area of the Church of the Holy Trinity. Dr. Royce was everywhere, treating the stricken, praying for the dying, burying the dead. On Sunday, June 9, he died of the disease after an illness of only a few hours. His ministry is an uplifting part of the history of South Nashville. The church building was completed and consecrated on May 27, 1888.

The Reverend Charles Tomes was a persistent man. He had hoped to install the free-pew system in Christ Church, but, unable to reach the goal, he proceeded to establish another church. It was the Church of the Advent, started in 1857 in a room over William T. Berry's bookstore. Mr. Walter Stokes of the city has a note written by his father in 1857: "We collected $300 for the new church at the meeting last night." One of the conditions on which the church was established was that it should depend as nearly as possible on weekly offerings. Dr. Tomes very appropriately was called to the rectorship, but survived the call only a few months.

In January 1858 Dr. Charles Quintard was chosen rector. He served until the outbreak of the Civil War. During his ministry the membership rose to 300. He was a Pennsylvanian who had become fully and sympathetically identified with the South. At the beginning of the war he was chosen as chaplain of a regiment. By its end he had risen to the head chaplainship of the Army of Tennessee. His carefully kept journal gives some vivid pictures and otherwise unrecorded details of the closing days of the conflict. It was Dr. Quintard who provided the coffins for the five generals killed at Franklin. The journal, very fitly, found its way to the library at Sewanee. When the churches were restored to their congregations Dr. Quintard returned and took as his major assignment the completion of the church building. Very soon, however, he was made Bishop of Tennessee.

The church was completed and the Reverend James Moore took charge of the parish. He was succeeded in 1870 by the Reverend Thomas B. Lee, who remained ten years and yielded the rectorship to the Reverend W. C. Wray. During his tenure the debt incurred in building the church was liquidated. Dr. Prentice Pugh was rector of this church for thirty-nine years. Dr. James E. Savoy has been rector since 1955.

Saint Anne's Episcopal Church was organized in a school-house on Fatherland Street in 1858. The church building was erected two years later on a lot given by Dr. John Shelby. The first rector was Dr. W. D. Harlowe, but his term was less than two years. No services were held during the war, but when peace was declared the church was reorganized and Dr. J. H. Bowles made rector. The church which had been at first named Saint Stephen's was changed to Saint Anne's in honor of Mrs. Ann Shelby Minnick, a descendant of Dr. John Shelby. Dr. Thomas F. Martin, from Berryville, Virginia, was installed as rector on April 13, 1879. He remained at Saint Anne's for a long while, and his rectorship was perhaps the church's golden era. The site of the church was not satisfactory, and it was sold in 1880, and a new lot purchased on Woodland Street. The new building was consecrated in June 1885 with a sermon by Bishop Quintard. The present rector is Dr. George Gibson.

Saint George's Episcopal Church, on Harding Road, was dedicated in September 1849, Dr. Robert Shaw, rector. It started with a membership drawn in considerable part from Christ Church. There are now about 1,250 communicants. Dr. Arthur Fippinger succeeded Dr. Shaw, and remains as rector. The church property is valued at $650,000.

There are twelve Episcopal churches in metropolitan Nashville with a membership of about 3,750. The Episcopalians have not increased rapidly in numbers, but they have from their beginning maintained a steady and commanding influence on the life and affairs of the city.

THE LUTHERANS

The first Lutheran church in Nashville was established in 1859. The first pastor was the Reverend Herman Eggers, who had become well known for his preaching in several counties south of Nashville. Services were held mainly in the courthouse, though at times in the Second Presbyterian Church. During the Civil War the congregation met in the German Methodist Church. After the war they moved back to the Second Presbyterian Church until their new building on North Market was ready. That year Mr. Eggers resigned and was succeeded by the Reverend J. Bachman, who remained two years. He was followed by the Reverend C. A. Nolte, and he by the Reverend Johannes Heckel. In 1878 the Reverend F. E. Peschau conducted the first services in English. That language was continued when the Reverend H. Juilfs became pastor in 1882. After two years he was succeeded by the Reverend C. E. Raymond, under whom, in 1886, the Lutherans purchased the historic First Baptist Church, paying for it $10,000.

The First Lutheran Church's growth has not been the most significant part of it. It has always been an institution of great steadiness. Its attendance is surprisingly unwavering. A Lutheran is not likely to be absent from his church. Dr. William Gernert was the church's pastor for a long period, and he helped to bring it into a closer identification with the city. The present pastor is Dr. Paul Monroe, and the membership is about 800. There are eight Lutheran congregations in metropolitan Nashville, and the membership is a few above 1,800.

THE JEWS

The Orthodox Jews, in 1851, rented a room on North Market Street, near the L. & N. station, and in it they worshiped on the Sabbath. In 1853 Mr. Alexander Iser, a native of Polish Russia, was elected rabbi. He served five years. The congregation grew, and in 1854 rented Douglas Hall on the Square. In 1862 the first Reform congregation was organized, and Rabbi Labshimer was chosen minister. In 1868 the two congregations merged, and Dr. Kaleish was elected rabbi. His successor was Rabbi Rosenspitz, under whom the Vine Street Temple was begun. Rabbi Rosenspitz was succeeded by Dr. G. S. Goldnamer, and he by Reverend Isadore Lewinthal, who remained more than thirty years. After him came in succession Rabbi Sturn, Rabbi Julius Mark, Rabbi Schwartzman, Rabbi Silberman. Rabbi Falk is the present incumbent. The congregation now worships in an impressive new synagogue in Belle Meade. There are three Jewish congregations in and about Nashville, with a membership of about 1,500.

THE SEVENTH-DAY ADVENTISTS

There have been Adventist preaching and worship in Nashville since early in this century. The first church was on Fatherland Street, but is now located at Blair Boulevard and Natchez Trace. There are seven churches at present with a membership of 1,250. The headquarters of the Kentucky-Tennessee Adventist Conference is located in Nashville.

There are in Nashville, according to data assembled by the Chamber of Commerce, sixty-one churches of denominations not included above with a membership of about 5,500. There are 169 Negro churches with a membership of about 28,000. Many of these 230 churches are obviously of small membership, and yet they are the religious leaven that vitalizes for good a considerable area of Nashville citizenship.

Nashville has in all about 650 churches. Almost all of them are alert and vigorous. They believe something and work toward it. They give their money freely, and the total of it is all but unbelievable. They build great church buildings, and colleges, and hospitals. They carry on carefully developed church programs and missionary efforts. They care for the widows and orphans. Nashville churches can never reach the fullness of their hopes, but they manage to keep them clearly in sight.

7

THE ATHENIANS MARCH AGAIN

THE PEOPLE of Nashville and their friends frequently call the city the "Athens of the South." The figure has a pleasant flavor, and the people love to savor it. Indeed, the phrase is sometimes used with such fine inflection and emphasis as to leave the impression that Nashville is a sort of New World relocation of the famed Grecian metropolis.

As a matter of fact, Nashville was first called the "Athens of the West." It was President Philip Lindsley of the University of Nashville who so put it in 1840. A half century later there had been such a shift in political geography that Nashville wasn't in the West at all. The shifting seems to have been made formally at the Tennessee Centennial in 1897. There Governor Bob Taylor boldly and with characteristic fervor called the place the Athens of the South. His usage was contagious, and before long everybody seemed to be contriving a need to use it. Nashville was then, and remains, the Athens of the South.

But why Athens? Where is the fitness, the relevance? Is it something merely ornate, or is it rooted in some fine likeness between the towns so widely separated by miles and centuries? Very probably the two phrases, to begin with, were bits of shining metaphors used to recognize Nashville as an educational center. It has without doubt always been that, but it doesn't quite justify the "Athens," which wasn't in our sense any sort of college center.

170

But even if indirect the fitness is there. Not many communities have been so wholeheartedly committed to education, particularly higher education. Such an interest began early. Nashville had an institution of higher learning soonest in its career of all the nation's major settlements. The place was five years old when James Robertson, the Founder, himself without benefit of academy, journeyed to Raleigh and there besought the legislature of North Carolina to grant a charter for the founding of an academy available to the youth of the community. As usual James Robertson was convincing and the charter was granted. Immediately following Robertson's return to the settlement Davidson Academy was established. It was located on the Kentucky Road, six miles north of the main group of cabins. The site was chosen because it seemed better sheltered from the Indians, and on the strength of a vague feeling that the main town might ultimately emerge in that neighborhood. A one-room building of stone was erected and made ready.

Dr. Thomas B. Craighead was elected president and main teacher. He had been a member of the class of 1776 at the College of New Jersey. The decade of the 1770's, despite the interruption of war, was one of Princeton's golden periods. The great John Witherspoon, then president, was manifesting a special fondness for the South and West by sending to their wildernesses his finest young men. He sent David Rice to Kentucky, Samuel Doak to Tennessee, John Brown to the Virginia Valley. Those were great names on our pioneer pages. Their marks remain indelible on the sections.

Dr. Craighead came directly to Nashville from the newly established Presbyterian Church at Frankfort, Kentucky. He brought with him as bride a daughter of the famous Brown family, Elizabeth. The influence of the Browns is still apparent in the Virginia Valley, in the Bluegrass of Kentucky, in Louisville, in Maury County, Tennessee, and in Nashville. In time Mrs. Craighead impressed her nephew, John Preston Watts

Brown, with the educational advantages offered in Nashville. He came and was graduated at the University of Nashville in 1834. The advantage Nashville offered him was not a one-way matter. The Browns have been offering advantages to Nashville ever since, indeed since the arrival of Mrs. Craighead. The name has a fine continuity. Since the young man reached Nashville it has never been without a John Preston Watts Brown.

DAVIDSON ACADEMY

Dr. Craighead conducted Davidson Academy, located six miles to the north, as a sort of adolescent Princeton in the western wilderness. The boys of the settlement learned the rudiments at home and then enrolled in the academy. They had from the beginning great respect for Dr. Craighead, first out of the wonder for the learning he had, and then for the interest he could put into their lessons. He taught them long hours and six days a week. The same forefinger that pointed outward in accenting the truth of the world pointed upward on the seventh, for on that day he preached to them the Presbyterian gospel. He taught the classics and mathematics to the boys, jousted delightfully with their parents in conversation, ate pioneer food with great relish, discrimination and capacity, and lived a good life in all of his ways.

But the conditions that govern men and their institutions shift and make readjustments necessary. "Progress" is inescapable. The main town clung to and grew about the site that James Robertson had chosen for it. It was found that the Academy would serve its purpose better if it were less distant, and also if its title were a bit more pretentious. So, on September 11, 1806, it was rechartered as Cumberland College, moved into town and located about a quarter of a mile south of Broadway. A street was named College Street and run by the new buildings, erected under the guidance of a committee, the chairman of which was Andrew Jackson. Dr. Craighead moved into town with the institution but retired in 1808.

Dr. James Priestley was chosen to succeed him, in part on the recommendation of Felix Grundy, who had studied under Dr. Priestley at Salem Academy in Bardstown, Kentucky. Priestley had been graduated from Timber Ridge Academy in the Virginia Valley, and had taught at Liberty Hall Academy, the forerunner of Washington and Lee. He was for a time the head of an academy in Baltimore. From there he had shifted to Salem Academy at Bardstown, and, after four years there, to one at Danville, Kentucky.

CUMBERLAND COLLEGE

President Priestley and Dr. William Hume shared obligations at Cumberland College. The two men were complementary. Priestley was stern and austere. A scholar himself, he never trafficked in mediocrity. He sent Cave Johnson back to his home in Clarksville because the young man was careless with his Latin pronunciation. Cave, who later became Postmaster General of the United States, always claimed that his real worth began to show the day he was expelled, and was a great admirer of Dr. Priestley as long as he lived. Once the boys were rioting a bit because of some real or imaginary grievance. Dr. Priestley, arrayed in academic cap and gown, went out into the yard and stood before the rioters, his face rigid with monastic grimness, his eyes blazing with medieval fire. The lads looked at him for a moment. Then, fully sobered, they scampered for their rooms and Latin books.

Dr. Priestley, immediately after arriving in Nashville, bought a farm from Andrew Jackson, for which he paid $3,000, *cash*. Where did a schoolmaster in Nashville, in the first decade of the nineteenth century, get that much money? One is baffled by such opulence on the part of a pedagogue. The only possibility that one may summon up is that he married it. While he was at Salem Academy, at Bardstown, he married Sarah McBride, daughter of one of the ranking families of Mercer County, Kentucky. We do not know for certain how Dr.

Priestley came to have that much money, but in any case he had it and used it in buying some choice land lying on the east bank of the Cumberland, six miles above Nashville. There, on a bluff towering above the river, he built his house and christened in Montebello. His family lived at Montebello, but he lived in a room at the college with the boys.

In 1816 the college went into one of its several states of suspended animation. When the college disbanded, though all felt that it was but temporary, James Priestley did a strange thing. He opened at Montebello a school for young ladies. However, Nashville has always been forward-looking in the project of female education. Moses Fiske from Dartmouth College, a scholarly man recently established in Nashville, had just done a stranger thing. He had gone up into Overton County and at the village of Hilham opened a very pretentious school for young ladies. It did not last very long but it seems to have been of importance while it lasted.

The Nashville Female Academy opened the same year as Priestley's school at Montebello. It prospered greatly and at the beginning of the Civil War was the largest school for young ladies in the country, perhaps in the world. In 1818 Priestley is mentioned in a connection equally strange. He was elected secretary of the Cumberland Agricultural Society, a surprising office for a classical scholar to accept.

Felix Grundy led in the movement to reopen the college. His leadership was fruitful and in December 1820 the college made a new start, Dr. Priestley in charge, living again in his old room. Two months later he died suddenly. He probably was only sixty-one years old though there were several references to him as an old man. His funeral was held at the college, but it is not known where he was buried. The best guess is that Sarah McBride took him back to a family burying ground in Mercer County, though search there has been futile. His four sons and one daughter have spread his posterity over a wide range of the South. His children were of excellent mind, though slightly flavored with eccentricity. There exists a long poem written in 1813 by his son William, describing in excellent Walter Scott verse the marriage of the poet's brother John to Sarah Montgomery, at the William Montgomery home, Shackle Island, Sumner County. The Montgomery house was built in 1792, and happily is still in excellent repair. The poem is so vivid that it is a pleasure to match its descriptive powers against the stately house standing there, and to visualize the felicitous scenes presented.

All available reports affirm that Dr. Priestley was an excellent teacher for those with the best and most classically turned minds. He apparently had little concern for the others. Six counties in Kentucky are named for men who studied with him at Salem Academy. Although his work at Cumberland College was interrupted several times, some great Tennesseans emerged from his tutelage—as instances, Ephraim Foster, John Bell, Constantine Perkins, Edwin Ewing.

Craighead and Priestley had made Nashville college-conscious in all respects except money. For two years after Priestley's death nothing was done. Then again Felix Grundy took the lead. The college needed reviving, and the town needed the college. It was once said of Felix Grundy in a speech made at the courthouse that he could stand on a street corner and talk the cobblestones into life. There is no doubt that his talk was helpful in reopening the college. Andrew Jackson took time out from urging his claims to residency in the White House to add his voice to the demand. Ephraim Foster was vigorous in his support. So was young Francis Fogg, lately arrived in the city. And soon a good part of the town was lending its support. Means were made available to start the college on a new era.

Then a troubling matter intruded itself. Where was there a man available for the presidency who could meet all the demands raised by the college specially and the town generally? A mediocre man would likely defeat the whole purpose. Presi-

175

dent Horace Holley of Transylvania College in Lexington, Kentucky, was obviously of the quality wished for. He was tactfully invited to visit Nashville. He came bringing his wife and daughter. The Jacksons invited them to make the Hermitage their home while in Nashville, and the Holleys accepted. That was indirectly a most fortunate thing. There is printed on pages 257-258 a letter written by Dr. Holley to his father in Salisbury, Connecticut, which gives the best available picture of life at the Hermitage in 1823. The Holleys were charmed by the Jacksons, and by the town—but not enough to make the change.

On April 26, 1824, Dr. Philip Lindsley was chosen to administer the affairs of Cumberland College during its current effort at permanency. It was a choice of notable wisdom. Philip Lindsley was born in New Jersey in 1786. He was graduated from the College of New Jersey in 1804. From 1807 to 1824 he taught and administered there, serving as acting president the final year. He was of distinction both as preacher and as teacher of the classics. The Lindsley family arrived in Nashville during Christmas week 1824. The college opened with the new year. Twenty-eight students were present on the opening day and seven more enrolled during the session. President Lindsley conceived the time and place ready for the expansion of the college into a larger institution, the University of Nashville.

It is not clear why Philip Lindsley accepted the place at Nashville. From all accounts he was fitting well into the Princeton standards. It is known that he was offered the presidency of the University of Ohio, and that of Dickinson College, in Pennsylvania. At that time Cumberland College had no equipment of importance, and its total resources were meager indeed. He must have been drawn to his new post by the eager, compelling, insistent lure of the West, the lodestar that has drawn so many Americans to immortality, and some to destruction. And so the University of Nashville was born. The name Cumberland was not used because the new Cumberland

Presbyterian Church had just organized a college at Princeton, Kentucky, not over a hundred miles away, and had used the name Cumberland in its christening.

THE UNIVERSITY OF NASHVILLE

In some ways the University of Nashville was destined to achieve greatness, and in some respects to meet only with frustration. Although Philip Lindsley remained its head for more than a quarter century he was never able to secure the means for the expansion he coveted. After twenty-three years as president his soul overflowed with the bitterness of this statement:

When, in 1824, this college was revived there were no similar institutions within two hundred miles. There are now thirty or more within that range and nine within fifty miles of Nashville. These all claim to be our superiors, and at least the equal of Old Harvard. I have before me a list of twenty colleges in Tennessee alone. Several of them belong exclusively to individuals, and are bought and sold on the open market like any other sort of private property. They are authorized to confer all university degrees at pleasure. This is probably a new thing, but Solomon's geography did not comprehend America.

But there might have been rejoicing in Philip Lindsley's soul with just as much cause. The university was always small and poorly equipped. There were registered during Lindsley's tenure 1,059 different students. In that time 432 earned degrees were awarded. It is reasonably doubtful that a better selected body of students ever gathered on an American campus. The roster of the graduates is in major part a catalogue of the first citizens of Nashville. Several historic names are inseparably connected with the university. In that period there were graduated eleven Fosters, seven Ewings, six Nichols, five McGavocks, four each of Donelsons and Hayes, three each of Hardings, Goodletts, Overtons and Craigheads. Strong blood usually survives in long cycles. After more than a century these names are still potent in the city.

Lindsley found at the university a board of trustees, collectively about as able as any trustee group in our educational history. Not many trustees in the nation could match the tenure of Francis Brinley Fogg. He served the university fifty-seven years. He was one of the best lawyers in the town, and one of its most helpful citizens. Andrew Jackson was a trustee of Cumberland College and the University of Nashville for a combined period of thirty-two years. Felix Grundy served for thirty-one years; Thomas Washington for thirty-three years; Washington Barrow twenty-six years; Ephraim Foster thirty-one years; Felix Robertson fifty-six years; John Bell forty-six years; James Overton forty-two years.

President Lindsley chose well his faculty. He brought Nathaniel Cross with him from Princeton as professor of languages. Dr. Cross remained on the staff until his death in 1848. All the documentary references report him an excellent scholar and teacher, though he was generally in some sort of squabble with the president. It got so that Lindsley usually referred to him as "My Cross." Dr. James Hamilton taught mathematics for sixteen years and was the section's pioneer in meteorology. He kept a systematic record of the weather here long before anyone was officially assigned to that service. Girard Troost, a native of Holland, joined the faculty in 1828 and remained for twenty-two years. He was surely one of the great geologists and naturalists of his time. He was as scholarly as his great contemporary, Rafinesque, and of incomparably better poise.

Professional duties were most exacting, although it was almost a century before the term "teacher's load" entered the idiom. It is known that Lindsley taught twenty hours a week during most of his presidency. No teacher had fewer than five classes, and classes met six days a week. Discipline was an impressive word in the old days. Perhaps it had to be. The young men in the University of Nashville were of strong

178

bodies, alert and keen minds, and often of turbulent spirits. It is recorded that William Harding, later master of Belle Meade, entered the university, but finding his classmates "very wild" withdrew of his own volition and studied the situation at Princeton and Harvard. Evidently the young men in those colleges were also a bit on the wild side. He entered the American Scientific and Literary Academy at Middleton, Connecticut, from which he was graduated in 1829.

The official records of the University of Nashville bristle with accounts of expulsions. The minutes state of one who underwent summary dismissal, "Professor Cross saw him on the streets at two o'clock in the morning." What was Professor Cross doing at that hour? Was he abroad in the performance of required police duty? It is not at all unlikely.

Professor Troost's original contract somewhat oddly exempted him from disciplinary duties. This proved irksome to Troost's colleagues. They prepared and forwarded to the trustees a petition prepared by Professor Cross and signed by various colleagues setting forth the unfairness of such discrimination. The trustees were asked to impose similar duties on Dr. Troost, or to reduce his salary accordingly. It is not known whether the professor was moved by a sense of humor and fair play or the prospect of a reduction in income. At any rate a letter was received by the trustees and read at the next meeting in which Dr. Troost agreed to accept his share of disciplinary obligations.

The university was always financially embarrassed. It had no endowment, and it did not receive funds from state or town or church. Its source of revenue was simply tuition, and such contributions as occasionally were made by the citizens. There were not many students and the tuition was low. The cost to a student was twenty-five dollars a semester. For room he paid two dollars, for the use of the library two dollars, for servants two dollars, for damages one dollar. That would amount to a total gross income per student of sixty-four dollars per year.

For twenty-five years Philip Lindsley struggled, torn by the university's unrelieved poverty on the one hand and his ambition for a larger and finer institution on the other. No hint of conflict between him and the trustees is revealed by the records, though there was one matter in which he didn't see eye to eye with them. He opposed the removal of the university from the original site to the hilltop which the trustees had selected. They probably were right. Undesirable social conditions had developed in the school's environment, and the city had altered and disfigured the campus by extending streets across it.

President Lindsley resigned in 1850, but his relationship to the university was not terminated by his withdrawal. His son John Berrien Lindsley was chosen to succeed him. The son's scholarship while in not so sharp focus as his father's was wider and more varied. It may very well be said of him that he became Nashville's most versatile citizen. Philip Lindsley could see much farther than he could grasp. When the son saw something desirable he began straightway to grasp it. The father had had some thoughts about a school of medicine, but he never seemed to be able to get beyond the thinking and talking stage. When John Berrien became president matters moved fast. Within a year the medical department was opened. Within a decade the medical department was the third or fourth largest in the country.

In 1854 the Western Military Institute became the military department of the University of Nashville. The spirit of the time favored military instruction, and during its brief period the institute prospered. It was founded at Georgetown, Kentucky, but made two moves within the state: first, to Blue Lick Springs, and then to Drennon Springs. Its next move was to Tyree Springs, not far south of the Kentucky border. It was in John Berrien Lindsley's imagination that the final shift was conceived, and it was he who made all the arrangements, legal and otherwise. When it was moved to the university the institute was placed under Colonel Bushrod Johnson, later to become a general in the Confederate forces. The enrollment of the institute averaged about 200 during its period in Nashville, almost all of whom joined the Confederate Army early in the war. It was from the institute that Sam Davis went to martyrdom.

In 1867 Montgomery Bell Academy opened as the preparatory department of the university. It was made possible by a bequest of Montgomery Bell, an iron manufacturer of great industry and vision. The original bequest was $25,000, but investments were so wisely made that the fund increased rapidly. The academy has had a colorful career. Now it occupies an excellent campus on the city's western border.

The University of Nashville never quite knew where the next semester's funds would come from. It was accustomed to lean years, but a belt may be tightened just so far. By 1873 the university had adjusted its belt to the least common diameter, so to speak. But there was to be a happy ending after all.

In 1867 George Peabody, of Massachusetts, Washington, Baltimore and London, established a fund for the help of "our stricken, sister Southern states." The amount was $1,000,000. Two years later, just before his death, he added a second million. Of that date Mr. Peabody's bequest was the world's greatest venture in philanthropy. The fund was placed under the direction of a board, appointed, quite likely after due deliberation, of equal membership from North and South. The immediate and detailed direction of the fund was assigned to Dr. Barnas Sears, at that time president of Brown University. The choice of Sears as secretary was an excellent one. He proved one of the nation's great educational diplomats. He was precisely the sort of friend the South needed most, sensitively discerning its educational needs, intelligently and bravely deciding the nature of the help to be given. He had succeeded Horace Mann as secretary of the Massachusetts Board of Education and so was intimately associated with the normal schools at Lexington and Bridgewater. This quotation from Sears in 1851 is pleasingly forward-looking for the time: "If there were a normal school of a higher order, persons already with a good literary education might repair to it and attend exclusively to the theory and practice of teaching."

There was, in Tennessee, nothing new in the notion of a normal school when Dr. Sears took up his residence in the South. Philip Lindsley approved the normal school in his inaugural address in 1825. In 1857 a vigorous though short-lived attempt was made to establish one; and again in 1865. In 1867 President John Berrien Lindsley recommended to the trustees of the university: "It would seem advisable to correspond with the trustees of the Peabody Fund with reference to co-operation in this field." A month later the board presented to Dr. Sears a tentative plan shaped to promote the education of teachers. In the late fall of that year Sears proposed to the state commissioner of education that if Tennessee would establish three normal schools the Peabody Fund would pay $1,000 annually to each, or that it would pay $1,000 to one. Measures accepting both offers were introduced in the legislature but both failed. For a while the matter lay dormant. Then in March 1874 the trustees of the university, whose literary department was again about to suspend, appointed a special committee to revive the normal-school plan. In March 1875 a bill passed the state senate establishing a normal school, but making no mention of any aid from the state. A week later the house passed a similar bill. Governor James D. Porter signed the bill. But still there was no money. On March 24 the charter of the university was changed to give it authority to come to an agreement with the Peabody Education Fund. On May 10 Dr. Sears, in behalf of the fund, offered $6,000 annually on the condition that the resources of the university be transferred to the new institution. The trustees immediately accepted the offer.

And so began the State Normal College, known after 1889 as the Peabody Normal College, and after 1906 as George

Peabody College for Teachers. Eben Sperry Stearns of Massachusetts was chosen president of the new normal school. He was a graduate of Harvard and had succeeded Cyrus Peirce as second president of the nation's first state normal college at Lexington, Massachusetts.

GEORGE PEABODY COLLEGE FOR TEACHERS

It was not called that at first; in fact, not for thirty-one years. The State Normal College opened December 1, 1875. Thirteen students enrolled on that first day, sixty during the session. The normal turned its entire effort to the preparation of teachers, particularly for the public schools. However, only two of the courses offered were, from their titles, obviously professional. Two years later an additional $2,000 annually was voted by the Peabody Fund. And at the same meeting the board voted an impressive number of scholarships, each one awarding $200 annually. These scholarships came to be a major influence in raising the standards of the public schools of the South. In 1881 the Tennessee legislature appropriated $10,000 annually to the school. In 1883 this was raised to $13,300.

President Peirce died in 1887 and was succeeded by William Harold Payne. Dr. Payne was a native of New York, but at the time of his election was professor of pedagogics in the University of Michigan. He may very accurately be called the nation's first professor of education. He served the college for fourteen years, an era of great distinction. He raised the enrollment from 177 to 607. He knew intimately many of the educational leaders of the day. His correspondence with Soldan, Harris, Edwards, Parker and Herbert Quick of England affords keen discussions of educational values then correct.

President Payne resigned in 1901 to return to the staff of the University of Michigan. He was succeeded by James D. Porter, who during the Civil War had been a staff officer under General Nathan Bedford Forrest. Porter had been governor when in 1875 the shift was made from the university to the normal. His administration was a troubled one, though in many ways one of lasting profit. His troubles were those of transition. There had developed under President Payne a strong demand for graduate work, and there was much talk among the more ambitious students about the advantages which a graduate degree might offer. President Porter was sensitive to the mistakes that an overambitious program might involve and for a while resisted entering the graduate field. But finally a year of graduate study was worked out.

That matter was barely settled when the feeling developed rather generally that the situation at the college demanded a removal to a new campus. There were good reasons for the change. There was also a great deal of sentiment against it. President Porter resigned in 1909. J. I. D. Hinds, professor of chemistry, served as acting president for a year, and Dr. Charles E. Little, professor of classical languages, for another.

Early in 1911 the decision was made to move from the campus then occupied across the town to the Hillsboro section, and to a site adjoining that of Vanderbilt. From 1911 to 1914 the classes were discontinued and the work of the institution limited to the erection of buildnigs on the new campus and making ready for the opening June 15, 1914. Dr. Bruce Ryburn Payne, a native of North Carolina and then on the faculty of the University of Virginia, was elected president. In many senses the college was new. But its welfare depended a great deal on the loyalty of the alumni in the various states. That question was answered when 208 former students, most of them graduates, enrolled the first day. About 900 others came, but the 208 gave proper linkage to the school's ancestry.

The master's degree was offered from the first, and the first doctorate to be given by any Southern college of education was awarded in 1919. Now, forty-one years later, 657 have been awarded the doctorate. Now thirty-five graduates of Peabody are presidents of colleges, seventy-five are college deans, more than a hundred direct libraries, about 60,000 are principals and teachers in schools.

President Bruce Payne died suddenly in April 1937, and Professor S. C. Garrison of the department of psychology succeeded him. In January 1945 he too died suddenly. Dr. J. E. Brewton served in the interval following. In September Dr. Henry H. Hill moved from the superintendency of the schools of Pittsburgh to the presidency of George Peabody College for Teachers and today remains in that assignment.

This then is the sequence of four institutions of learning, the changes being made to fit better into the conditions involved. It is a story that actually begins with the beginning of Nashville, the story of a classroom in which instruction was being given more than a decade before Tennessee became a state. The narrative continues through three other sets of classrooms, each serving in its own way the needs of Nashville. These institutions have survived crisis after crisis, temptation after temptation to stop altogether. Not one of the nation's depressions have they escaped. They have felt the impact of every war the country has waged and participated in it. The final institution of the series now occupies the fourth campus, and each one, in its own way, has added to the attractiveness, the traditions and the culture of the city.

VANDERBILT UNIVERSITY

Very likely Vanderbilt University comes first to mind when the phrase "Athens of the South" springs into visibility or audibility. It is the largest of Nashville's institutions of learning, and it occupies the widest front. It has prestige in medicine, in law, in engineering and in its school of religion. Its college of liberal arts has from the beginning carried shining names on its roster. The leadership of the city is dominantly of the posterity of Vanderbilt. The university sets the pattern for much of Nashville's thinking.

Five years after the close of the Civil War, the Methodists made a determined though short-lived effort to establish in the city an institution of learning to be called "The Central University of the Methodist Episcopal Church, South." A charter was secured and a campaign to raise a half-million dollars was begun. But the war had left the people so impoverished that the merest fraction of the amount was pledged. Happily the cloud, dark though it was, came in its maturity to bear a silver lining. Victory, arrayed in splendid drama, emerged from defeat. Bishop Holland McTyeire, one of Methodism's commanding figures, had been prominent in the effort to establish Central University. It was in the alert mind of the bishop that the first lines of the drama were composed. His wife and Mrs. Cornelius Vanderbilt were cousins, a most felicitous connection. In February 1873 there came to the McTyeires an invitation to visit the Vanderbilts in New York, which was very promptly accepted. The bishop was of consummate skill in presenting a plan and a plea. During the visit he dramatized with telling effect the disaster involved in the defeat of the Central University project, and the vitalizing power that a good university could exercise in kindling the hope of the South and in recreating its substance. At any rate when the McTyeires left New York City to return home the bishop bore a letter addressed to the Board of Trustees of Central University. The letter authorized the purchase of a campus, the erection of suitable and needed buildings, and the setting aside of such money as might be left from the offered $500,000 as an endowment fund to be held forever inviolable.

There is a story which fits into character, though documentation is not available. It relates that Dr. A. L. P. Green, one of Methodism's best preachers and strategists, had maneuvered matters helpfully before the visit of the McTyeires. Sometime earlier McTyeire had carried on a debate with another Methodist minister named George Pierce. They had debated with vigor the merits of the proposed Central University,

Pierce declaring in effect that education above the secondary level tended to weaken the ministry. The bishop strongly affirmed the opposite. Dr. Green saw to it that a full account of the debate was given to Vanderbilt before the McTyeires arrived in New York. It so shocked Vanderbilt to find that anyone high in Methodist councils should regard education in such a light, that it rendered him all the more responsive to the bishop's plea.

No grass grew under McTyeire's feet after he reached Nashville. On March 26, 1873, the Board of Trustees met and accepted all conditions of the Vanderbilt offer. It withdrew from the earlier name and christened the institution Vanderbilt University. Then the Board set about looking for a site. It wasn't easy. There were many desirable sites available. They considered them all. In the end they chose the Litton place, occupying an elevation on the city's western border, with a clear and unobstructed view of the Capitol and main buildings downtown, two miles away. No question has ever been raised as to the wisdom of the selection.

The cornerstone of the main building was laid on April 12, 1874. In the early autumn of 1875 the buildings were ready for the university to open. The main building contained the chapel, the library (with over 6,000 volumes then on the shelves), the classrooms, the laboratories, and offices for the professors and administration. The board to begin with had set aside $300,000 for endowment. The grounds, buildings and equipment, after the immemorial tendencies of such matters, had moved somewhat deep into the endowment. So Mr. Vanderbilt raised his original gift to $1,000,000.

On October 3, 1875, Vanderbilt University opened with appropriate ceremonies. The choices of administrators and instructors were good from the first. The selection of Landon C. Garland as chancellor was an understanding one, indeed an inspired one. "The full value of a college president is not revealed until the second or third generation." So wrote F. A. P. Barnard, at that time president of the University of Mississippi, and later of Columbia University. The generations have amply revealed the worth of Chancellor Garland to Vanderbilt University and to Nashville. It discredits no one to say that the students of the university during its first two decades were as well instructed as they have been since, or likely ever will be. The canniness of Garland in his selection of teachers is still a tradition at Vanderbilt. He brought in good teachers, and by his own teaching he set them an impressive example. The war was so close in the background, and so negative were its effects on education generally, that admission was rightly more in terms of instinct and sympathy than in terms of the standards which later were put in force. On the teaching staff were Nathaniel Lupton, chemistry; Milton Humphreys, Greek; B. W. Arnold, Latin; Edward Joynes, modern languages and English; A. A. Lipscomb, philosophy; James Safford, botany, mineralogy and geology; William Brown, mathematics; Alexander Winchell, zoology. In the Biblical department were T. O. Summers, A. M. Shipp, J. M. Granbery and R. M. McIntosh; in law: Thomas B. Malone, Ed Baxter, and W. B. Reese; in medicine: Thomas Menees, Paul Eve, W. T. Briggs, T. L. Maddin, W. M. Nichol, Van S. Lindsley, T. A. Atchison, T. O. Summers, John H. Callendar and C. S. Briggs.

Chancellor Garland managed things so well that the whole university was sensitive to the challenge of good teaching. There were few, if any, loafers among the students and they matched their zeal against the teaching power of the faculty. There are many choice stories connected with those early days. A charming one has to do with Miss Kate Lupton, daughter of the professor of chemistry. She had a thirst for learning and more than anything else wanted to study at the university. But the services of the university were designed exclusively for young men. She visited the dean and requested admittance. He mentioned very tactfully his regret that no provision had been made to admit young ladies. Miss Lupton then called on the chancellor. He listened to her with patience and sympathy. But what could even a chancellor do under the circumstances? There were excellent schools for young ladies in Nashville. The chancellor doubtless felt that he had handled the matter most effectively. He was surprised to find Miss Lupton back in his office before the week was over. And this time her approach was from a new and confusing direction. Of course she would like to have academic parity with the young men, but if she couldn't, why, that was that. Her desire was for learning. She therefore asked for permission to sit in such classes as seemed to her to offer special promise. She would take no part in the discussions of the class. She would merely sit unobtrusively in the rear and ponder such matters as were presented. The young men could have no reasonable objection to her gathering up such crumbs as fell in the back of the room. The chancellor frowned, then pondered, then smiled. Very well, he would present her request to the faculty when it met, and the majority would decide. He was in position, however, to offer her very little hope. He presented the matter, and the professors voted unanimously—having been approached individually by Miss Lupton in the meantime—to grant the request.

Kate Lupton sat in the classes four years, saying nothing, missing nothing. She had deliberately selected those classes required for graduation. She asked for an examination on all the subjects. Again the professors voted consent. She finished everything for her baccalaureate degree. But there was one more hurdle. She would not be permitted to march with the graduating class. There would be too much overt femininity in that. Her father carried her diploma to her. One wonders whether gratitude is a vanishing virtue when he discovers that the young women now freely admitted to classes have erected no monument to their great forerunner.

There are a number of fine stories of the "discovery" of Vanderbilt men and their subsequent advance to fame. In 1882 E. E. Barnard, later to become a monumental figure in the field of astronomy, entered college. The "discovery" of young Barnard was a bit dramatic. He was found by Mrs. Alexander Koscis, who was on a mission of mercy to a very poor home in a very poor section of the city. Mrs. Koscis's husband was in charge of a school for boys at Vine and Bell streets. He was an exile, a Magyar patriot and scholar. Mrs. Koscis was an Overton, a member of one of Nashville's foremost families. She became so interested in the boy that she carried him to her husband's school. His work in the school, and in Poole's Photographic Gallery, in which Mrs. Koscis secured for him part-time employment, was of an excellence to admit him quickly to Vanderbilt. His record there was from its beginning prophetic of his later career.

The year 1886 was especially rich in additions to the Vanderbilt staff. J. H. Kirkland, a South Carolinian bristling with the lore of German universities, was added then. So was J. J. Tigert and William L. Dudley, all inseparably associated with Vanderbilt's career.

During its first year Vanderbilt enrolled 307 students in all departments. And that for the first year of a Southern institution of learning was a student body to be noted. After this impressive beginning Vanderbilt's growth was slow, but there was a certainty about it. Ten years later the enrollment had risen to 553. In 1879 a school of pharmacy was added, and the next year a dental department. Both of these were subsequently discontinued.

The high schools of the section then were new and untried. All too often they didn't exist at all. In the first period Vanderbilt's freshmen came largely from the academies. Later, under Vanderbilt's vague sponsorship several "training schools" were added. From them the university drew some of its best students. In time the high schools became the main source of freshman supply.

The McTyeire-Pierce debate, in a sense, forecast an issue

which in time would lift its visage on the Vanderbilt scene. The emotions stirred by the controversy over the theory of evolution did not fail to push school and church somewhat apart. Professor Winchell was likely more scholarly than discreet in his lectures in zoology. The anti-evolutionists formed for battle. The professor was "tried." It wasn't an agreeable episode, and the conclusion of it all was that there was still a great deal of highly prized ignorance in the world, and that it was unwise and unsafe to try to lead people faster than they could safely go. For that matter it still is, but travel is better now. In time the accumulated strain of that and other matters pushed the university and the Methodist Church into a formal separation. That was in 1914. There were wounds of course, but they have healed. And the flavor of Methodism remains about the university.

Those 307 students have stretched into more than 4,000, and the Litton farm cannot hold many more buildings. The campus throngs with those who envision careers in hospitals, in courthouses, in churches, in laboratories, in the various phases of engineering, in schoolrooms, in the making of homes. Vanderbilt has deep sentiment for its great dead. They are not forgotten. Garland and Kirkland live in Vanderbilt's memory. So do Dr. Dudley, Dr. Tolman, Dr. McGill, Dr. Mims, Dr. Tillitt, Dr. William Witt, Dr. Benton and many others whose minds and spirit helped create the university.

In 1893 Dr. James H. Kirkland succeeded Garland as chancellor. His administration lasted forty-four years. Dr. Oliver C. Cromwell was inducted into the office in 1937, and nine years later Dr. Harvie Branscomb.

The idiom of the Vanderbilt campus is an exciting thing to hear. It is compounded of basic English, flavored with the drawls and lingering cadences of the South, and conditioned by a half-dozen specialized vocabularies.

Bishop McTyeire is buried on the campus, and a great part

of the university passes daily by his grave. It would please the bishop to know that John Wesley still abides at Vanderbilt. And, for that matter, so does Socrates.

FISK UNIVERSITY

The main purpose of the American Missionary Association, founded in 1846, was to establish schools for the Negro slaves in the South. With the close of the Civil War that purpose became an emergency.

There came to Nashville in the summer of 1865 the Reverend E. M. Cravath and the Reverend E. P. Smith, agents of the association and assigned to open here an institution of learning for the freedmen. After considerable search they bought some buildings lying near the depot of the Chattanooga Railroad, just released by the Federal forces from service as hospitals.

General Clinton B. Fisk, of the Federal Army, took such an active interest in the founding of the school that it was christened with his name. It opened January 9, 1866, Professor Ogden serving as principal. A year later the title of the school was enlarged to Fisk University. There was no question of persuading the Negroes to attend school. More than 1,200 enrolled the first two years.

The available buildings fitted the needs of the school most poorly. A new campus seemed the only solution. That problem was solved in considerable part by Fisk's teacher of music, George L. White, a man remarkably gifted in the development of singing groups. In his mind was born "The idea of coining the melodies of the slaves into gold and silver." He chose his singers and trained them with infinite patience. He borrowed on his personal note the money needed to take his singers to Cincinnati for a concert. It was not a financial success, nor were several other concerts he gave in Ohio. Professor White was greatly depressed. And then there came to him a name for his band, the "Jubilee Singers."

It was pure inspiration. The crowds began to come. The title drew them and the singing held them. The seasons of 1872 and 1873 netted $40,000. Professor White brought the money back to Nashville and deposited it to the credit of a new campus. Then, in a great exclamation of faith, he took his singers to England. Queen Victoria heard them and endorsed them. So did Prime Minister Gladstone. The Jubilee Singers carried $50,000 more back to Nashville. Twenty-five acres were bought on the site of Fort Gillem, something over a mile northwest of the Capitol and in plain view. On January 1, 1876, Jubilee Hall was dedicated. But the Jubilee Singers were not there for the dedication. They were back in England, singing for money, all, except for a considerable sum given by Mrs. Valeria Stone of Massachusetts, that was needed to erect on the new campus Livingstone Missionary Hall, ready for use in 1882.

Fisk made rapid progress and at the beginning of the present century was the leading college for Negroes in the nation. It has developed steadily under the presidencies of E. M. Gravath (1875-1900), James Merrill (1901-1908), G. A. Gates (1909-1912), F. A. McKenzie (1915-1925), Thomas Elsa Jones (1926-1946), C. S. Johnson (1947-1956) and S. J. Wright (1957 on). The present value of campus equipment is approximately $4,500,000, the endowment approximately $7,000,000, the enrollment approximately 900. Fisk offers one graduate degree. Happily the spirit of music is still dominant on the campus. The curriculum has spread into all the major fields of thought and performance, but the posterity of Professor White's Jubilee Singers still sets the pitch.

TENNESSEE AGRICULTURAL AND INDUSTRIAL STATE UNIVERSITY

This was opened mainly as a state normal school for Negroes on June 19, 1912, though special courses were offered in agriculture and manual arts. Ten years later its curriculum was raised to meet standard baccalaureate requirements, and in 1951 it officially was given university status. It is supported by state funds, supplemented by Federal funds provided in the Morrill Act. The university is composed of five schools: agriculture and home economics, education, arts and sciences, engineering, and a graduate school offering work leading to the master's degree. There were enrolled during the year 1959-60 3,120 students. At commencement June 1960, 243 baccalaureate degrees were given and 29 masters. Property and equipment are valued at $15,500,000. Dr. W. S. Davis has been president since 1951. This school has gained national prestige in athletics, especially in the victories won by its alumni in the 1960 Olympics.

SCHOOLS FOR YOUNG LADIES

Nashville has always favored schools on the various levels for girls. Moses Fiske, a New Englander but then a resident of Nashville and a trustee of Cumberland College, gave thought in 1805 to the establishment of such a school. On September 11, 1806, he had a charter issued for a school to be started at Hilham, in Overton County. Fiske Academy, conceived on a grandiose scale for one located in the pioneer fringes, was for a while very successful, then it gradually wound to a close. When Cumberland College suspended in 1816, its president, James Priestley, opened a school for young ladies at his home high on the Cumberland River bluff, six miles up the river from Nashville. Very little is known of this school except that it was liberally attended for a while.

Some leading men of Nashville, Robert Whyte, Robert Searcy, John P. Erwin, John Baird, James Trimble and Joseph Elliston, decided early in 1816 that it was both desirable and feasible to establish within the limits of the town an academy for young women. They bought three acres from David McGavock within the vicinity of Spring and McLemore streets. Two more acres were subsequently added and a building erected. On August 4, 1817, the Nashville Female Academy was opened with Dr. Daniel Berry as principal. Two years later Dr. Berry resigned and Dr. William Hume succeeded him. Dr. Hume died in 1833 after fourteen years of rich leadership both in the academy and in the cultural and religious life of the town. He was followed by Dr. R. A. Lapsley, and he in 1839 by Dr. Collins D. Elliott, a native of Ohio but immediately from Florence, Alabama. Under his guidance the academy continued to flourish, until in 1860 the attendance was 513, making it the largest girls' school in the nation, perhaps in the world. The Nashville Female Academy was in excellent condition on that Sunday morning in February 1862 when the news reached Nashville that Fort Donelson, seventy miles down the Cumberland, had surrendered to the Northern forces. No lights blazed in the academy when dark came that night. The girls had scattered to their homes. An attempt was made to reopen the academy when the war was over, but it proved futile. The war had claimed another casualty.

WARD'S SEMINARY

In 1865 Dr. William E. Ward opened a seminary for young ladies in buildings at the corner of Summer and Cedar streets. The school had been under consideration for some time, but Dr. Ward had waited to see whether the Nashville Female Academy would reopen. He was a Presbyterian preacher, well educated, and well endowed with the qualities of leadership. The school was favorably regarded from the beginning, but not the location. It was moved within the year to new buildings erected on Spruce Street, between Church and Broad, at a cost of $125,000. The seminary grew steadily. In 1874 there were forty-eight graduates. Special courses were offered in art and dramatics, and in 1875 a course in physical education. The Ward's Seminary basketball team was the first girl team in the South, one of the first in the nation. Dr. Ward was a classical scholar, but willing, even eager, to give the new a trial. He died in 1887. The seminary was bought by a stock company and continued with little change in staff and none in curriculum. Dr. John Diell Blanton became president in 1893 and continued until the seminary merged with Belmont College in 1913.

BELMONT, WARD BELMONT, AND BELMONT AGAIN

The mansion which Adelicia and Joseph Acklen built in 1848, '49 and '50 never quite fitted its function as a home after the Civil War. It was magnificently conceived, constructed and used during the decade of the fifties. Joseph died during the war, and his wife never regained her enthusiasm for the place. She traveled a great deal and was absent from Belmont for long periods. In 1889 she died in Washington, and within the year the place was sold to Miss Ida Hood and Miss Susan Heron. These ladies, originally from Philadelphia, had for five years conducted Martin College at Pulaski. They were ambitious, alert, cultivated and notably industrious. They lost no time in making Belmont ready. They added an electric-light system, a private water system and a gas machine. The announcement went out that the college would open in September 1890. The people shook their heads a bit doubtfully. They were not used to hurry like that.

The spring and summer of that year was a busy period at Belmont. The college opened on schedule. The enrollment was favorable to begin with and increased steadily. Poverty had retreated obviously by then and those who wished to go to college could very likely find the means. New buildings were added as required, including those now so pleasingly visible from Belcourt Avenue. Miss Hood and Miss Heron conducted a good school and offered an abundance of extracurricular events. In one season the following appeared on a Belmont College lecture series: Margaret E. Sanger, President James M. Taylor of Vassar College, President John F. Goucher of

Goucher College, Russell H. Conwell and William J. Bryan.

The college ran well and with some distinction, but Misses Hood and Heron began to feel its wear and tear. In December 1912, after twenty-two years of service as the college's guides, they sold it and all properties connected with it to a purchasing corporation, which in the meantime had bought Ward's Seminary. On June 1, 1913, Belmont College and Ward's Seminary were merged, chartered as Ward Belmont School, and located on the Belmont campus. Dr. Ira Landrith, who had been on the Belmont faculty for eight years, was chosen president. But within the year Dr. J. D. Blanton succeeded him. Dr. Blanton continued as president until his death in 1933. He was followed by Dr. John W. Barton, formerly an associate in the Methodist Publishing House. Three years later President Barton died. Mr. A. B. Benedict served as acting president for three more years, and then Dr. Joseph Burk, of Dallas, Texas, became president. His administration lasted six years, after which Dr. Robert Provine was president until the school closed in 1951.

Ward Belmont School offered excellent living conditions and good teaching. At first it omitted nothing that seemed to offer an advantage to girls. For a decade it maintained in the southern part of the town a historic dwelling named Woody Crest, used with good effect as a sort of students' club. The "Lecture and Artist" series brought to the Ward Belmont auditorium the best available speakers and musicians. Consider the impressiveness of this list for one season: Woodrow Wilson, G. Campbell Morgan, Walter Hines Page, William Howard Taft, Stephen Wise, Hamilton W. Mabie, Maude Powell, Fritz Kreisler. The school drew to its courses and to its life some very fine young women. But not enough of them. The school was more ambitious than the enrollment justified. It outbuilt its prospects. In its surge of optimism it erected a number of excellent and costly buildings. In 1951 the indebtedness incurred caught up with it. The banks foreclosed and the Baptists of Tennessee took over the property. Ward Belmont

School had greatly endeared itself to Nashville, and its loss was heartbreaking. The Baptists very wisely decided to start another college on the campus. It proved a bit difficult to settle on a name. After some experimentation the christeners came back to the original Belmont.

Belmont College, as a phase of a new era, opened September 1951. President Warren Jones was asked to divide his administrative time jointly between Union at Jackson and Belmont. It was a difficult matter, but he got the college under way. In 1953 Dr. Kelly White, for eighteen years pastor at Belmont Heights Baptist Church, was elected president. The college was extended to full baccalaureate stature, and young men were admitted. At the meeting of the Southern Association of Colleges and Secondary Schools on December 3, 1959, Belmont was granted full admission. Under the new president, Dr. Herbert Gabhart, the enrollment has touched 450.

A great deal of history clusters about the Belmont campus. It was on a noble eminence but had little part in the life of the city that was in full view two miles to the north. On what mysterious errands does history travel. A bride and her groom went on their wedding journey to a far and classic country. A house they saw gripped them. They returned home and there rose immediately on this hill a house full of Mediterranean flavor and magnificence. For a rich and colorful decade life in that home was lived by the standards of the most cultivated. Then war sounded its alarms, and enemies took over the house. The cycles pass and the shrill commands of the soldier yielded to the quiet tones of the teacher. Belmont was ordained to outwear time.

As has been mentioned, almost from the beginning of the settlement Nashville has been preoccupied with the problem of female education. The Nashville Female Academy set a pattern to which the city has been surprisingly responsive. Some of the schools for young ladies survived for only a brief period.

Others were more durable. Now acceptance of the principle of coeducation has become so widespread that only three schools still hold to their original commitment—Harpeth Hall, Saint Cecilia and Saint Bernard. We will mention for this record some that in their day burned brightly before shifting to a flicker, and then to darkness.

In 1824 a Mrs. Scott opened on Cedar Street a seminary for young ladies. It lasted seven years. The courses were taught by Mrs. Scott, Mr. Peticolas and Mrs. DeForges. Almost nothing is known of the details of Mrs. Scott's school. Dr. Philip S. Fall opened a female seminary on Spring Street in 1828. The attendance soon required a faculty of five, and a sixth was added the third year. For some reason the school closed in that year. Little is known of the Davis Female Academy except that it was opened in 1829 and lasted fifteen years. The Cross Classical Seminary was organized in 1833 and closed in 1851. Dr. George Weller, assisted by Mrs. Margaret Warren and a Mr. Kemp, in 1834 opened Weller's School for Young Ladies. There are some contemporary comments as to the excellence of instruction, and the severe discipline practiced. The school lasted five years.

Mr. Alexander Villeplait, a native of France, established in 1836, in the same block as the Nashville Female Academy, the English and French School for Young Ladies. It closed at the end of its sixth session. Dr. Wheat, rector of the Episcopal church, in 1840 opened in the basement of the church a female seminary, but it does not seem to have been in existence three years later. In 1838 a Female Institute was begun in the basement of the new Baptist church on Summer Street. It lasted three years. In 1844 a Mr. Kennedy opened a Select School for Young Ladies on Vine Street. Six years later Varian's Seminary for Young Ladies was located in the same quarters. Minerva College for Young Ladies, located in the outskirts of Nashville on the Murfreesboro Pike, opened in 1848, the instructors being Elder S. E. Jones and his wife. One claim for Minerva was that both its discipline and its instruction were "rigorous." The school was one of the casualties of the Civil War.

In 1848 fourteen women founded the Tennessee High School for Girls. A statement in the articles of incorporation provides an interesting commentary:

... the object of the school being the education of poor young ladies of good character, for the purpose of sending them out into the world as school teachers.

This was in all probability an early approximation of a public high school. The duration of the school is not known.

In 1852 Professor R. A. Lapsley withdrew from the staff of the Nashville Female Academy to emphasize his opposition to the introduction of dancing. He was immediately chosen principal of the Nashville Ladies College. The available information indicates that Professor Lapsley managed well and that the enrollment was favorable. The school was another casualty of the news that Fort Donelson had surrendered.

In October 1860 the Sisters of the Dominican Order established Saint Cecilia Academy. It was located on Mount Vernon Heights in North Nashville, and afforded a superb view of the city. The house in which the academy was opened had been the home of John Beck, the husband of James Robertson's youngest daughter Lavinia. The school was not interrupted by the war but its affairs reached a crisis in the dismal days after Appomattox. In the summer of 1868 all but two of the Sisters left. These two, Sisters Ann Hanlon and Frances Welsh, carried on patiently with the encouragement of Bishop Feehan. Their alertness, good judgment and untiring devotion rescued Saint Cecilia from threatened closure. Prosperity again favored the school, and in 1880 a large building was completed and other needed equipment added. While in its original location Saint Cecilia never offered courses above the academy level, but now its new site on Overbrook Street in the Harding Road section has been planned and arranged for service as a junior college. Saint Cecilia is today the oldest school for girls in Nashville.

Saint Bernard Academy was opened in 1868 on Cedar Street, near the Capitol, in the house which Andrew Johnson had occupied during his period as military governor of Tennessee. It remained there more than thirty years. In 1905 it moved to a new location just west of the Hillsboro Road at the edge of the city. Mother Mary Xavier Young almost singlehandedly raised funds with which to equip the new campus. Saint Bernard remains active and competent in the service it offers.

Dr. Blackie's School for Young Ladies was established in 1875 at 55 South Cherry Street. This was the house in which Dr. Felix Robertson, Nashville's first-born, had lived, and in which he had died in 1865. Dr. Blackie was a graduate of the universities of Edinburgh and Bonn. He was a man of sound scholarship and true culture. Mrs. Blackie, who assisted in the management and instruction, was a great-granddaughter of James Robertson, the Founder. The school prospered for a while but closed after six years.

Nashville Academy opened in 1878, flourished for two years, languished for one, and closed in 1880. It was managed and taught by the Misses Mary and Martha O'Brien, on Spruce Street, only one house separating it from Ward's Seminary.

In 1880 Dr. George Washington Fergus Price opened the Nashville College for Young Ladies, also on Spruce Street. He was a competent and colorful man, a native of Butler County, Alabama. It was his plan to study medicine, and he spent some time in a doctor's office. Then he shifted his direction and entered the University of Alabama, being graduated with honors in 1847. He taught in various schools for five years, and then entered the Methodist ministry. However, some weakness developed in his voice, and he resumed teaching at Selma. In 1856 he became a teacher in the Female College at Tuskegee and, three years later, its president. In 1872 he transferred to the presidency of the Methodist Female College at Huntsville. He held that post until he moved to Nashville in 1880, where his school was conducted under the general sponsorship of the Methodist Church, and under the special guidance of Bishop McTyeire, chairman of the Vanderbilt Board of Trustees. It was successful from its beginning and during the year enrolled 147 young women. The relationship with Vanderbilt proved very favorable to the College for Young Ladies. So close were the connections that it was more or less regarded as a female branch of the university. Vanderbilt opened its library, its museum and its lecture courses to girls. This closeness was a in 1882 the school moved to its new quarters at Vauxhall and helpful influence in the solicitation of funds for a new site. So Broadway. Ten years later it had grown to an enrollment of 425, reaching ambitiously for the record set by Nashville Female Academy. But the school had committed a basic error in that it was built around one man. Dr. Price died in April 1899. His school survived him less than a year, but it left its mark enduringly on Nashville.

Mrs. Clark's Select School for Young Ladies opened in 1885. Its location was in east Nashville, two miles from the heart of the city. The building, four stories high, stood in a grove of fine trees. The enrollment was never large, thirty boarding pupils and about 100 day pupils. The instruction was generally held to be of good quality. Mrs. Clark died in 1896 and the school closed.

In 1889, the Baptists, under the leadership of Dr. C. S. Gardner, founded Boscobel College for Young Ladies. It was named for the historic house which it occupied. Dr. John Shelby, in his day one of Nashville's most influential and wealthy citizens, had favored his daughters with fine homes as wedding presents, one being Boscobel. Though then approximately two thirds of a century old, Boscobel was a most elegant place. Apparently the school got off to a good start. The

Baptists were crowding the Methodists for first place in the city. Boscobel reached its peak about 1911, but the era of schools for young ladies was about over. Boscobel closed in 1914.

Buford College was moved from Clarksville to Nashville in 1901, Mrs. E. G. Buford, principal. She had taught in Martin College at Pulaski under Miss Hood and Miss Heron, and for a while in Dr. Price's school. Buford College was at first located in the Glendale section, just south of the city. Then in 1911 it was moved to the present site of the Midstate Hospital. It moved again in 1917 to the Bransford house, near the Gallatin Road. In 1920 Mrs. Buford died, and with her the school she had founded. It had contributed to the literacy of the community, but it had come to the end of its way. When it closed only three of its contemporaries were left, Ward Belmont and the two Catholic schools, Saint Cecilia and Saint Bernard. Now Ward Belmont is gone.

In 1951 Harpeth Hall, an academy for girls, was established, with Mrs. Susan Souby, formerly with Ward Belmont, as principal. The school has an excellent standing, and there is always a waiting list for admission. For a full century Nashville's commitment to girls' schools was a phenomenon of considerable significance.

DAVID LIPSCOMB COLLEGE

Several colleges have been started in Nashville since the beginning of the twentieth century. David Lipscomb College, in the Granny White section, has achieved a favorable standing among the colleges of Nashville. It was dreamed into existence by two men, James A. Harding and David Lipscomb, ministers of the Church of Christ, then a small but active religious body. That existence was achieved in the summer of 1891, under the title Nashville Bible School. The formal opening of the school occurred on October 15, 1891, on the second floor of an old frame building on Fillmore Street. On the first day there were no chairs, no desks, no tables and only seven boys. Some equipment was secured and the boys were taught mathematics, Greek, Latin, natural science and the Bible. Harding was principal and the classes were taught by David Lipscomb and his brother William. When no classes were being taught the Lipscomb brothers solicited students. The general notion was that the school would close at the end of the first year.

But it didn't. In a rented building on South Cherry Street it began its second year, and on the opening day thirty-four boys were present. David Lipscomb smiled a bit grimly. "Within one year we have increased our enrollment almost 400 per cent," he said. The school moved to a site on South Spruce between Reed and Olympic streets at the beginning of its third session. Slowly but surely the attendance grew. In 1902 David Lipscomb deeded to the school his home and his farm of sixty-five acres, lying between Granny White Pike and Belmont Boulevard. A brick dormitory was erected for boys, a brick structure for recitation rooms and an auditorium, and the Lipscomb house was turned into a girls' dormitory.

David Lipscomb died in 1918, and that year the name of the school was changed to David Lipscomb College. It has encountered some difficult periods. At one time debt became so pressing that the part of the Lipscomb farm lying west of Belmont Boulevard, approximately twenty acres, had to be sold. Now the college owes no money whatever. On its campus are eighteen buildings, ranging in age from the Lipscomb house to the Acuff Chapel, completed in 1958. The auditorium is the largest college auditorium in the city, and in its gymnasium are played the section's basketball tournaments. The enrollment is about 1,300.

Lipscomb College happily is in favor with a group of patrons of substantial means. The leader of these is Mr. A. M. Burton, founder of the Life and Casualty Insurance Company. His generosity has been adding new buildings, new endowment and new devotion to Lipscomb for forty years. At a dinner given lately in his honor a speaker said: "Brother Burton has given more money to Lipscomb College than any other Tennessean ever gave to anything." The next morning at the libraries, the banks and the Chamber of Commerce this statement about Brother Burton's philanthropy was being checked. The checkers didn't believe it at all then. Later they did. Such generosity set a very contagious pattern among the friends of Lipscomb College. President Athens Clay Pullias has the knack of using it to the utmost.

MADISON COLLEGE

Madison College, sponsored by the Seventh-Day Adventist Church, evolved from Battle Creek College in Michigan. There developed some reason to move the college. So it was shifted to Berrien Springs in Michigan. The name of the school was changed to Emanuel Missionary College. Again the college found something to be lacking at Berrien Springs. The decision was made to move the school to the South, and the search for the proper site began. Gradually the survey narrowed to the vicinity of Nashville. The college was to be self-supporting, taking its living right from the soil, so to speak. The search was long and painstaking.

One day in 1904 the locating party was scouting the land lying near the Cumberland River a few miles up from Nashville. It was late in the day and they were a bit depressed. Suddenly one of the women, Sister Ellen White, stiffened into rigidity. "There it is," she said, and there was awe in her voice, "there it is. That is the place. I saw it in a vision."

There was some debate, but her vision was convincing. They bought the land, a small tract then, but now grown to 816 acres. They worked out the beginnings of Nashville Agricultural College, changed to Madison College in 1919.

From the beginning health was a major concern. In 1906 it established a sanitarium which has grown to a 200-bed hospital. The fields are used mainly for crops best adapted for human food. The laboratories have performed well in turning peanuts and soybeans into new, pleasing and beneficial experiences for diners. All students work a part of each day on the farm, in the dairies or the bakeries or the hospital. Necessary expenses are held at the lowest.

E. A. Sutherland was president until 1946; since then, E. A. Sandborn. There are now nine buildings, a teaching staff of thirty, and an enrollment of 325. The degrees awarded are the B.S. and the standard one in nursing. A full course is offered in pre-medical work and for X-ray technicians. The lady's vision has been justified.

TREVECCA COLLEGE

In its first stage Trevecca Nazarene College was the Bible and Missionary Training School. It was established in 1901, mainly through the efforts of the Reverend J. O. McClurkan. Its mission was to provide training for those with evangelistic leanings. It was located on Fourth Avenue, north of Broadway. In 1910 the school was reorganized with an enlarged curriculum and given the name it bears now. In 1914 President McClurkan worked out a plan for the removal of the college to the Gallatin Road near the city's eastern border. Not long after that the president died. Dr. C. E. Hardy served, first for ten years, and after a brief interval for nine more. In 1937 Dean A. B. Mackey was made president. He fitted with credit into the assignment and has guided the college safely through several crises. In 1935 the college was moved to its present excellent site on the Murfreesboro Road. The enrollment is about 400.

THE WATKINS INSTITUTE

The Watkins Institute is a unique school that for about eighty years has been occupying an area left vacant by the other schools. Samuel Watkins was born in Virginia in 1792.

Soon his family moved to Nashville, and not much later both his parents died. The boy learned the art of brickmaking. He was thrifty and before very long went into the brick business for himself. His whole life was a masterpiece of business canniness and frugality. When the Civil War began he was worth more than $300,000, but the war wasted all of it. Although past seventy years of age he started over again. When he died in 1880 he left by bequest $100,000 in cash, and a lot on the corner of Church and High streets (the site of the home of Francis B. Fogg), "for the diffusion of knowledge among the youth of Nashville, otherwise without means." This set a good example.

Mrs. Ann Floersh Webber was a teacher in the Nashville schools who had turned milliner and prospered. She supplemented the resources of the Watkins Institute by leaving it real estate of considerable value on Summer Street between Church and Union. Today the institute is conducted on the second and third floors of the building at Church and Sixth, now new. The remainder of the building and the Summer Street properties now yield close to a quarter of a million dollars a year. More than 4,000 students enroll annually, most of them in noncredit courses. Others use their evening hours to accumulate the credits required for a high-school diploma. It is not an uncommon thing for a woman of thirty-five or forty—the "youth of Nashville" has been liberally interpreted—to sit there, a quiet baby held on her lap, listening intently to every word spoken by the teacher; or for a retired professor from one of the colleges to use the institute to supply something hitherto neglected in his training, but desired. An excellent library is maintained, and special laboratories and studios are provided to meet all needs.

SCARRITT COLLEGE

Scarritt Bible and Training School was established in Kansas City, Missouri, in 1892. The institution was the result of the zeal of Miss Belle Bennett and the generosity of Mr. Nathan Scarritt, who gave $25,000 and the real estate on which to build it. Its original purpose was to train those preparing for missionary service under the sponsorship and auspices of the Methodist Church. It did well enough, but time revealed that it was too far removed from the center of Methodism to give its maximum service. Nashville was in effect such a center, and at Nashville Scarritt could find the co-operation from other colleges that it sorely needed, and carry on its work in one of the nation's leading centers of Methodism.

The move was made in 1824 to a site in immediate proximity to both Vanderbilt University and George Peabody College for Teachers. In Kansas City Scarritt had been directed by Miss Maria Gibson and Dr. Ed Cook, and after 1921 by Dr. Jesse Lee Cuninggim, who helped to wind up affairs there and establish the school at Nashville. The Scarritt campus is one of the most fitting and beautiful of the country's small colleges. Dr. Cuninggim was a man of great devotion, of learning, of quiet and pervasive humor, and one of modern Nashville's most significant leaders. Dr. Hugh Stuntz succeeded him. He was president until 1956 when he retired to take the ministry of a church in Brazil. Dr. Foye Gibson was president for three years and was succeeded in 1960 by Dr. D. D. Holt.

THE DRAMA

Churches and colleges have always been major preoccupations, but Nashville has never been without interest in the drama and at times has found it, in its varied forms, most exciting. There was a theater as early as 1817, but of the performances given there very little is known. The nearest consistent approach to the drama offered in early Nashville was the programs open to the public at Cumberland College, the University of Nashville and the Nashville Female Academy. The literary societies flourished at Cumberland College and the university, though the main drama at their meetings was that inherent in oratory, the debate and the declamation, of which the programs were almost entirely composed. However, they were popular among the town's better citizens. At the Nashville Female Academy the programs came closer to the drama, usually including some music, some declamation and a dramatic skit. There is record of some violin playing by Dr. Boyd McNairy at the academy. He was accompanied by his wife at the piano. The report held that the music was "very uplifting." These academy events were very popular among the townspeople. It could hardly have been otherwise when their daughters and their neighbors' daughters were the performers.

There were turkey shootings, barn raisings and log rollings for the men just as there were such events in most pioneer settlements and towns. The ladies got together at quiltings and things like that. Nashville was always a great place for dining and visiting—for instance on New Year's Day when everybody called on everybody who was anybody.

Considered as a whole, the theater, in any advanced degree, has not imparted an Athenian quality to life in Nashville. But there has been the evidence of it, at times quite obvious. That was definitely true in the decade of the 1850s. That may be accounted for in part by the European travel which began in some mass in the late forties, and became almost a passion in the fifties. The visitors attended the theaters in Paris and London, and the interest which they found there was to make its demands on Nashville.

The Adelphi Theater, on Cherry Street near Cedar, was the most important theater here. The second was the Olympic, on Union Street between Summer and High.

Perhaps the first play to become a pronounced success in Nashville was *Lucille*, by William Boyle Bernard. The drama critic of the *Gazette*, Mr. John L. Marling, was a bit hard to please, but *Lucille* caught his fancy, "embellished with all the beautiful garniture to be found in the kingdom of Nature, Poetry, and Art." Doubtless a little later, when the plays of

William Shakespeare began to come to Nashville, some strain was put on Mr. Marling's eloquence. They came in profusion: *Henry IV*, *Richard III*, *Othello*, *The Merchant of Venice*, *Hamlet*, *Macbeth*. Those starring were James Murdock, J. B. Roberts, Eliza Logan, Julia Dean, Charlotte Cushman and Edwin Booth. *Rip Van Winkle* was first played in Nashville in 1851—the main player, Charles Burke. The play was not enthusiastically received then, but it was later when Burke's half brother, Joseph Jefferson, presented it in revised form.

One of the time's most popular players was Solon Shingle in the *People's Lawyer*. There can exist no doubt that Charlotte Cushman was a great actress. The critics of the Nashville press with unanimity and eloquence affirmed her greatness in portraying Rosalind and Lady Macbeth. "There was never such acting done in Nashville," exclaimed the *Banner*. "Or anywhere," echoed the *Gazette*. J. B. Roberts and Julia Dean were most popular in their Shakespearean repertoire. Eliza Logan in *The Lady of Lyons* was one of the town's favorites.

It was on March 29 and 30, 1851, that an event occurred both very comic and very artistic. P. T. Barnum brought to Nashville the Swedish Nightingale, Jenny Lind, for two concerts. The incongruity involved in joining those two names is apparent at first thought, and the two principals played nobly their parts in that incongruity. Barnum was in rare form, even for Barnum. He arranged to sell the tickets for the two concerts at auction. The novelty of this sales technique apparently caught on, as this account by Barnum himself suggests:

After the auction was over one of my men happening in at the main dry goods store heard the proprietor say, "I'll give five dollars to any man who will take me out and give me a good horsewhipping. I deserve it, and I am willing to pay for having it done. To think that I should have been such a fool as to have paid forty-eight dollars for four tickets for my wife, my two daughters, and myself to listen to music for only two hours makes me willing to pay somebody to give me a thundering good horsewhipping."

The showman continued in rare good form. On April Fool's Day he sent faked telegrams to many of his party. Several received offers at fabulous salaries from banks, opera managers, etc. One man was informed that his wife had unexpectedly given birth to twin sons. Even Barnum's daughter was told that her sister and several cousins were awaiting her arrival in Louisville. The alleged father of the twins sent his wife an answering message telling her to be of good cheer, and expressing the hope that the boys would grow up into images of their mother. There was never a dull moment in the Barnum entourage.

But what about the music itself? The reports lack unanimity. Some claim that the Nightingale was in excellent voice and sang marvelously. Mr. Marling, the critic of the *Gazette*, didn't think so at all. His dislike of Miss Lind's singing leaves a sort of hint that he must have bought his tickets at the auction. But Miss Lind liked Nashville. She found her stay an exciting one. She and several other members of the party went out to the Hermitage. She liked it. It was there that the Nightingale first heard a mockingbird sing.

The seasons passed with some very good plays coming to Nashville. There were some of which the mere announcement remains the only record. In 1856 the Adelphi shifted to a less ambitious but more appropriate name, the Nashville Theater. It was repainted throughout and generally improved in appearance. Jean Davenport, one of England's brightest stars, was secured to open formally the refurnished and renamed theater. The play was *Adrienne the Actress*, a drama unknown now but greatly admired then.

Mr. and Mrs. John Drew gave *The Irish Emigrant*, and again the drama columns of the papers overflowed with superlatives. At that time Ireland was making itself felt in the affairs of Nashville. For ten years the Irish had been reaching the city in numbers that increased annually. The play was as manna to them. Drew's rich brogue, his unmistakable mannerisms, the never-failing buoyancy of his spirit were what they needed most. They practically mobbed him every night. Not only the Irish but the other people of the town liked him too. His gay lilt, the hint of a swagger without letting it materialize into one, his jaunty touches were never failing. But the manager of the Nashville Theater, Mr. Joel Davis, could be a trifle niggardly at times. The Drews and Cushmans cost a great deal of money, and Mr. Davis tried to use only just enough talent that costly to hold his patronage. So he would fill up the spaces with cheap plays and players. The town brought such a complaint against Mr. Davis that he resigned his office. The name of the theater was changed to the Gaiety, and William Crisp was named to succeed him.

Mr. Crisp made an obvious effort to keep a constant run of good plays. On March 8, 1859, Edwin Booth opened an engagement. The play was *Richard III*, and the audience that gathered for the event was the largest that till then had ever assembled for a play in Nashville. The engagement lasted two weeks, and at no performance was there an empty seat in the Gaiety Theater. Booth opened and closed the series with *Richard III*, but it was *Hamlet* that the people remembered longest. Booth was born for the theater, the great theater. His father, Junius Booth, was one of the stage's great figures. In Edwin Booth's body was the grace and carriage that could be shaped to the play's message, and his mind caught the full meaning of the lines he spoke. In the words of the *Gazette*, "He was Hamlet."

In that decade too opera came to Nashville. On May 26, 1854, Arditi's Italian Opera Company performed *Lucia di Lammermoor* at the Adelphi. It is not known whether opening with that opera was a strategy shaped for Nashville, but it might well have been. The city was then most sensitive to

Scottish affairs. It was more a Scottish town than an English one, and Walter Scott was the prime favorite among authors. Many of the great estates were named from Scott's books: Rokeby, Mansfield, Glen Leven, Melrose. But a considerable part of the large audience which filled the Adelphi was not quite prepared for the technique of the opera. The novel they could have understood, or any play derived therefrom, but words sung in an alien tongue were all but baffling to some of them. A live and well man might be entitled to sing, but it wasn't quite the proper procedure for one who was dying. There must have been much talk about it, since a week later the *Gazette* lectured operagoers mildly but firmly.

Those who attend opera must not find fault because they cannot reduce the performance to any rule of reason. If a man in his death agony is heard to sing the hearer must not become disgusted at the outrage thereby inflicted, but must catch in the mystic flow of song the spirit of the dying man.

In addition to *Lucia* the company presented *Lucretia Borgia*, *The Barber of Seville*, *Norma* and *Ernani*. Rosa DeVries was the prima donna, and gained steadily in Nashville's affection. She might not reach the high notes that were so easy for Jenny Lind, but she was the greater artist. She did a wise and gracious thing. There were many good people in town whose religious scruples would not permit them to attend the theater. She arranged for them a special program to be given in Odd Fellows Hall.

Early in 1858 the New Orleans Opera Troupe came to Nashville for eight days, opening with *Fra Diavolo*. They continued with *The Daughter of the Regiment*, *The Barber of Seville*, *The Bohemian Girl* and *Il Trovatore*. In January 1860 Parodi's Italian Opera Company arrived and opened with *Ernani*, followed by *Don Juan*, *Norma*, *La Traviata* and *Il Trovatore*. The prima donna of the Parodi Company was Carolina Alarmo, referred to by the Nashville *Patriot* as "the greatest lyric cantatrice."

In the fifties some important concerts were given in Nashville. In April 1853 Ole Bull, the great Norwegian violinist, gave a concert which by the records was a thrilling event, though few, if any, of his pieces were familiar to Nashville ears. Three years later he came back for another performance. Obviously by then the audience had made some advance in their acquaintance with violin pieces. Adelina Patti, then a child of ten, sang several numbers at the first Ole Bull Concert; two of them had been sung by Jenny Lind when she was in Nashville, "The Echo Song" and "Home, Sweet Home." The *Gazette* rose to the Patti occasion: "No one can conceive of the power, richness, and perfection of voice of the little prodigy until he has listened to her." On June 3, 4 and 5, 1858, the violinist Vieutemps and the pianist Thalberg appeared in a joint concert. These artists made a very favorable impression on the music lovers of Nashville. The two artists very generously gave a free concert to 1,200 school children of the city and to the teachers and the members of the board of education.

Nashville had taken great strides in its artistic development when the Civil War came on. War had been hovering over the city for a decade. It was topmost in everyone's thoughts. The people talked and debated long and insistently as to the nature of the times and the prospect of conflict. They simulated war out at the Western Military Institute. The children played at war on the vacant lots. Yet when it came the people were not ready for it. The suddenness of its advent threw all of their ways out of joint. When the tragic news came they hurried with might and main, but it was too late. In a little while the enemy came steaming up the Cumberland and occupied the city. Then the people, most of them, could go no more to the Gaiety, no more to their churches, for the doors were barred. All they could do was to spend four long tearing years waiting and hungering, and wondering if peace would ever come again.

In time the theater was made available for the army of occupation and for the citizens who joined in their cause.

General Grant made a visit to Nashville—and its theater—in December 1863. In honor of his presence Duffield and Flynn gave a special performance. We do not know what the play was, but the general apparently was pleased by it. The star was Mr. Edwin Adams. A little later Miss Bella Golden drew more than 2,000 in two performances, *A Husband at Sight* and *Pocahontas*. Then came the Ravel troupe for an extended stay. Yankee Locke followed in *A Wife for a Day* and *Green Mountain Boys*. On the evening of February 1, 1864, John Wilkes Booth played *Richard III*. There is massive irony in the patronage the Union troops gave this actor. He was likely even then, in a vague way, planning the death of the President.

The war ended leaving the people halfway between joy and numbness. They would have to carve out new paths, live by new rules. Some had been rich before the war; they were now poor. Many had been poor; they were now much poorer. It was a matter of starting all over again. The grandparents of many of them had started new at Nashville. The old determination still held. They looked back at the past with glowing eyes. Then resolutely they turned them toward the future. There was no theater going during the remainder of the sixties. Too many other things took priority over the arts. There wasn't much going on in the seventies except the founding of colleges. The campus of Vanderbilt University was being carved out of the Litton farm. Peabody was making its transition from the University of Nashville. The Fisk Jubilee Singers were composing the song that would swell into a university. Nashville had been left weak. The best way to become strong was through learning.

But in the eighties the artistic impulses were stirring. The Vendome Theater opened October 3, 1887, J. O. Milson proprietor and manager. The occasion was a gala one. The Abbott Opera Company presented *Il Trovatore* with Emma Abbott singing the role of Leonora. Before the curtain rose there was a moderately long and entirely fulsome address by Colonel Thomas B. Craighead (of the posterity of Nashville's first preacher and teacher), who reviewed the cultural life of the city and emphasized the significance of the event. Other operas performed by the Abbott company were *Faust*, *The Bohemian Girl*, *Mignon* and *Ruy Blas*.

The flavor of the theater was upon Nashville all the time. The Little Theater of Nashville was organized in the spring of 1926. Miss Jane Crawford, from whose devotion the Little Theater sprang, was president, and Mr. Lark Taylor was director. Mr. Taylor was an actor of wide and rich experience and for several seasons had been one of the leading players with Sothern and Marlowe. The Hillsboro Theater, erected as a movie house at Carlton and Hillsboro, was leased and remodeled to serve the new function. Eight plays were presented the first season. Among them were *The School for Scandal*, *Passing of the Third Floor Back*, and *Outward Bound*. The Hillsboro Theater was discontinued in 1932 but reopened three years later as the Nashville Community Playhouse, Fritz Kleibacker, director. The Playhouse prospered dramatically and, in reasonable degree, economically through a series of directors. The name was changed again in 1958, this time to the New Theater Nashville. The present director is Barrett Owens. Many names of distinction have appeared on the *dramatis personae* of the New Theater Nashville, such names as Fred Coe and Delbert Mann, but the one whose devotion and acting ability stands out in shining letters is Sam Tarpley.

Another institution of importance to Nashville's theatrical interests is the Circle Theater, established in 1950 and located in the Green Hills village of Hillsboro.

THE NASHVILLE SYMPHONY ORCHESTRA

Nashville, as a whole, is not as willing to pay for its classical music as it is for its country music. It has spent more money for

"Sourwood Mountain" than it has for Schubert's "Unfinished." Eddie Arnold has far greater box office appeal than does Brahms. "The Tennessee Waltz" has more economic standing here than *Aida*. The income of the Grand Old Opry is at least three times that of the Nashville Symphony Orchestra and the Community Concerts Series combined.

But the record would affirm that for more than a century Nashville has had a persistent core of citizens, not large but growing, whose fondness has been for great music. They were not organized. They faithfully attended concerts given in the city, and wrote letters to the papers stating that the music was fine, and there should be more of it. But that was as far as they went.

It was within this generation that Nashville's music lovers formed themselves into an aggressive and articulate body. The leader in the organization was, and is, Walter Sharp, now director of fine arts at Vanderbilt. He came back from the war convinced that the need and the time had drawn fitly together. He brought into a series of conferences some who were similarly convinced. Among them were Kenneth Rose, violin teacher, Mrs. Fitzgerald Parker, harpist and housewife, Reber Boult, lawyer, Dr. Irvin Wolfe, director of music at Peabody. And so, on December 10, 1946, the Nashville Symphony Orchestra was born. For all the leaders in the movement the ensuing period was a time of great drudgery. A symphony orchestra of good talent, good discipline and well directed is costly. It was costly then and it has grown steadily more so. There have to be more players, more rehearsals and generally a soloist of national prestige. But the orchestra has met its full schedule for each season. Now a season carries six concerts, each presented twice. There are seventy-five players in the Nashville Symphony Orchestra. They come from the colleges of the city and section. Some are professional musicians in the city, music teachers, members of radio and television staffs, etc. Some are citizens with the talent and desire to perform. There have been three directors, William Strickland, Guy Taylor, and Willis Page. The annual budget has risen from a little over $40,000 to a little over $90,000.

Once established the Nashville Symphony Orchestra proved a proliferating body. Within two years the Nashville Youth Orchestra had been formed under the sponsorship of the parent group. Its membership is selected from the public and private schools' most promising instrumentalists. They play three concerts a year, one at Christmas, one in the spring and one at the Arts Festival. Twenty-five members have already graduated into the senior orchestra. Andrew Ponder directed the Youth Orchestra until his death. Don Cassell succeeded him and continues.

The Nashville Symphony Orchestra goes further than the artistic service mentioned above. It schedules and plays twenty-four concerts a year in the schools of the city and county to a total audience of about 20,000. The schools are good ground and the seeds sown there are good seeds.

It may be a bit overhopeful to think that in Nashville grand opera will ever overtake the Grand Old Opry. One can engage in a fraction of wonder as to whether it should. But a discerning person can find here an ever-improving good taste in music, and an ever-increasing ability to recognize it, and an ever-growing eagerness to hear it. Those things that are permanent in music will find an anchor in Nashville.

PAINTING

Any record of Nashville's art should begin with Ralph E. W. Earl, who for seventeen years served as Andrew Jackson's private portrait painter. Earl was descended from a family of painters, and his portraits were dependable though never great. He married Jane Caffery, niece of Mrs. Jackson. Mrs. Earl died a few months after her marriage, and thereafter Earl lived at the Hermitage and painted such portraits as the General might direct. He was obviously not often unemployed.

The town's most popular artist of all time was Washington Cooper, born in east Tennessee in 1802. The family moved first to Shelbyville and then to Nashville. He had no training in the use of paint until he was twenty, though during his teens he spent all of his money for it, and used all the available flat surfaces to spread it on. His father finally became convinced that he would never make a farmer out of his son, and yielded to the boy's plea. He was sent first to Murfreesboro to study under Earl, and then to Philadelphia to study under Thomas Sully. He came back to Nashville, set up an office and invited all who yearned for portraits to call. A great many called, and his artistry became very much sought for. He averaged about thirty-five portraits a year as long as he lived, and these have become the prime artistic exhibits of the section. He sent his brother William, similarly committed to painting, to Italy to study under the Italian masters of the time. William settled in Nashville but within a few years moved to Chattanooga. His portraits are held in high esteem, though not quite ranking in favor with those of his brother.

Peter Calvert was born in England in 1855, but came to the United States early, settling in Nashville. He painted a great deal and his work was of good quality, but his fame rests mainly on photography, which he developed into the best. George Dury was born in Bavaria in 1817. He was early inclined to art and excelled in it. He painted portraits of some of Bavaria's rulers. Then he left his country and came to Nashville where his prestige still holds. William E. West, born in Lexington, Kentucky, in 1788, also studied under Sully in Philadelphia. He painted portraits of Byron, Shelley and Mrs. Hemans. He came to Nashville and was successful during the few years of life he had remaining.

William Strickland's reputation in Nashville rests mainly

on his architectural service to the Capitol, the Presbyterian Church, Saint Mary's Cathedral, and some homes. But it is known that he left some excellent water color sketches.

Among Nashville's painters of the ensuing period were Sara Ward Conley, Mayna Treanor Avent, Willie Betty Newman and Ella Sophonisba Hergesheimer, great-great-granddaughter of Charles Willson Peale. Nashville today has an impressive array of portrait painters, architects, sculptors, landscape artists and practitioners of the fine art of flower growing. The eyes of Nashville have always been sensitive to Beauty, and its hands skilled in creating it.

RYMAN AUDITORIUM

Ryman Auditorium has been the scene of the city's leading dramatic, oratorical, musical and political events since it opened in 1892. These uses were not foreseen in its planning and construction. The Reverend Sam Jones was then the South's leading approximation to Dr. Billy Graham today. His fame had spread to the extent that he was asked to assist Dr. DeWitt Talmage in a revival held in Brooklyn in 1885. Not long after that he came to Nashville and held a meeting in a tent at Eighth Avenue and Lee Street.

At that time one of Nashville's best-known men was Captain Thomas Ryman. His early career was spent on the Cumberland River, and he rose in time to the captaincy of various steamboats plying the river. Ultimately he became the owner of a line of steamboats. He was a vigorous, intelligent man, with the rough spots typical of a river career showing plainly. His attendance at the Jones meeting is not explained, though it seems that everybody was going. He went, was converted and spent the rest of his life as an active churchman. That involved several shifts in his estimates of fitness. He found the crudity of a tent for the use of a preacher of the high type of Sam Jones to be specially offensive. When Captain Ryman became that interested he put himself into action. He decided on the erection of a tabernacle appropriate for the use of the Reverend Sam Jones. He put down his own contribution first, an impressive one. Then he set about to collect from his friends what more was needed. He got it. In 1892 the building, a great, hulking, ungraceful, commodious affair, was finished. It was to be used for religious meetings, with Sam Jones given preferential priority. The first time it was used for another purpose was in 1898 when the Confederate Veterans held their annual reunion in Nashville. Those reunions were impressive. Every veteran who had the money for a railroad ticket—and there were a lot of them—rode by train. If not, and he had a horse or was an able walker, he still showed up for the reunion. Before the week was over the city became aware that it was being an eye and ear witness to a reunion.

When there was no further excuse to remain longer the veterans departed, fully convinced that the wrong report had got around as to the outcome of the war. Nothing else in Nashville was of the size to accommodate the reunion, so the use of the Ryman was requested, and granted. But when they counted the seats it was plain that some excellent veterans would have to stand during the programs. The United Daughters of the Confederacy rallied and met the emergency. They collected money and had the gallery built. It has always been known as the Confederate Gallery. The reunion was by unanimous vote a great success. After that, the Ryman, while still holding to its ordained function, began to offer its facilities to secular talent.

Here Bob Taylor, the owner of the golden voice and the user of the golden adjective, enters the Ryman story. The Rice Lyceum Bureau, of which he was the owner, moved to Nashville and made considerable use of the Ryman. In 1914 the Bureau was dissolved and Mrs. Lula Naff leased the building for independent purposes. She had been connected with the Bureau and was familiar with the work it did. For thirty-five years, without interruption, she remained as manager, and to the Ryman she brought prodigious talent. The building is large, the seats are comfortable, and by some felicitous accident of construction the acoustics are unsurpassed. By the time he had turned his first phrase an orator knew that the place was perfect for speaking. After the first few measures the musician relaxed. Here the music would sound as hoped for. William Jennings Bryan's compliments were spontaneous and fervid. So were John McCormack's. Most of the great ones of this century have appeared at the Ryman. Adelina Patti sang there almost a half century after she had sung at the Adelphi. Elman, Heifetz and Maude Powell played concerts there, and Fritz Kreisler played three. Season after season DeWolf Hopper brought Gilbert and Sullivan to the Ryman. Schumann-Heink was there often. Among the others were: Paderewski, Gans, Rachmaninoff, Galli-Curci, Farrar, Caruso, Martinelli, Hempel, Alda, Ruth St. Denis, Ted Shawn, Pavola. Almost no artist with any prestige whatever went unacquainted with the Ryman.

Lately the main attractions offered at the Ryman are road shows and the regular Saturday night programs of the Grand Old Opry. This institution which is almost forty years old is the nation's most important organization committed entirely to country music. The Saturday night program is the senior of all the radio and television series. For many years all seats in the Ryman have been taken long in advance, and three fourths of the patrons come from outside the state. The Ryman was well built, else it would have been worn out long ago.

Nashville has more park area per capita than any city in the nation. The people are park-minded and make free and frequent use of their parks for recreation, sightseeing, and picnicking. There are thirty-three parks belonging to the city with a total of 3800 acres. They are well equipped for games, for serving food, for horseback riding, for use by boy scouts and girl scouts, and for those who wish merely to commune with beauty.

The Children's Museum is one of Nashville's most unique and helpful institutions. Its obligation is to children, and yet one out of five of its visitors is a child no longer. It deals with many areas of life and the universe, and its lessons are not likely to be tedious and boring. Every year something over 95,000 visit the museum. They have come from seven states and from seventy of Tennessee's counties. They generally come in school busses, accompanied by their teachers.

The building is 108 years old. It has known all the stresses of time and war. It was the main building of the University of Nashville from 1852 to 1862, after which it was used as a war hospital by the Union forces. Then for a decade it again served a crippled and starved university. In 1875 it became the main building of Peabody College (then called the State Normal College), and continued in that function till 1911, when Peabody began building on its new Hillsboro campus, two miles to the west. For twelve years, Vanderbilt University's classes in medicine were taught in the building. Then, in an odd adjustment, the state of Tennessee came into possession of the building. For a while it was used as an armory, but this too was discontinued. There seemed nothing left for the old building but its destruction.

Rescue came from an unexpected and surprising quarter. Sergeant John Ripley Forbes was stationed in an army post near Nashville. In civil life Mr. Forbes was associated with the Hornaday Foundation. The foundation existed in major part to assist in the establishment of children's museums. Sergeant Forbes had been duly indoctrinated in the value of such institutions. So, in his spare time, he hunted up persons in strategic positions and had talks with them. He had no ax to grind. His was purely a missionary effort, and his listeners found him convincing. On June 22, 1944, a meeting to discuss plans for a museum was held. Those present were: Dr. H. S. Vaughn, Mrs. Rufus Fort, Dr. George Mayfield, John Sloan, Vernon Sharp, G. H. Waters, James Armistead, Miss Margaret Cate, W. A. Bass, A. S. Ganier. The conference spread contagion, and at a meeting held on September 27 the project of the Children's Museum went into organization with Vernon Sharp as president; as vice presidents, Mrs. Battle Rodes and W. A. Bass; as treasurer, Maxwell Benson. The members of the advisory committee were Stanley Horn, Mrs. F. C. Lasky, Bascom Jones, Mrs. Robert Cheek, Charles Mitchell, Alfred Starr, Dudley Gale. The main function of the committee was to interest the officials and citizens of Nashville in the museum. The members of the board were: Vernon Tupper, Mrs. David Stein, J. E. Windrow, Tony Sudekum and E. B. Walker.

Governor Gordon Browning listened to the story and was convinced. He, in turn, convinced the proper members of his administration. Soon the building was made available, and, in modest degree, funds for its operation. Dr. Harry Vaughn was named director of the museum. It was got into order for service and the doors opened. Dr. Vaughn was succeeded in 1946 by W. G. Hassler, and he in turn by Philbrick Crouch. Miss Louise Davis is director of programs. In its fifteen years the museum's equipment has multiplied. It now includes these features: the Tony Sudekum Planetarium, the Alfred Starr Memorial Art Gallery (for and by children), the Joseph H. Thompson Mammal Hall, the Dan Maddox African Waterhole Diorama, the Rudolph Light Bahama Reef Diorama, the Davidson County Agricultural Society Plant Hall, the Live Animal Room, the Historical Section, the Natural History Section, and a fabulous arrangement of toy trains planned and installed by the city's railroad engineers.

That building which the state was planning to demolish has become—through the help of the state, through vision and planning, through the contagion of a moving idea, through hard work and generosity—one of Nashville's great centers of learning.

THE PILLARS

Nashville is Athenian in another sense—its pillars. It is a pillared town in pleasing degree. Its era of pillars began about 1830, though a few were standing in their "gray glory" before then. There were fine pillars for the main building of Cumberland College, completed in 1809. They were placed under the direction of Andrew Jackson and James Robertson, who composed the building committee. It is not known what became of the columns—they were there in 1850—but the capitals are kept on the campus of Peabody College. They are of sturdy effect and well carved; they tell not only of classic Greece but of their own primitive and perilous time and place. The conventional egg-and-dart pattern has been shifted into one obviously stone-club-and-Indian-arrow. By the beginning of the Civil War an Athenian echo could be caught from the pillars standing in front of most of the great estates—Belle Meade, Belmont, the Hermitage, Tulip Grove.

It isn't merely an echo at the Parthenon or the Capitol. The Capitol has been called with some justice "the most Athenian building in the country." It is two buildings brought from Athens and ingeniously compounded, the Erectheum and the Choragic Monument to Lysicrates. There are porticos on both sides and ends of the building. On the north and south sides there are eight Ionic columns, and six each on the east and west sides, a total of twenty-eight. The tower is supported by eight columns of pure Corinthian style. More than a century of wear and weather left heavy marks on these columns, and they have been entirely replaced. No state Capitol in the nation is more reminiscent of great Grecian art than Tennessee's.

The Parthenon came much later. It was first constructed in 1896 and served as the great central building of the Tennessee Centennial in 1897. It follows in the closest possible measurements the immortal structure on the Acropolis, and it was deliberately chosen to lift the building ideals of the people above the level of the General Grant style of architecture, dominant since the war, back once more to the grace and dignity of Fairview and Riverwood. The choice seemed to serve its purpose. There was at first no plan to use the building further than for the duration of the Centennial, but the people had become so fond of it that there was a reluctance to tear it down with the rest of the buildings. That reluctance hardened, but the money to give it permanence wasn't readily available. However, in 1920 the Nashville Board of Park Commissioners assumed the task of restoring the Parthenon with permanent material. The interior of the building was completed in 1925 and the exterior in 1931. The Parthenon affords one of the great displays of columns not only in Nashville but in the nation. Nowhere are there pillars finer or more fitting than those used in the War Memorial Building.

All the buildings on the campus of Peabody College except two are fronted by magnificent columns, some Corinthian, some Ionic, some Doric. The college song is "Pillars of Peabody." A great many of the churches of the city by their pillars acknowledge a kinship to Athens. In its houses, in its churches, in its colleges and in its public buildings the pillars of Nashville betoken the sensitivity of the people to ancient beauty.

This is not inclusive of the full repertoire of Nashville's associations with Athens. There is in particular one that time, the great weakener, has tended to dissolve. Athens was the city of Demosthenes, and in Nashville the orator was a great force during a long period of the city's life. Some of that era kissed their words good-by with as much fervor as ever did William Jennings Bryan or Henry Clay. Their mellowed phrases still echo in the memories of some of the older men here. But alas for a full half a century the fine art of oratory has been losing its fineness. Gone from Nashville are the stentorian voices, the lingering cadences, the great climaxes of Felix Grundy, of John Bell, of Ephraim Foster, of Bob Taylor, and none have appeared to take their places. The legislative voices on Capitol Hill have become stereotyped and dissonant. The resounding voices of the courtrooms have sunk to tinny echoes.

A little more than a century ago, when the word went out that Edwin Ewing was to speak in a case, the courtroom was packed long before the court opened. Ah, there was a voice and a vocabulary! There were others, many others. But now the crowds gather to hear a crime re-enacted, not to hear the lawyers speak. The response to the pleadings of the politicians now is only skin deep, too often bearing strange hints of a mutual plagiarism. The least loss has been in the pulpits, but even there the eloquence of the successors of Dr. J. H. Otey, of Dr. John T. Edgar, of Dr. R. B. C. Howell, of Dr. Phillip Fall, of Dr. Holland McTyeire seems to have become a bit forced.

Oratory has been one of Nashville's great arts, indeed one of the nation's. But it is not now. The old spontaneity, the old feeling for the poetry of words, the merry quips untouched by the grossness of the wisecrack, the old magnificence of gesture, all have weakened lamentably.

What has brought this loss upon us? Was it the schools demanding more facts and less fancy? Was it television, or the public address system, crowding too many into the category of the orator; or the thousand and one sideshows that cry aloud for our attention? Has the true orator disappeared permanently from our platforms? One who will not ever lose the thrill he felt one October afternoon when for two short, short hours he sat upon a steel-tired carriage wheel and heard William Jennings Bryan speak, hopes not.

8

PEN AND PRESS

As a matter of fact Nashville is a good business town. Its academic, religious, artistic and professional life is becomingly supported by the manufacture of shoes, bags, tires, glass for automobile windows, vacuum bottles, overalls, hosiery, etc. It is a distributing center of importance for everything that is sold in the section's stores.

The country's third largest shoe manufacturing company was founded here, and still is administered from here. It is no longer just a shoe company. The imagination of its officers could not be limited merely to service to feet. So it has spread its production and inventory upward from the pedal extremities to include outer clothing for gentlemen, underclothing for ladies and jewelry for everybody.

In Nashville are located two major insurance companies, and three more are on the way up. The financial district guides and guards a great deal of money in transit or lying in wait. The stores are ample, and some of them are colorful. Some of the nation's largest and most dependable construction companies are here. A great deal of meat is prepared and marketed from here. The hotels and motels care for an amazing lot of guests, tourists, conventioners, and those on business.

With most of the town's industrial and business life the writer has too little acquaintance to be either fluent or factual. But his acquaintance with the business of printing and publishing is more personal and dependable. It is the town's foremost business. From its earliest period Nashville has manifested an affinity for the printing press. And, from its beginning, Nashville has been eager to provide its presses with something to print. To produce and to peruse the printed page have always been complementary excitements in Nashville.

The pen and the press have ever been companions here. The pen has written and the press has printed. In a very valid sense Nashville has lived by their combined efforts. The newspaper, the pamphlet, the magazine and the book for more than a century and a half have ranked high in Nashville's esteem and achievement. Here are a public library and its branches, a state historical library, about thirty church libraries, ten college libraries, more than seventy-five school libraries. One unique and remarkable institution is the Joint University Library, serving Peabody College, Scarritt College and Vanderbilt University. This concentration of materials and service is a new and effective effort in library administration.

The *Tennessee Gazette*, Nashville's earliest publication, was first printed when the settlement was seven years old. Of Mr. Henkle, the editor, very little is known. After two years he sold the paper to Benjamin Bradford, who changed the paper's name to the *Clarion*. He sold it, soon after that, to his cousin, Thomas Bradford, whose printing activities in early Nashville were of significance.

The best-known paper of the town's pioneer period was the *Impartial Review*, established by Thomas Eastin in 1805. The motto carried on the masthead was a bit ambitious and suggested more the classic than the pioneer: *I, from the Orient to the drooping west, making the wind my post horse*. The price of the *Review*, published weekly, was two dollars a year, two and a half if paid later. It was issued for four years and is the source of many glimpses of early Nashville, otherwise lost.

In September 1812 the Nashville *Whig* made its appearance. It was owned, edited and published by the Norvell brothers. The Nashville *Banner* was first published in 1822. Four years later it was consolidated with the *Whig*. The product of the merger was the Nashville *Banner and Whig*, William G. Hunt, editor. In those days the title "Editor" suggested an inclusive assignment. He got the news, wrote the copy, set the type, ran the press, folded the papers and frequently delivered them. How exciting it was to see one's own composition flow out of a pen into a press and then spread into the public view!

Nashville's first author of importance was Judge John Haywood, an able jurist, interested in just about everything. In 1809 Thomas Bradford printed for him *A Revisal of all the Public Acts of North Carolina and Tennessee Now in Force in Tennessee*. He wrote many books, some in Nashville but more in Knoxville. All those bearing a Nashville imprint were published by Bradford, located "next door to the Talbot Hotel." In 1819 appeared the judge's work, *The Christian Advocate*, and in 1823 his *Natural and Aboriginal History of Tennessee*.

In 1812 Bradford published for Isaac Clark, of Gallatin, *A Miscellany of Prose and Verse*. In 1813 he issued *A Compendium of Useful Information*, probably edited by himself.

The pulpit got into the press early. In 1814 the Reverend Barton W. Stone produced in Nashville *An Address to the Christian Churches of Kentucky, Tennessee, and Ohio*. Stone was a Marylander who had recently come to the Southwest. After a period of itinerant preaching in Georgia and Tennessee he became pastor of the Cane Ridge Presbyterian Church in Bourbon County, Kentucky. For several years he had felt some twinges of conscience as to the church's Calvinistic theology. At Cane Ridge this uneasiness swelled to a crisis. When it subsided, a new denomination was well on the way to formation—the Christian Church, or the Church of the Disciples. In the main its theology was compounded of the beliefs of Barton Stone and Alexander Campbell, both able Presbyterian preachers to begin with. And both were fluent writers. Much of what they wrote found its way into print.

In 1814 W. W. Cooke wrote a book for use in the courts, *Supreme Court of Errors and Appeals*, which was printed by Norvell. In 1817 Grier's *Tennessee Almanac* was printed by Bradford. Judge John Overton's book, *Tennessee Superior Courts of Law and Equity*, appeared about the same time. The judge was a very remarkable man. He was an excellent lawyer, though his study of the law had been informal indeed. He was an excellent judge of property values, as the fortune he amassed suggests. He was an excellent political strategist, and the wisdom of his long-continued counsel to Andrew Jackson is most convincing proof of it. He was the founder of one of the section's great estates, Travelers' Rest, five miles south of Nashville.

In 1820 Adam Clarke wrote a small book, *Letter to a Methodist Preacher*, published by G. Wilson. In 1820 the section's first song book, *Western Harmony for Singing*, was published by Cary Harris. Wilkins Tannehill's *Masonic Manual* came out the same year. This was an important book in the fraternity of Freemasonry, used as a text in various study courses.

Tannehill was of enough importance to deserve some further notice here. He was born in the outskirts of Pittsburgh in 1787. He attended a preparatory school, and later the institution which developed into the University of Pittsburgh, from which he was one of the first to graduate, perhaps the very first. He had three uncles named Wilkins who owned the Saline Salt Works in southern Illinois. Young Tannehill was sent there as a clerk in 1799. Then his kinsmen began to develop the salt industry in northeastern Kentucky. So he was transferred there with headquarters at Lexington. He soon was made sales manager, and in that capacity made trips to Natchez, Memphis and New Orleans. In 1810 he was sent as the representative of the company to Nashville. He brought with him a bride, who had been Eliza DeWees, of Lexington. Her grandfather had provided the headquarters used by General George Washington at Valley Forge. She was a niece of the famous Judge John Coburn of the early days. To the Tannehills were born seven children. Their posterity, bearing the names Berry, Bryan, Pilcher, Avery and Callicott, is potent in Nashville today.

Salt was in great demand and the business prospered, but Tannehill soon withdrew from it and entered public and literary life. He served two terms as mayor, beginning in 1825. He became the area's outstanding Mason. He was Tennessee's Grand Master from 1817 to 1824 except two years served by Andrew Jackson. When Lafayette visited Nashville in 1825 Tannehill delivered an address of welcome in behalf of the Masons. He directed the formation of a Masonic college at LaGrange, Kentucky, and three years later one at Clarksville, Tennessee. On July 4, 1845, he presided in due and ancient form at the laying of the cornerstone of Tennessee's Capitol. In 1818 he became editorial writer for the *Whig*. In 1830 he moved to Louisville and there edited a paper which performed yeoman service in exploiting Henry Clay. His breadth of interest was such that he became secretary of the organization which in time matured into the Kentucky Educational Association.

In 1827 Tannehill published *The History of Literature from the Earlier Period to the Revival of Letters in the Fifteenth Century*. In 1847 he produced a *History of Roman Literature*. In October 1845 he became editor of the *Orthopolitan*. This was likely conceived to be a political organ, but it never was. The essay was more at home in its columns than the advocacy of a political candidate or measure, the essay flavored with classic epigrams or with polished Latin phrases. The spirit of the *Orthopolitan* was quite detached from petty moves on a political chessboard. For its loftiness of thought it was so penalized by a prejudice-fed public that it died of inanition at the end of a year. In June 1847 Tannehill began the *Portfolio*, in large part a journal of literature. It survived for three years.

One of Tannehill's daughters married William T. Berry, an early printer and a renowned bookseller. His store became a gathering place for those throughout the South whose libraries were in process of accumulation. A prominent feature was a well-stocked reading room available to all at no cost whatever. This according to one writer of the time was "a commendable offset to the patronage of the barrooms."

Tannehill died June 2, 1858.

In June 1824 Maury and Harris established the Nashville *Republican*. The next year they purchased the Nashville *Gazette* and combined the two. In 1837 the two papers evolved into the *Republican Banner*. This newspaper had a series of important editors, among them Felix Zollicoffer, later to rise in the Confederate Army to the rank of brigadier general, and to fall at Fishing Creek, a casualty of one of the Civil War's earliest battles. Apparently the Whigs of Nashville took their politics seriously. It seems that the Nashville *Whig* was not of the political robustness desired, so the Nashville *True Whig* was brought out in 1845 and continued until 1856. Then it was changed to the Nashville *Patriot*. The Nashville *Union* published its first issue on March 30, 1835. The *Union* supported General Jackson with vigor as long as he lived. Harvey Watterson, father of Henry Watterson, the famed editor of the Louisville *Courier-Journal*, came into the possession of the *Union* in 1850. In 1853 it and the Nashville *American* were merged and thereafter published under the title Nashville *Union and American*. The Nashville *Gazette* was established in 1844. There ensued a succession of editors until 1854, when Henry Maney took the chair. He was one of the finest literary figures of a city that had been literary from its founding. (John Donelson's journal of his journey by the rivers would rank high as literature anywhere.)

Maney was born in Franklin, Tennessee, in 1832. Three years later the family moved into a Nashville home erected at Broadway and McLemore, where Christ Church now stands.

When he was eighteen he was graduated from the University of Nashville, officially designated as the ablest student of the class. He was very probably President Philip Lindsley's favorite student, an honor set apart for the one most facile in the classics.

We may wonder what the president thought of Maney's growing fondness for the poetry of Byron. In the end it became his favorite literature. At the time of his graduation it was his plan to enter the Episcopal ministry. But just then his heart manifested some alarming symptoms, and his physicians suggested a European trip. So in July 1851 he left Nashville for a ten-months stay abroad. When he returned he wrote a delightful travelogue under the title *Memories over the Water*. It was promptly published and proved very popular. It is a genial story of his visit to most of the countries of Europe. But the pages of the book bear, too, the romantic flavor of old Nashville. Much of the time Bishop Otey was a traveling companion. And Henry Fogg, Randall McGavock and Edwin Ewing were in the party abroad.

Even before the book was published Maney had assumed the editorship of the *Gazette*. He loved the paper and gave it his characteristic industry and erudition. In 1856 he represented Davidson, Robertson and Montgomery counties in the state legislature. There he helped elevate Andrew Johnson to the national Senate, little expecting the relations which would come to exist between the Maneys and the "Tailor from Greenville" a scant half-dozen years hence. His old trouble began to reassert itself, and this time the physicians ordered him to take a Gulf Coast trip. Before he had been gone two weeks he knew it was too late. He came home to die—which he did, though somewhat slowly. He still had time to write some excellent poetry. The end came on April 5, 1858.

Randall McGavock also recorded his experiences and impressions of the trip to Europe in a book—*A Tennessean Abroad*. Both men were of superior minds but very different.

234

Maney was quiet, reflective, poetic. McGavock was robust, always hurrying, commanding in appearance and performance. McGavock kept a journal, with daily entries, for sixteen years of his life. There were eight volumes of it, but one of them was a casualty of Fort Henry, taken by the Yankees, of whom McGavock wrote, "They will doubtless sell my journal and apply the proceeds to help pay for their unholy war." The McGavock journals have lately been edited and published by Dr. Herschel Gower and Dr. Jack Allen under the appropriate title *Pen and Sword*. An excellent biography of the diarist serves as introduction. The journals are, among other things, the best social and political commentary on Nashville for the decade of the fifties.

Edwin Ewing never wrote a book, but he made many public addresses, several of which remain in print. They are notable for their classic distinction and for their eloquence.

Henry Fogg neither wrote books nor made speeches. But this young patrician, with a look of soft sadness on his face, was perhaps finest-grained of them all.

If Henry Fogg wrote no books, his remarkable mother more than supplied the lack. In 1799 Henry Middleton Rutledge, of Charleston, South Carolina, son of Edward Rutledge the Signer, married Septima Sexta Middleton, daughter of Arthur Middleton, another Signer. She had been christened with the Latin words for the immortal years of the signing. The Middleton home was one of Charleston's great places, and the Middleton Garden today is visited by a great many beauty-loving Americans. As an award for his service Edward Rutledge was given by congressional grant a large body of land in what are now Coffee, Grundy and Franklin counties, Tennessee. His son inherited the land, and the couple came to occupy it in 1814. One of the family was Mary Middleton Rutledge, then thirteen years old. In the proper course of time Mary Middleton Rutledge met Francis Brinley Fogg, a young lawyer who arrived in Nashville in 1818 from his home in Brooklyn, Connecticut.

In 1824 they were married. Success came to the Foggs in every way but one, and there tragedy touched them sorely. Their oldest child died on the eve of his scheduled wedding. Their daughter died at the age of twenty-three while her brother was on the European trip mentioned earlier. In January 1862 at Fishing Creek, Kentucky, Henry was mortally wounded within a few minutes of the death of his commanding officer, Felix Zollicoffer.

The bereaved mother sought relief from her accumulated sorrows by writing poems in which she poured out the anguish of her spirit. These were published under the title, *The Broken Harp*. The only known copy of the book is in the Boston Library, and was once the property of Edward Everett. A copy of her second book, *A Mother's Legacy*, also belonged to Mr. Everett, and it too found its way to the Boston Library. The inscriptions indicate friendship, though the details are not known. Perhaps the New Englander met the Foggs when he was Nashville's guest in 1829, or the acquaintance may have begun on one of their numerous trips to the Northeast. Mrs. Fogg published a book on *Sunday School Teaching*, and a novel, *Mary Ashton*. Her versatile pen reached a surprising climax in *The Elements of Natural Science, Comprising hydrology, geognosy, geology, meteorology, botany, zoology, and anthropology*, published in 1858. Her authorship of such a book is a bit baffling. Just where had she learned science? Not at the Nashville Female Academy where she was graduated. Not at the University of Nashville. President Lindsley's university was many years distant from any gesture toward co-education, and also from any course in physical geography. There is no record of Mrs. Fogg's ever going away to college. So the best guess is that she studied physical geography at home, though one is still without any more than vague inference as to what she might have used for textbooks. Her book must have been a good one. Matthew Fontaine Maury wrote of it from the National Observatory in Washington, on March 30, 1858:

"Physical geography, in our own day, has grown to be one of the most beautiful, interesting, and useful departments of human knowledge. In no department of science are good school books more wanting. This is decidedly one of the best I have ever seen."

The storytellers, the scholars, the pamphleteers, the almanac compilers and their kind have always been busy in and about Nashville. Girard Troost, one of the great scholars of his day, whose teaching of science in the University of Nashville remains a high point in the section's record, published *The Tennessee Geologist* in 1841, McKennie, printer. Later Troost was to revise and enlarge the book several times. In 1841 the Tennessee Silk Company published a manual on the culture of silk, arousing considerable interest in an industry which did not survive a full decade. In 1842 M. Deavenport published a forty-two-page poem with the perfect touch of a cynic in the title *Humbuggiana*, Cameron and Fall, printers. The next year Mrs. R. J. Avery collected her poems and published them in a volume of 204 pages, also printed by Cameron and Fall. In 1843 the fourth of Henry Maney's traveling companions, Bishop James Otey, published *The Unity of the Church*, W. F. Bang, printer. The same year Stanhope Shannon gave birth to what was probably the area's first cookbook, *Shannon's Useful Receipt* (sic) *Book*, "Upward of 500 receipts gleaned with great care from many sources," Cameron and Fall, printers. In 1846, Green Grimes published two books, *A Secret Worth Knowing*, and *The Lily of the West*. No printer is indicated, though both books identify the author as "an inmate of the lunatic asylum." In that year Reverend Fountain Pitts published *Zion's Harp*, Nashville's first attempt at a song book.

As for periodicals established in this period, 1844 saw the appearance of the *Baptist*, edited by R. B. C. Howell and W. C. Crane; the *Christian Review*; and the *Southwestern Law Journal and Reporter*, Milton Haynes, editor. In 1845 came the *Southwestern Literary Journal and Monthly Review*, Judson and Kidd, editors. In 1846 arrived the *Naturalist*, "printed at Franklin College, five miles east of Nashville." The year 1847 gave birth to the *Southern Ladies Companion*, McFerrin and Hinkle, editors. In 1852 was the first issue of the *Ladies Pearl*, "published monthly and devoted to the interest of ladies," W. S. Langdon and J. C. Provine, editors. The *Ladies Pearl* proved very popular, but to serve editorial advantages it was moved to Saint Louis in 1856. The *Southern Medical Journal* was first published early in the year 1853. It survived four years. The *Banner of Peace*, an organ of the Cumberland Presbyterian Church, had moved several times before reaching Nashville in 1853. It became a casualty of the Civil War. The *Parlor Visitor*, a literary organ of the First Baptist Church, was published from 1854 to 1857. The *Southern Homestead*, a farm periodical, lasted from 1858 till the surrender of Nashville. Two prewar music publishing houses, Benson's and McClure's, flourished until disrupted by war.

THE METHODIST PUBLISHING HOUSE

The Publishing House of the Methodist Church has lived an exciting life. The Methodists have been engaged in printing for a long time, certainly from as early as 1769 when Robert Williams, a Methodist preacher, undertook the printing and selling of some of John Wesley's sermons in Virginia and Maryland. On May 28, 1789, a conference was held in New York to plan the establishment of a printing business, but no funds were provided. The Reverend John Dickins lent £120 to get it started. It was then that the Methodist Church entered the business of printing and selling books. The church asked of the Reverend Mr. Dickins more than the loan of his money. They asked him to supply guidance in spending it, which he did for ten years. After that, various ones were in charge of the church's printing business: Ezekiel Cooper for nine years, John Wilson for two, Daniel Hitt for six, Joshua Soule for four, Nathan Bangs for eight, John Emory for four, Beverly

Waugh for four. That brings the publishing business up to 1836.

Some confusions and tensions were beginning to develop within the Methodist Church. The foretaste of the Civil War was beginning to turn bitter in men's mouths. At the General Conference in 1844 it was plain that the Northern and Southern areas of the denomination would be unable to adjust their accumulated differences. So, with whatever brotherly love could be summoned, a plan of peaceful separation was agreed on.

At Louisville, Kentucky, in 1845 plans were approved for the organization of the Methodist Episcopal Church, South. One section of the plan, fully accepted by both factions, called for an equitable division of all properties. That, of course, included the book concern. But the Conference of 1848 withdrew from the Plan of Separation and repudiated any provision to divide the properties. The next year the Methodist Church, South, brought suits in the United States Circuit Courts of Ohio and New York for its share of them. Finally the suits reached the Supreme Court, and on April 25, 1854, a decision was rendered in favor of the Southern church. The printing establishments in Richmond, Charleston and Nashville were given to the Southern Methodists, and in addition $270,000 in cash.

At the Conference of the Southern Church, held in Columbus, Georgia, in May 1854 the book concern was located at Nashville. A. L. P. Green, John B. McFerrin and N. Hobson were appointed a committee to select a site for the publishing house and to solicit subscriptions from the citizens of Nashville to assist the project. The committee worked diligently and late in August reported subscriptions amounting to $20,000, and recommended the purchase, for $30,000, of a building located on the northeast corner of the Public Square. It was bought and altered for printing use, and in April 1855 the first periodical was issued, the Nashville *Christian Advocate*. The first books published were Watson's *Apology*, the *Life of Carvosso* and *The Discipline of the Methodist Church, South*. Dr. John B. McFerrin was appointed editor of the *Christian Advocate*, but soon he was made general agent for the publishing concern, and Dr. H. N. McTyeire appointed to succeed him as editor.

But dark days were ahead for the publishing business, as indeed for everything else. On February 25, 1862, the Northern army occupied Nashville. Immediately the plant of the book concern was confiscated for use as a printing office for the Federals. There were no religious publications issued in Nashville during the war years. During that time Dr. McFerrin served as missionary with the Army of Tennessee. But within two weeks after the war's end he was back in Nashville trying in vain to persuade the military authorities to release the property. Failing there, he shifted his supplications to a higher authority, President Andrew Johnson. In a little while the Southern Methodists were again in the publishing business.

In February 1872 the building was destroyed by fire, but the Methodists wasted no time in lamentations. They erected another building almost before the ashes of the old one were cold. It served until 1906 when the building at Ninth and Broadway was secured and occupied. It was used until, fifty years later, the magnificent new building at Eighth and DeMonbreun was completed and ready for use. Many great and historic names belong on the roster of the Methodist Publishing Company. Here are a few: A. L. P. Green, John B. McFerrin, Holland N. McTyeire, T. O. Summers, J. D. Barbee, D. M. Smith, A. J. Lamar, John W. Barton, B. A. Whitmore.

In 1939 the old sectional scars were declared healed, and the three branches of Methodism were brought into a state of unity under the simplified title, The Methodist Church. All main offices were located in Nashville. Lovick Pierce is president of the publishing house, and Emory Bucke chief editor. The business has now grown to massive proportions. In 1959 ninety-five different books were issued with a total of 5,750,264 volumes. The total number of periodicals and church school literature was in excess of 120,000,000 pieces. The head office of all Cokesbury Book Stores is located in Nashville, as is one of its most important stores. Robert Williams was indeed a prophet.

THE BAPTISTS AS PRINTERS

The Baptists entered the business of printing and publishing much later than the Methodists. For a considerable period there had been some demand for the denomination to print the materials it used, but there had been enough objection to block it. Such an astonishing increase in Sunday schools in Southern Baptist churches had gone on that a Sunday-School Board was established and located in Nashville in 1891. And that same year a resolution was passed by the Convention which authorized the publication of Sunday-school literature, but endorsement of anything further was withheld. The demand grew and in 1897 the Board, after prolonged consideration, sanctioned the issuance of a biography of Matthew Tyson Yates, the great missionary. The book met with such favor that authority was granted to publish such books and materials as seemed specially appropriate.

In 1910 the Southern Baptist Convention authorized the establishment at Nashville of a publishing house. For a while matters moved slowly. In 1922 Dr. John L. Hill, then dean of Georgetown College in Kentucky, was chosen book editor, an assignment he held with distinction for twenty-seven years. It was Dr. Hill who chose the name the Broadman Press, a joining of the names of two great Baptists, John A. Broadus and Basil Manly. It has been a demanding performance for the press to keep up with the increase of the Baptists in the South, but it has met the challenge in a degree even surprising to its supporters. Its books, periodicals and pamphlets have gone into all parts of the South, and in great quantity. Exact figures are not available for a later year than 1957, but it may be assumed that since then there has been a marked increase in distribution. That year, 73,202,000 copies of seventy-nine periodicals were issued; also over 14,000,000 tracts were printed and delivered; 1,618,341 volumes of first-edition books, and 2,355,581 volumes of books reprinted. Fifty bookstores are directed from Nashville headquarters, all dealing largely in Broadman books. Dr. William J. Fallis is book editor, and the director of distribution is Dr. Harold Ingraham.

Let us return to wartime Nashville. Five newspapers— weekly, three-times-a-week and daily—were issued at the beginning of 1862: The Nashville *Patriot*, the Nashville *Gazette*, the *Republican Banner*, the Nashville *News* and the Nashville *Union and American*. But that output of printed pages could not survive the fall of Fort Donelson, seventy miles down the Cumberland River. Suddenly the city was without benefit of printed news. And, for a people nurtured on news, that was an additional agony. The newspaper for seventy years had been a vital part of the city's life. The desire for news was so great that many newspapers and periodicals were maneuvered in from other cities, specially Louisville. Some paper runners developed quite a business of it. The news-hungry people went to a great deal of trouble to secure these, and read them with great eagerness. But that didn't last long. It is not the part of conquering armies to provide the vanquished with newspapers, and soon the Federals had all sources of supply plugged up securely.

From March 1862 on, no news in any manner favoring the South was printed in Nashville. But when the war ended newspaper publishing again became one of the city's prime occupations, and reading one of its passions. The *Union and American* began appearing again in December 1865, under the ownership of Dunnington and Jones. A year later it was bought out by the *Dispatch*, and so it became the *Union and Dispatch*. The first number of the *Banner*, in its modern form, was put on the streets in April 1876. It continues to this day as the city's afternoon paper. The *Tennessean*, descended from several newspapers, made its first appearance in 1907. It continues as the morning paper. The two dailies have a combined circulation of more than 200,000. The *Gospel Advocate* resumed publication, under new management, in 1867. The Advocate Publishing Company was the forerunner of the McQuiddy Printing Company. The *Gospel Advocate* continues as an organ of the Church of Christ. The *Southern Lumberman*, first issued in 1880, has continued without interruption since, and is a trade journal of wide patronage and importance.

The Cumberland Presbyterian Church, before its merger in 1906 with the Presbyterian Church, U.S.A., issued under its sponsorship seven periodicals. Three men did the main editorial work: Dr. R. V. Foster, Dr. Marcus B. DeWitt and Dr. J. I. D. Hinds. The *Southern Practitioner*, devoted to medicine and surgery, was established in January 1879, editors, George S. Blackie, Dr. Chalmers Dow and Dr. Deering J. Roberts. This was published until about 1890. Nashville's main attempt at a literary journal was perhaps the *Round Table*, with an announced list of 6,000 charter subscribers. Its printing was well done and its authorship auspicious, but it could not maintain its excellent beginning.

Historians, novelists, poets and textbook writers have abounded here. The concentration of colleges in Nashville has induced an almost fantastic increase in the city's output of books. The concentration of churches and church agencies has added similarly. Books inevitably flow from newspaper offices. All of these have greatly lengthened the city's literary catalogue.

One literary center and contagion of Nashville has been the Fugitives, a group of gifted young poets appearing in Vanderbilt between 1915 and 1928. They were John Crowe Ransom, Donald Davidson, Jesse Wills, Alfred Starr, Sidney Hirsch, Walter Clyde Curry, Merrill Moore, Allen Tate, Alec B. Stevenson, William Yandell Elliott, Stanley Johnson, Robert Penn Warren and the lone woman member, Laura Riding. Of these the only ones to remain in Nashville for their full literary careers were Donald Davidson, Jesse Wills, Alfred Starr, W. C. Curry and Sidney Hirsch. All the Fugitives wrote poetry, some a great deal of it. Almost all have engaged in other fields of literary creation, some with remarkable success. Donald Davidson's two-volume history of the Tennessee has high rank in the "River" series, as does *Lee in the Mountains* as poetry. Jesse Wills' recently published book, *Early and Late*, while not widely publicized, is as moving poetry as any done in Nashville. Dr. Curry's *Shakespeare's Philosophical Patterns* is a book of major significance for scholars.

By 1930 the Fugitives were well scattered, but they remained close personally, and their reputation has cohered and lasted. In 1956 the Rockefeller Foundation provided for a Fugitive reunion on the Vanderbilt campus. For four days they lived the old days over with full literary undertones and overtones. They set to sounding the old personal and poetic echoes, and they tried their declamatory powers to create some new ones. The preservation of such solidarity after a third of a century is a remarkable matter.

The literary excitement of the Fugitive days sent another group of talented young men scurrying to their typewriters, the Agrarians. They were Andrew Lytle, Frank Owsley, Lyle Lanier, Donald Wade, H. C. Nixon, John Gould Fletcher and H. B. Kline. Some of the Fugitives found their theme attractive and joined them. The Agrarians stuck to prose and with skill and quixotic fervor attacked industrialism and the evils it evoked. In 1930 the Agrarians published a symposium titled *I'll Take My Stand*, calling for a return to the old and basic ways of life. It was widely read and quoted.

A college teacher frequently has a great desire to write a book. There are many reasons for him to write one, or more. No one knows how many books or periodical studies have been composed on the Vanderbilt campus, and still less is there likely to be knowledge of how many have been inspired there. The list would be impressive. Perhaps the most widely read and discussed book during the decade of the forties was *The Advancing South* by Dr. Edwin Mims. Before that he had written several books about various phases of literature, and later he wrote the biography of *Chancellor James H. Kirkland*. A scholarly study is Dr. Claude Finney's *The Evolution of Keats' Poetry*. Dr. Randall Stewart's *American Literature and Christian Doctrine* is thoughtfully written and fits well into the times. Dr. Sam Clark's *The Anatomy of the Nervous System* is standard in the study of anatomy.

Dr. George Pullen Jackson's *White Spirituals of the Southern Uplands* is the only book of note in a rich field. Jesse Stuart wrote *The Man with the Bull-Tongue Plow* while a student at Vanderbilt. Dr. Walter Sullivan has recently published two novels, *Sojourn of a Stranger* and *The Long, Long Love*. Dr. Richmond Beatty has gained distinction in the field of biography with his *Bayard Taylor*, *James Russell Lowell* and *William Byrd of Westover*. Dr. Norman Munn's *Psychology* has met with much favor as a college text. Dr. George Bennett has published a biography of *William Dean Howells*, and Dr. Dewey Grantham one of *Hoke Smith*. Douglas Leach has had published *A History of King Philip's War*, and Dr. Charles Delzell one on *Yalta*. Dr. W. H. Nichols has to his credit *Southern Traditions and Progress*. In the School of Religion these books have been published lately: by Dr. J. P. Hyatt, *Jeremiah, Prophet of Courage and Hope*; by Dr. Lou Silberman, *Prophets and Philosophers*; and by Dr. Landon Gilkey, *Maker of Heaven and Earth*. In political science there is Dr. Avery Leiserson's book titled *Parties and Politics*.

These are by no means a complete listing of books produced at Vanderbilt, but they do show that the university is a veritable inkshed, and that the sound of the typewriter is abroad in the offices.

On the Peabody campus book writing is a familiar scene. In 1953 Dr. John E. Brewton listed the books written by staff and alumni since 1914. There were 576 books by 129 authors. These represented a wide range, the largest group being texts in almost all the subjects taught in the public schools, books on arithmetic by Dr. F. L. Wren and Dr. John L. Banks; on geography by Dr. A. E. Parkins and Dr. J. R. Whitaker; on spelling by Dr. Arville Wheeler and Dr. S. C. Garrison; on science by Dr. H. A. Webb, Dr. Jesse Shaver, and Dr. R. O. Beauchamp; on reading by Dr. Ullin Leavell, and Dr. Arville Wheeler; on music by Dr. Irvin Wolfe; on children's poetry by Dr. and Mrs. J. E. Brewton; a book on English by Dr. C. S. Pendleton; several on modern languages by Dr. A. I. Roehm; a text on economics by Dr. O. C. Ault; and books on history and political science by Dr. Fremont Wirth, Dr. Jack Allen, and Dr. Kenneth Cooper. Of these last, Dr. Wirth's *Development of America,* for use in the high schools, leads in popularity with a sale of about 1,850,000 copies. Dr. Shores contributed several texts on library management; Dr. Charles McMurry several on type studies in teaching. There is a one-foot shelf on agriculture by Dr. Kary Davis, a pioneer in the field; several books on school buildings by Dr. F. B. Dresslar, another pioneer; a college text on the teaching of reading by Dr. H. L. Donovan and Miss Julia Harris; a book on college psychology by Dr. S. C. Garrison; books on education and teaching by Dr. Clifton Hall, Dr. Sam Wiggins, Dr. W. M. Alexander and Dr. Michael Demiaskevich; President Henry Hill's *Changing Options in American Education.* These outside the textbook field are by Peabody authors: Dr. L. W. Crawford's *Rivers of Water;* Dr. J. E. Windrow's *Life and Works of John Berrien Lindsley;* Thurman Sensing's *Champ Ferguson, Confederate*

Guerrilla; Dr. Charles Little's *Quintilian, the Teacher*, in two volumes.

The following are the best-known books issuing from Fisk University: James Weldon Johnson's *Along This Way* and *The Book of American Negro Spirituals*; Dr. John Wesley Work's *Folk Songs of the American Negro*. It was Dr. Work who introduced music at Fisk. Dr. Arna Bontemps, the librarian, published *Black Thunder, Chariot in the Sky* and several books for children.

But let us move away from the campuses to the city itself. Opie Read never called Nashville home, but during a part of his life, when he was living nearby, he spent much time in the city. Certainly parts of *The Jucklins* and *A Kentucky Colonel* were composed here. Mary N. Murfree (George Egbert Craddock), author of *The Prophet of the Great Smoky Mountains*, lived in Nashville from 1856 to 1873. Maria Thompson Davies lived in the outskirts of Nashville during much of her productive period. She wrote many novels, but is best remembered here for *Rose of Old Harpeth* and *Over Paradise Ridge*. Corra Harris, who wrote *A Circuit Rider's Wife* (used in the motion picture *I'd Climb the Highest Mountain*), lived several years in Nashville, her husband being employed at the time by the Methodist Board.

John Trotwood Moore, an Alabamian, moved to Maury County, Tennessee, to raise blooded horses. But he soon shifted to literary work. He and Bob Taylor, Tennessee's colorful governor, author and orator extraordinary, organized and started the *Taylor Trotwood Magazine*. It was a good magazine, filled with Tennessee vitality and color, but it could not survive after 1911. In 1919 Mr. Moore became director of the Tennessee Historical Library. The assignment only stirred his pen to greater action. Among the books he published were *The Ghost Flower, The Bishop of Cottontown, Red Eagle and White, Hearts of Hickory* and, with A. P. Foster, *Tennessee the Volunteer State*.

Mrs. Gladys Barr wrote *Monk in Armour* and *Cross, Sword and Arrow*. Wirt A. Cate is the author of *A Biography of L. Q. C. Lamar*. Margaret Cate wrote *Without a Sword*, and Robbie Trent, *The First Christmas* and *What Is God Like*.

Gates P. Thurston came south with the Federal army. He spent some time here with the occupation forces. He rose to the rank of brigadier general. At the end of the war he married Miss Ida Hamilton, one of Nashville's choice young ladies, and remained in Nashville for an illustrious career as lawyer and citizen of varied cultural intersts. His book, *The Antiquities of Tennessee*, remains an authority in the local prehistoric field. John Berrien Lindsley's *Annals of the Army of Tennessee* is an excellent source for materials on the Tennessee personnel of that great fighting force. Judge Thomas E. Matthews' biography of his great-grandfather, General James Robertson, is filled with valuable data on Nashville's early days, and it carries the only organized genealogy of a most distinguished family. Without Stanley F. Horn's books, Nashville would be lacking some eloquent pages, indeed chapters, of its past. His biography of *The Hermitage*, his *Decisive Battle of Nashville*, his definitive story of *The Army of Tennessee* and his *This Fascinating Lumber Business* present unforgettable facts and figures.

Joseph B. Killebrew's *Tennessee, Its Agriculture and Cultural Wealth* and *Elements of Tennessee Geology* give vivid pictures of the resources of the state. Mrs. Martha Morrell's *Young Hickory, the Life and Times of James K. Polk* helped greatly to recall interest in a great Tennessean. John Allison's *Dropped Stitches in Tennessee History* fills in interestingly, and sometimes excitingly, certain gaps in our record. Jesse Burt has recently published a fact-filled volume entitled *Nashville, its Life and Times*.

Robert Selph Henry, temporarily assigned to Washington, has added some stirring books to Nashville's list: *The Story of the Confederacy*, *The Story of Reconstruction*, *"First with the Most" Forrest* and *The Story of the Mexican War*. Mr. Henry also wrote *This Fascinating Railroad Business* (which had been his business, as lumber is Stanley Horn's).

Henry McRaven wrote *Nashville, the Athens of the South* and a very good biography of Edward Swanson, who came into Nashborough during its first year, immediately took up land on the Harpeth River in Williamson County and established himself in the founding of that county. Will Allen Drumgoole wrote on a theme always pleasing to Nashville readers, *The Heart of Old Hickory*.

One interested in the history of Nashville may refer with profit to these books, all written there or near by: W. T. Hale and Dixon Merritt, *History of Tennessee and Tennesseans*; A. V. Goodpasture and W. R. Garrett, *History of Tennessee, Its People and Institutions*; Robert H. White, *Messages of the Governors of Tennessee*; Robert H. White and W. T. Alderson, *A Guide to the Study and Reading of Tennessee History*.

Not all of these books, by any means, were printed in Nashville, but a great many were. And, of course, not all of the books printed here were of local authorship. The Broadman Press prints books generally by Baptist preachers and high-ranking laymen over the entire range of the South. Lately there has been some tendency to break across sectional lines. The Methodists, having dissolved all geographical boundaries, draw more freely from a wider area. The professors in the colleges, having no presses immediately assigned to their use, are likely to search abroad for their publishers. Vanderbilt University does maintain a press, but not on the scale of the University of North Carolina, or Louisiana State University, or the University of Kentucky. Peabody College has at times published books, but not often.

There are in Nashville, besides the two religious presses, thirty-four printing companies. A few are rather small, some unbelievably large. All seem busy. Some hold on steadily to straight job printing; others have developed specialties. There are twenty-two companies whose business it is to supply the printing companies with paper, ink, engravings, etc. There is in the city the Southern Institute of Graphic Arts, which in its career has trained more than 6,000 young men and women to serve in the more skilled phases of printing. The printing companies now employ more than 3,800 workers and pay them about $13,500,000 annually. There is no sort of printing, nor of color work, nor of binding, that cannot be done as well in Nashville as anywhere. There are enough type-casting machines and operators here to set *Gone with the Wind* in three hours.

Of the printing companies, the oldest is Marshall and Bruce, which opened October 25, 1865, on Deaderick Street, then a narrow lane usually either muddy or dusty. The company grew with the times, adjusting itself to the printing needs of the town. It has moved several times, finally to an excellent and adequate plant on Twelfth Avenue, South.

Some of the companies have developed expertness in various departments of printing that occupy much of their effort. Cullom and Ghertner print business forms used by I.B.M. and kindred machines. They have gained prestige also in the printing of promotional literature for business houses. They formerly printed tickets—train, bus, airplane and theater—but two years ago they sold their ticket-printing business to Rand McNally, whose new plant here prints an infinite number of tickets and maps. Williams Printing Company accepts any printing business offered, but takes special pride in their color work. They printed all the Duncan Hines dining and lodging books until the death of Mr. Hines.

Ambrose Printing Company specializes in printing state and corporate bond blanks. Baird Ward does no job printing but specializes in periodicals and telephone directories. Of these they print an incredible number, a mountainous heap. McQuiddy prints everything for which there is need, but carries on a specialty in periodicals. Benson's specialty is school and college annuals. The firm of Brandau, Craig and Dickerson is a general printer and highly specialized lithographer. Stoddard's specialty is engraved and embossed materials.

All thirty-four of these companies, whatever their specialties, rest on a solid base. They all exist to give a degree of permanency, great or small, to materials which serve some good purpose in the life of the city. There has been printing done here, in almost ever-increasing amounts, for about 175 years. It is the great enricher of our days. Without it life would be desolate, if not impossible.

9

ANDREW JACKSON'S HERMITAGE

AT SUNDOWN, Sunday evening, June 8, 1845, very quietly Andrew Jackson died. He had been sick a long time, but even consumption found Old Hickory a doughty man of surprising endurance. He had been ever a fighter, fierce and intrepid, but disease had given him time for meditation. So he had come to recognize and accept the inevitable. Toward the end he was calm, even placid. Dr. Esselman, knowing that it was a matter of hours, remained at the Hermitage on Saturday night. Toward morning he retired for a little sleep. Sometime before nine, Sunday morning, he came back into the room. The General was sitting in an armchair, a servant on either side. The first look told the physician that the hand of death was upon his patient. He had him put back into bed.

Jackson asked for the entire household to be summoned. In turn he told each good-by. Then he delivered what was in nature and effect a quiet sermon lasting over an hour. With an odd lack of emotion and with entire coherence he talked about the various phases of immortality. He finished and fell into a sleep. The slaves left the room weeping.

Jackson's long-time friend Major Lewis arrived at noon. The General took a long look at him, then said, "I am glad to see you, Major, but you like to have been too late."

In the late afternoon Andrew, Junior, took his hand. "Father, do you know me?"

"Of course I know you. I would know all of you if I had

my spectacles. I want to meet all of you in heaven, all of you both white and black."

Then, in the room and about the windows, there arose the sounds of low weeping. "Oh, do not cry! We will all meet in heaven." And the General slept again.

Those were the last words he spoke. At sundown he died.

So passed Nashville's most remarkable and unfading citizen. The sickness had been on him for many years, even before he had gone to the Presidency, but his spirit had risen high above it. It is more than merely possible that the trouble had its beginning in the bullet that Charles Dickinson fired into his chest on that May morning in 1806, or it might have been Jesse Benton's bullet in 1813, or it might have been both. In any case, his health was somewhat precarious during the last third of his life. But Andrew Jackson never yielded to his infirmities any more than Herodotus' postmen were stayed by theirs. Bereavement, wars, political campaigns, presidential pressures— all, compounded with disease, left him unscathed till toward the end.

At the moment of Jackson's death General Sam Houston was hurrying along the Hermitage road, hoping to get there in time to bid his old comrade good-by, though they had told him in Nashville that he probably would not. When he arrived, he led his young son to the bed, telling him to look hard at the General, for he would not see his like again.

On Monday morning the visitors started coming early to the Hermitage, and throughout the day there was a continuous stream of them. A great man had gone, and friends and neighbors wished to acknowledge their bereavement. Behind all the coming and going arrangements for the burial went on.

On Tuesday morning at ten the funeral sermon was preached. The minister was Dr. John T. Edgar of the Presbyterian church in Nashville. It was a fine morning, filled with June at its freshest and greenest. A good rain had fallen three days before, and the countryside bloomed and flourished. A great crowd gathered, the papers said more than 3,000, and spread out fanlike before the preacher standing on the front porch.

The text of the sermon was the Scripture beginning, *These are they who have come up through tribulation.* Dr. Edgar was perhaps Nashville's most eloquent preacher of all time. He had come from a pastorate in Frankfort, Kentucky, in 1833. Once Henry Clay was asked who of all the preachers of the day was the most eloquent. He replied, "Go to the Presbyterian church at Frankfort and you will hear him."

Dr. Edgar's sermon that morning was an hour in length and gripped everyone within his hearing. He finished and they sang one of the General's favorite hymns. Then they carried his body back through the garden and lowered him into the new grave under the magnolias. There he rejoined Rachel, who had left him more than sixteen years before. The people reluctantly scattered for their homes, feeling certain that a great man had died, and vaguely that an era had passed too. There was much talk about the sermon that Dr. Edgar had preached.

"Ah, but that was a sermon Old Hickory himself would have liked," said one.

"It was a sermon God Almighty did like," answered his companion.

The usual salutes and memorials to the departed leader were given in Washington. For a season the centers of the nation echoed with the voices of orators paying their praise to Andrew Jackson. Later that year twenty-five of those addresses were collected and printed in an impressive volume. A few discordant notes were heard in Nashville. "He will be forgotten within five years," a member of an anti-Jackson faction said the afternoon of the funeral.

But those who thought that Andrew Jackson's funeral represented any sort of finality were wrong. Though he has been dead 115 years it does not seem likely that any city in the nation has been so much influenced by one man as he has influenced Nashville. He was not quite twenty-one years old when he arrived in the settlement. He immediately became a major influence, and he still is. To an almost incredible degree he shapes the thinking and behavior of the place today.

Very few addresses whether by local or brought-on orators—and no Nashville day passes without its quota of addresses—are delivered without a long, sonorous, well-metered eulogy to the memory and majesty of Andrew Jackson. All candidates for local office find it advisable to appeal to the electorate in a manner calculated to leave the impression that a favorable vote would not only support the best man, but would conform to the ideals and policies of Old Hickory himself. All printed descriptions and interpretations of Nashville toast Jackson as the city's main claim to fame. Which he surely is.

The name in Nashville seems to be self-perpetuating. There are five Andrew Jacksons in the telephone directory. There are in Nashville the Andrew Jackson Hotel, the Andrew Jackson Courts, the Andrew Jackson Business College, the Andrew Jackson Liquor Store, the Andrew Jackson Grammar School. There are twenty-nine business institutions using the name *Hermitage*. The shelves of the food stores overflow with canned and packaged goods labeled *Hermitage*. Old Hickory, a suburb of Nashville, is the seat of a major Dupont industry. There are eight business enterprises bearing the name *Old Hickory*. Old Hickory hams, sausages, bacon and a full line of cured meats are produced and marketed by Neuhof's, a subsidiary of Swift. The Cumberland River, near Old Hickory, was dammed six years ago under the sponsorship of the Tennessee Valley Authority. Now Old Hickory Lake has become a center of year-round homes and vacation homes and a leading resort for fishermen and vacationists. Old Hickory the man still sheds vivid colors on Nashville and its entire periphery. The daily press still uses daily fragments of the Jackson story. An uninformed visitor might very well infer from the immediacy of the references to Jackson that he is still around, and be quite surprised to learn that he was buried in the Hermitage garden more than eleven decades ago. During the fifty-eight years of his life in Nashville, Andrew Jackson never did an unnewsworthy thing, nor many things whose news value tended to fade.

The original Hermitage into which Andrew and Rachel Jackson moved in the fall of 1804 still stands about 600 feet north of the present building. It was a two-story log building then, but as the years passed the lower story rotted. So the upper one was lowered intact to the ground. The memories that cluster about this humble building, the history of which it was a part, make it worth the effort to pay the cabin a visit. The cabin is redolent with history. It was to it that Jackson, wan and wounded, returned from his duel with Dickinson. It was to it that the General, a conquering hero, returned from New Orleans in 1815. It was there that Aaron Burr spent a four days' visit in 1805, and privately told his daughter that he would have had pleasure in extending his stay to a month.

The Jacksons lived in a log house until 1819. They were then in position to build a larger and more befitting home. The site, the present one, was chosen and the house built. It was much finer and more commodious. Its hospitality was one of the section's fine traditions. Any important visitor was almost certain to receive a bid to the Hermitage. Dr. Horace Holley, president of Transylvania University, in Lexington, Kentucky, visited Nashville in the summer of 1823. It wasn't exactly a social visit, though it turned out to be one. Dr. Holley made the trip to consider the presidency of Cumberland College, then vacant. Quite naturally they were invited to the Hermitage and spent two days there. A letter from Dr. Holley to his father in New England sparkles with an erudite description of life in the home. Very few have read the letter, so it is given here in full.

Dear Father:

We have just returned from the Hermitage, General Jackson's residence in the country, thirteen miles from town. We went out on Sunday evening and visited there delightfully. The General called on us in town on the evening of our arrival. He is one of the most hospitable men in the whole state. Mrs. Jackson is not a·woman of great cultivation, but has seen a great many people, has fine spirits, entertains well, and is benevolent. She is short in her person and is quite fat. The General is lean and has been in ill health, but is now invigorated and promises to live out his three score and ten. He has built him a good brick house in the last three years, and has furnished it handsomely. My wife has made three sketches of it in her view book. We looked at all the presents that have been made to the old warrior in honor of his military achievements, and were gratified not a little. The gold box which contains the freedom of the city of New York, presented by the Mayor and aldermen, is rich and finely wrought. A large silver vase with various engravings upon it was given by the ladies in South Carolina. A sword was given by Tennessee, and was made in Middleton, Connecticut. It is the most beautiful of all the presents. A sword of different kind was sent him from a rifle company in Louisiana. He has a bronze statue of Napoleon sent by somebody in Paris. Mrs. Jackson has the grass bonnet made in Philadelphia by two young ladies, both under twelve. This was talked about so much in the papers eighteen months ago. It is as good as any leghorn I have ever seen. The General receives newspapers from most parts of the union, and his study is loaded with piles of them. Considerable company was at his home every day, and our ladies danced every evening in the entry to the sound of the flute. Our daughter seemed to be as well amused as I ever saw her. The General gave me many anecdotes of his wars with the Indians, particularly with the Creeks. The General is a planter and has 110 acres of cotton the present season. He expects 1200 pounds of rough cotton to the acre. He does not like Mr. Clay, and he likes Mr. Crawford still less. He prefers Mr. Adams to any of the candidates for President. The General is a prompt, practical man with very correct moral feelings. Governor Carroll called upon us yesterday. He was elected this year without opposition. He was with the General at the battle of New Orleans.

My arrival has been noticed by the papers with compliments. I am to preach on Sunday next. It is seldom that I preach, but I sometimes do it for the benefit of the University. I encounter for the same reason many public appearances which I would otherwise avoid. I have been asked and have consented to sit for a portrait here by Mr. Earl, a distinguished painter here from the east. He has quite a gallery of heads including Mr. Monroe, Governor Shelby, Governor Carroll, an Indian chief named Chenivi, and others. Mine is to go among them. I am to visit a female college on Monday and make an address to the members.

Nashville is agreeably situated on the Cumberland River, 200 miles from the mouth. Steamboats of large size navigate it for seven months in the year, and batteaus go 400 miles farther up. The river is deep and is a fine stream. A new bridge is thrown across it at this place and is well covered. The center of the town is a courthouse and market square. The market ought not be upon it. The courthouse does well enough. The soil is washed off and the rock is left bare. The sun, falling upon the rock, is bad upon the eyes and makes heat. The hills about the town offer agreeable sites for homes, and many are well filled. Cumberland College is about prostrated for want of funds, but an effort is being made to revive it. Two new buildings are going up, but there are neither teachers nor scholars. Both Governor Carroll and his wife are plain people. Mr. Earl has promised to send Transylvania a portrait of General Jackson. We have a report here that Mr. Clay is very ill and given over by his physician. Our best love to Mother and all the families.

Your son,
HORACE

Luther Holley Esq.,
Salisbury, Conn.

There is a similar picture of the Hermitage, written four years later. On June 7, 1827, Congressman Henry Workman Connor of Iredell County, North Carolina, married Juliana Courtney and started on a wedding journey which happily included Nashville in its itinerary. Mrs. Connor kept a daily journal filled with well-recorded events and impressions. Mrs. Connor liked Nashville very much, and was much thrilled by their visit to the Hermitage. An arrangement had been made for Mrs. Eaton, mother of Senator Eaton, who was later Secretary of War, to accompany the Connors. Mrs. Connor's impression of Mrs. Eaton was: "A fine old lady, quite of the old school, very dignified in her appearance and manner." But Mrs. Eaton became indisposed and could not go. Here we take up Mrs. Connor's journal:

Dr. Davis, Mr. Connor, and myself went in the barouche, servant-mounted. It is rather more than twelve miles from here. We arrived before dark, rode up a long avenue, and on alighting were met at the hall door by Colonel Ogden. The General and Lady were in the act of descending the stairs. We of course remained until they reached the hall, and were then presented. He is a venerable, dignified, and fine looking man, perfectly easy in manner. But more of that anon. Mrs. Jackson received us with equal politeness, then led me into a drawing room, and insisted on my taking some refreshments. One would have supposed from the kindness of her manner that we were old friends. I rested for a few moments and then she proposed walking into the garden, which is very large and quite her hobby. I never saw anyone more enthusiastically fond of flowers. She culled for me the only rose which was in bloom, and made up a pretty nosegay. After an agreeable stroll we returned to the drawing room, and were joined by several gentlemen. The conversation was kept up with spirit till supper was announced. I was handed in by the General and seated at Mrs. Jackson's left. He occupied the right opposite to me. He pronounced with much solemnity of manner a short grace. Then he performed the honors of the table with that attentive politeness which usually characterizes a gentleman. Everything was neat and elegant; a complete service of French china, rich cut glass, damask napkins, etc. After supper Mrs. Jackson, Senator Eaton, and myself formed quite a social trio till we retired.

Tuesday, July 4

I shall claim a writer's privilege and quite in journal style enter into all the details of my visit. First, a description of the house. You enter a large spacious hall, or vestibule. The walls are covered with a very special French paper—beautiful scenery, figures, etc. A fine oilcloth is on the floor. There is a handsome sofa, chairs, table, etc. To the right are two large handsome rooms, furnished in genteel style as drawing rooms—rich hangings, carpets, etc. To the left is the dining room and their chamber. There is no splendor to dazzle the eye, but everything elegant and neat. After breakfast we went into one of the drawing rooms where there is a number of elegantly framed portraits of the friends of the General, one of his wife, and one of himself. I have never yet seen one which did him justice. They want the spirit and expression which the original possesses in great degree. We then examined, as they were shown us, the offerings which have been presented him from every part of the Union. The sword presented at New Orleans is the most splendid piece of workmanship I ever saw. It is in the antique style, and would require an armor bearer in attendance. The one from Tennessee is in the modern style, most elegant and rich, but adapted for use. On the mantelpiece are placed the pistols which were presented to General Washington by General LaFayette, used by the former, and presented to General Jackson by his relative Mr. Custis. They are preserved with almost sacred veneration, and except a small pocket spyglass which was used by General Washington during the whole of his military career, appear to be more highly prized by the owner than all besides. On looking around the room my eyes rested on a rich elegant silver urn, and it was with a feeling of gratification that I read the inscription "From the ladies of South Carolina." It was the only female offering which I saw.

There was an elegant gold snuff box presented by, and with the freedom of, the city of New York. Also other offerings which would be endless to enumerate.

The manners of the General are so perfectly easy and polished, and those of his wife so replete with kindness and benevolence that you are at once placed at ease. I was seated at a small table playing chess with Colonel Ogden. The General stood at my side and being an excellent player he frequently directed my moves, apparently much interested in the game. There were no traces of the Military Chieftain, as he is frequently called. You saw him as a polished gentleman, dispensing the most liberal hospitality to all around him. In the morning Mrs. Eaton, several other ladies and several gentlemen joined the party. At noon about twenty of us sat down to a sumptuous and excellent dinner. The General saw all of us arranged and then seated himself at the foot. Senator Eaton was on his left. The General was Mrs. Jackson's aid for carving, helping, etc. Before leaving the table he proposed that all join him in drinking a toast to *Absent Friends*. I did not drink the toast but the sentiment was deeply felt.

We had our arrangements made to return to Nashville immediately after dinner, as it is a long ride. The General and Mrs. Jackson urged us much to stay, but we were to leave the next day for the Western District. So, we felt obliged to decline their polite invitation. When the General heard that we were going to the Western District he observed that he had several friends there and would be glad to give us letters. Mrs. Jackson would not permit me to leave without a bouquet which she arranged very tastily. The General drew my arm through his and conducted me to the carriage.

The Connors' Western District proved to be Jackson, Tennessee. So a little more than two weeks later they were back in Nashville. They did not return to the Hermitage, but the General and Mrs. Jackson came in to see them. Mrs. Henry M. Rutledge and her daughter, Mrs. Francis Fogg, called and took Mrs. Connor to the Sulphur Spring where there was much partaking of the health-giving waters. The legislature, newly convened, was causing much excitement, but the overwhelming event of the Connors' second visit was the marriage of Dr. John Shelby's second daughter to Washington Barrow.

Dr. Shelby was the town's richest man, and his house, already large and fine, was made larger and finer to accommodate the 200 favored with invitations. It was a grand affair, related in humorous and vivid detail by Mrs. Connor. She was most grateful to the Jacksons since she felt that it was through them that they were invited. At the wedding she saw the new governor, General Sam Houston. She was disappointed. She had expected an Apollo, but he turned out to be a Samson instead. She observed specially another gentleman she saw at the wedding, Judge Hugh Lawson White: "A man generally allowed to possess the greatest talents in the state. He is of diminutive size, with scarcely enough flesh to cover his frame. He wears his hair in the Methodist style, hanging down his neck. But he has eyes which redeem all." The Connors found Nashville a charming place, but to them, very specially to her, the visit to the Jacksons at the Hermitage was excitement at its peak.

What a magician is Time! How quickly changes can come! And yet those changes for a long time have been maturing into reality. A year from then Andrew Jackson was a candidate for the Presidency of the United States. It was very likely the most venomous national campaign ever conducted in the country. The air was filled with scurrilities directed against both candidates. Characters were assailed and home life desecrated. It was Jackson's time to win, and in November he was notified of his election. That was prelude to tragedy. In Christmas week his wife died. She was a gentle and peace-loving woman and that unbridled campaign was a strain she could not bear. With her death ended an era at the Hermitage. On January 19, 1829, the President-elect left for the White House without her. Since

1791 she had loved him devotedly, made a home for him, steadied him when he needed it. He was to need sorely her steadying counsel and presence.

But another change was to come into the Hermitage. In 1831 Andrew Jackson, Junior, Mrs. Jackson's nephew, legally adopted when an infant, married Sarah Yorke of Philadelphia. The marriage pleased all concerned. The President decided that it was a fitting time to recast the house, to build it a bit better and a bit larger. Two wings were added and the front and back porches. A new kitchen and a new smokehouse were built. This was the home of young Andrew and his wife. The President spent a part of each summer there. There are very few accounts of life at the Hermitage during that period. That Hermitage was short-lived and historically of least importance of all the Hermitages. It burned on the last day of October 1834. The walls were not vitally damaged and practically all of the furniture was saved.

As soon as word of this disaster reached the President, then at the White House, he ordered that immediate steps be taken to rebuild. He politely rejected several offers of help in the rebuilding, saying that it was his responsibility, and that he was able to meet it. The house was rebuilt as it is today. The two stories were made somewhat higher, and the windows rearranged in better proportions. The President took an intense interest in the building, and almost daily correspondence arrived from Washington for the builders. The President's judgment determined finally all selection. For instance, he personally chose the wallpaper that still remains in the great hall. He was greatly irked by the delay in building, but finally it was finished and ready for occupancy.

The General's Presidential tenure was completed March 4, 1837. Then he returned immediately and eagerly to the Hermitage. It was in the summer of that year that he directed the construction of the guitar-shaped driveway, and the setting out of the cedars that line the drive. He knew exactly what he wanted, but the technical phases required the help of his daughter-in-law and the artist Ralph Earl.

The tumult and the strain of the Presidency were over. Jackson had often spoken of his longing for the rest and quiet of the Hermitage. But any continuity of rest and quiet always galled the man, violated his very nature.

He had eight years of life remaining when he returned home, but they were not to be quiet and passive years. He was never well, but his crops were always calling to him, his stock always awaiting his scrutinizing eye, and he was always answering. The political issues of the day were still unfinished business, and the leaders still sought his counsel. There was in his diseased body an amazing amount of vitality that lasted till the end. There were no quiet days at the Hermitage while Andrew Jackson lived there.

He joined his wife under the magnolias, and the lights in the Hermitage grew somewhat dim. Andrew, Junior, and his wife inherited the place and lived on there, but eleven years after the General died they sold it to the state of Tennessee for $48,000 and moved to a plantation in Mississippi.

They did not stay long in Mississippi. At the beginning of the war Governor Harris asked the Jacksons to return to the Hermitage and serve as custodians. They accepted the assignment and moved back. Andrew, Junior, died from an accident in 1865. His widow lived at the Hermitage until her death twenty-two years later. Andrew Jackson III was born there in 1835. He grew up, was graduated from the University of Nashville and then from West Point Military Academy. At the beginning of the war he enlisted in the Confederate Army, and rose to a colonelship of artillery. He was twice captured and spent ten months in a war prison. He assumed care for his mother when his father died in 1865, and was well along toward mature bachelorhood when he met Miss Amy Rich of Hamilton, Ohio. It was a matter of love at first sight for both of them, and in 1885 she came as a bride to the old homestead.

In Amy Jackson's mind was born the idea of transforming the Hermitage into a shrine. The Jacksons could not remain on the place indefinitely. Sooner or later the state would have plans for it. It was too heavily laden with historic memories to permit them to fade out. Mrs. Jackson developed a tentative plan for the preservation of the home which she confided to her husband, to Mrs. Mary Dorris and to Mr. Alex Donelson. Mrs. Dorris was the wife of a newspaperman and a woman of unswerving devotion to any project to which she committed herself. Mr. Donelson was a kinsman and near neighbor of Colonel Jackson.

The three saw the matter in a single light. They gathered into the movement others of similar qualities of devotion. An organization was formed and a measure introduced in the legislature to turn the Hermitage over to the sponsorship of the "Ladies Hermitage Association." There was opposition and a furious legislative battle ensued. In the end the Ladies outmaneuvered and outargued their opponents, and on April 5, 1889, won a shrine for posterity. In translating their dream into reality the Ladies performed incredible labor.

The place was in poor condition when they got it. The whitewashed fences had faded and rotted. Trees had fallen and there they had lain until they had dwindled into uneven mounds of dust. The old mansion languished for paint and repairs. The roof leaked. Weeds had grown up in a grossness that Old Hickory would never have tolerated. The Ladies raised money by all the honorable devices yet discovered. Slowly they put the house and fences and garden back in order. Amy and Andrew Jackson III had taken the furniture when they left the house. There could be no complaint about that. It was their property. Then the furniture had been sold. The Ladies slowly began buying it back. It wasn't easy to get the money, and it required detective work of a high order to locate it all.

But today all the rooms are furnished as they were on that

June evening when Jackson died. Of all the nation's home shrines the Hermitage is the most complete. The house is almost exactly as it was in Old Hickory's day.

The memory of Rachel Jackson lingers gallantly about the Hermitage. She was the only woman in whom Andrew Jackson ever had any romantic interest. Her marks are as indelibly on the Hermitage as his. A slight mention of Rachel Donelson's first marriage already has been put on these pages. Matters reached such an impasse that it finally became necessary for Mrs. Robards to move permanently away from Harrodsburg. Matters on the Cumberland then were so urgent that none of the Donelson menfolk could be spared for the trip. Andrew Jackson volunteered to go and escort the lady to her mother's home. After a family consultation his assistance was accepted. Jackson went and Rachel came back with him to Nashville. The episode kindled a fury among Jackson's enemies that was not to die away during his lifetime. The Donelsons, themselves highly sensitive to such matters, found no wrong in the arrangement and said so emphatically. Suits for divorce were decided by legislative action in those days. Robards applied for one to the legislature of Virginia, Kentucky being a part of the Old Dominion.

Rachel's stay with her mother did not seem to lighten her distress. So it was decided for her to spend time with the Thomas Marston Greens at Natchez, the Greens being old and valued friends of the Donelsons. There she could relax from the pain and confusion that had beset her. Word reached Nashville that the divorce had been granted and Andrew Jackson set out in haste for Natchez. They were married at Springfield, the home of the Greens, sometime in August 1791. They remained for a while in Mississippi, and then came back to Nashville, hoping that all would be well.

Indeed for two years the current of their lives was disturbed by nothing more than ripples. Then came the news that there had been no divorce. The only action the legislature had taken was to grant Robards the right to sue for one. Obviously he thought there had been one since nothing else could explain his inaction for so long a period. But then he set about in a fury to use the right granted him two years before. The Jacksons came into Nashville and were remarried by Dr. Thomas Craighead, which Jackson thought to be a superfluity but was persuaded otherwise by his friend John Overton.

After that the matter lay dormant for a while, then sprang venomously alive. Scandalous allegations were a major commodity in the Presidential elections of 1824 and 1828. The treatment of both Andrew Jackson and John Quincy Adams remains a blot on the record of our political behavior. There can be little doubt that Mrs. Andrew Jackson went to a premature grave because of it.

Nor can there be any doubt that Rachel, in considerable degree, made her husband ready for the Presidency. She had the qualities he needed most in a wife. He never denied her anything, even a request to quiet down from a state of anger. He had great determination and a keen vision for opportunity. She was wholeheartedly hospitable, a good homemaker and devoutly religious. Both of the Jacksons had definite inclinations to culture. Let the furniture at the Hermitage or the correctness of the garden affirm that statement. Or the letter of President Holley, or the journal of Mrs. Connor.

It was surely Rachel's quiet, subtle influence that helped her husband to form his estimates of a home, of a garden, of furniture, of social relationships. In such matters he was an apt pupil. Together, they built a home of great distinction and filled it with furniture of museum quality. Together, they planned and made a lovely garden. Together, their lives were brightened with touches of elegance. Together, they suffered a great deal. Who can know what seeds she planted in his fertile mind?

She didn't teach him ambition. He came to Nashville because he was ambitious. But she added her strength to his strength, turned his ambition to larger and fitter directions. She taught him discretion, though in that he was less apt as a pupil. She was ambitious for him but not for herself. The prospect of life in Washington was for her, even as mistress of the White House, a dismal prospect. For Rachel Jackson the good life was to be found at the Hermitage. There she could do the work of the home she had helped to build, and which she deeply loved. There she could receive the visits of her kinfolk and dear friends. There she could put on her Sunday finery and go to the little church across the road to hear Dr. William Hume preach. If only her husband went with her she would ask of life no greater boon. When young Rachel Donelson went aboard her father's boat, the *Adventure*, on that winter day in 1779, Destiny began to direct Andrew Jackson's life along new ways.

Life sometimes seems to delight in the ironic. Rachel Jackson did not have to go to Washington after all. Her husband received official notification of his election to the Presidency in November 1828. Six weeks later Mrs. Jackson died very suddenly. She was buried out in the garden in the grave the site of which she had chosen.

If is a potent word. Sometimes it is a whimsical one. May we make a little such use of it here? Suppose Rachel had lived and gone on to the White House with her husband. What differences would it have made in the pages of history? For instance, there would hardly have been any Peggy Eaton episode. Mrs. Jackson would have known how to avoid that. There probably would have been strain in the official family, but not to the degree it reached. With his wife's counsel available the President would likely have avoided several other crises.

Andrew Jackson returned to the Hermitage in the spring of 1837. Henceforth he lived there with his acres, his books and newspapers, his friends and his memories. He was a sick man, but his activities at times were those of a robust man. He sat in his library or on his front porch and blew a mighty breath on the political sails of the time. More than any other man he elected Martin Van Buren to succeed him. More than any other man he elected James Knox Polk in 1844. In his mind party fealty was a prime virtue, and he could not forgive one of frail loyalty.

One of the most ironic cases of American politics is that of John Eaton, Secretary of War from 1829 to 1831. Twelve years before he entered the cabinet Eaton completed a biography of Jackson which flattered and pleased the General. It was, however, much too florid and uncritical for permanence. The year after he wrote the book Eaton was appointed senator and continued in office until he took his seat in the cabinet. Soon a great storm developed with Mrs. Eaton at its center. The Peggy Eaton case was one of Jackson's major crises. It was a time when he greatly needed Rachel. He defended Mrs. Eaton with characteristic vigor, but the cabinet yielded no ground, and the storm didn't subside.

Finally, in desperation, the President dissolved the cabinet. But he took care of his biographer, sending him to Florida as governor and later as minister to Spain to Madrid. A copy of the biography which Eaton wrote is in the library at Peabody College. It was obviously Old Hickory's personal copy. On a flyleaf Jackson wrote and signed his statement of Eaton's subsequent career, a masterpiece of irony. Here it is as he wrote it on a blank page of his own biography, and about his own biographer:

Major John H. Eaton, after having received every honor and emolument that he was capable of filling in this country, at last received from the General Jackson the office of *Charge d'affaires* to the court of Spain. He continued to hold this office under the administration of Mr. Van Buren until the latter part of the year 1839 when he was recalled on account of alleged misconduct. Arriving in this country, and finding that his hopes of political advancement were blasted on account of his misconduct, he basely abandoned his principles and party, hoping to obtain office in the event of the success of the opposite party. In this he was disappointed. The Whigs used but never trusted the traitor, and after the termination of the campaign of 1840 he was suffered to sink into just and merited contempt and obscurity.

ANDREW JACKSON
August 23, 1842

Nashville found Andrew Jackson a very exciting man, though there were some who didn't thrive on the Jackson sort of excitement. He was a rugged man, a homespun man, a canny man in a trade. He was a man sensitive to culture in its varied forms. He had a flair for elegance. His was not a complex personality, and he was generally predictable. He never flinched from getting into a quarrel, and usually was entirely competent in the performance of his part of it. He was a doughty man in the practice of warfare, a trait in which Nashville found, and finds, great satisfaction. For the first century of its life Nashville had a great fever for war, which to this day hasn't wholly subsided.

The year 1845 was a very exciting one. On March 4 a citizen of Nashville was inducted into the office which Andrew Jackson had surrendered eight years before. On the night before Mr. Polk left for Washington he stayed at the Hermitage. There was much for him and Old Hickory to talk about. It was clear that the General's disease was in its last stages, but he wanted to talk. They talked about many things, surely about Texas and Mexico. Polk left at midmorning. He never saw the General again. The two men saw eye to eye in the Texas matters. War was declared against Mexico in June of 1846. And the men of Tennessee stood in line all over the state to volunteer their service. The spirit of Old Hickory was holding.

Not many men grip the imagination and seem as near and lifelike as Andrew Jackson. He and his wife had built the Hermitage, and lived in it, and loved it. So it became a vital part of the Jackson epic. There is very little chance that a visitor to Nashville will not be taken out to the Hermitage and told the story with varying degrees of accuracy and embellishment. It is a prime gesture of the city's hospitality.

But most of the visitors come to the Hermitage of their own choice. They come from all sections and states. Even on a stormy day one may see in the parking lot there a surprising number of cars from a surprising number of states. One does not visit the Hermitage casually or accidentally. It is not on a major highway and only those go there who have chosen to go. Last year the average number of visitors to the Hermitage was 405 a day. The place is twelve miles distant from Nashville. Those visitors went to some trouble to get there. They went, for the most part, because they wished to establish a closer connection with the personalities of Andrew and Rachel Jackson.

They kept saying at the funeral and after it that the death of Andrew Jackson marked the end of an era. Perhaps it did, but his life marked the beginning of an era much greater. If Thomas Jefferson's power of mind led him to a formulation of the rights of the common man, it was Andrew Jackson's power of feeling that applied the formula to the ways of the common man. Surely, after the manners of those who begin eras, he was in too much of a hurry, a bit unwilling to wait the slow instruction of Time. A difficult thing for us to grasp is that men never come into their eras with the discipline required for gracious conformity. Andrew Jackson's common men shouted when silence would have served them better. They walked noisily and roughly down forbidden paths. They broke up receptions and public gatherings. But a hundred and fifteen years have taught them in considerable degree that the common man need not be the uncouth man, that a common man must yield to the demands of civilization in precisely the same way as any other man. Andrew Jackson's common men have a great deal to learn yet. But they are learning. And Old Hickory was the first one to open wide the door of that opportunity. He could pronounce and defend the life and rights of the common man, but he lived and died a most uncommon one.

IN ACKNOWLEDGMENT

It is impossible to write a book of this sort without a great deal of help. I have had my full share of such help. Indeed, almost everyone with whom I have had serious conversation during the past two years has added something, small or large, to these pages. The willingness of people to lend help to one struggling with the manifold problems that inevitably arise in the writing of a book is one of the delightful phases of literary endeavor. I fear that information and counsel have gone into these pages whose sources, to my shame, I cannot now explicitly identify. A complete listing of the many people who have helped me would be too long to be crowded into the space available, but there are some whose assistance was of such a nature as to demand recognition here.

All the mistakes in the book—and the number of them concerns me—are mine. My special thanks goes to:

Miss Annie Loe Russell, Reference Librarian, Peabody College; Miss Clara Brown, Reference Librarian, Joint University Library; Mrs. Gertrude Parsley, Reference Librarian, Tennessee State Library; Miss Bettye Brown, Reference Librarian, Nashville Public Library; Miss Isabel Howell, Director, Library Division, Tennessee State Library; Mr. Robert Quarles, Director, Archives Division, Tennessee State Library; Mr. Isaac Copeland, Librarian, Peabody College; Mr. William Alderson, Editor, *Tennessee Historical Quarterly*; Mr. Charles Britton and Miss Joy Bayless of The Methodist Publishing House; Mr. Walter Sharp, Director of Fine Arts, Vanderbilt University; Mr. Henry Swint, Professor of History, Vanderbilt University; Mr. Edgar Duncan, Professor of English, Vanderbilt University; Mr. Robert McGaw, Director of Information and Publications, Vanderbilt University; Mr. Harold Ingraham and Mr. Homer Grice of The Southern Baptist Sunday School Board; Mr. Arno Bontemps, Librarian, Fisk University; Mr. Earl Shaub and Miss Alice Yeager, Department of Conservation, State of Tennessee; President A. C. Pullias, David

Lipscomb College; President A. B. Mackey, Trevecca College; Mr. Hugh Walker, *The Nashville Tennessean*; Mr. Forrest Reed, The Tennessee Book Company; Mr. Ed Huddleston, *The Nashville Banner*; Mrs. Walter L. Baggett, The Methodist Board of Education; also Mrs. Sam Orr, Mrs. Roy Avery, Mrs. George Frazer, Mr. Walter Stokes, Mrs. Claude Finney, Mrs. Alfred Sharpe, Mr. Henry Goodpasture, Mr. Reba Goff, all of Nashville.

The following books and pamphlets have been specially helpful:

The History of Davidson County, by W. W. Clayton, 1880

The History of Nashville, Tennessee, edited by J. Wooldridge, 1890

Tennessee: A Guide to the Volunteer State, Federal Writers Project, 1939

General James Robertson, Father of Nashville, by Judge Thomas Matthews, 1929

The Life of Andrew Jackson (3 vols.), by James Parton, 1860

History of Homes and Gardens of Tennessee, edited by Mrs. Roberta Seawell Brandau, 1932

Life of John Berrien Lindsley, by J. E. Windrow, 1937

History of the Methodist Publishing House, by J. M. Batten, 1954

First Presbyterian Church, A Century of Service, 1914

Christ Church, Nashville, edited by Mrs. Anne Rankin, 1929

The Army of Tennessee, by Stanley F. Horn, 1941

The Hermitage, by Stanley F. Horn, 1938

Historical Country Homes near Nashville, by Mrs. May Winston Caldwell, 1911

Andrew Jackson's Hermitage, by Mary French Caldwell, 1933

Nashville, the Athens of the South, by Henry McRaven, 1946

Nashville: Its Life and Times, by Jesse Burt, 1959

Old Days in Nashville, by Miss Jane Thomas, 1890

The Price of Sunrise, by Ed Huddleston, sponsored by *The Nashville Banner*, undated

The City Cemetery, by Ed Huddleston, sponsored by *The Nashville Banner*, undated

Nashville as a World Religious Center, by J. W. Carty, Jr., sponsored by *The Nashville Tennessean*, undated

Pioneer Medicine and Early Physicians of Nashville, by Dr. T. V. Woodring, undated

Cultural Life of Nashville (1825-1860), by Garvin Davenport, 1941

History of McKendree Methodist Church, 1933

Catholic Women of Tennessee, edited by Mrs. Herbert Haile, 1956

A History of the Vine Street Christian Church, by Eva Jean Wrather, undated

Pen and Sword: An Editing of the Diary of Randall McGavock, by Herschel Gower and Jack Allen, 1960

"First with the Most" Forrest, by Robert Selph Henry, 1944

The Story of the Mexican War, by Robert Selph Henry, 1950

Preservation of the Hermitage, by Mrs. Mary C. Dorris, 1915

The Life of General Simon Bolivar Buckner, by A. M. Stickles, 1941

A Guide to the Study and Reading of Tennessee History, by W. T. Alderson and Robert H. White, undated

Champ Ferguson, Confederate Guerrilla, by Thurman Sensing, 1942

Various issues of the *Peabody Reflector*, the *Tennessee Historical Quarterly*, and the *Filson Club Quarterly*

INDEX

Feehan, Rev. Patrick, 161
Ferguson, Dr. Jesse B., 157
Ferguson, John T., 148
Finney, Dr. Claude, 245
First Baptist Church, 93, 151, 167, 238
First Christmas, The, 248
First Lutheran Church, 167
First Presbyterian Church, 44, 63, 78, 137, 143
First Tennessee Regiment, 46
"First with the Most" Forrest, 248-249
Fisk, Gen. Clinton B., 192
Fisk Jubilee Singers, 215
Fisk University, 99, 192-193, 247
Fiske, Moses, 174, 194
Fiske Academy, 194
Flaget, Bishop, 84
Flanigan, Rev. George J., 162
Fletcher, John Gould, 244
Flippinger, Dr. Arthur, 167
Floyd, Gen., 58, 60
Fogg, Francis Brinley, 51, 56, 163-164, 175, 178, 207, 235
Fogg, Mrs. Francis, 57, 261
Fogg, Henry Middleton Rutledge, 51-52, 54, 58, 65, 234-236
Fogg, Mrs. Henry, 236
Fogg, Mary Middleton Rutledge, 52
Folk Songs of the American Negro, 247
Forbes, Sgt. John R., 223
Ford, Dr. John P., 93
Ford, Reuben, 153
Forrest, Nathan Bedford, 30, 67, 70, 183
Fort, Dr. Allen, 152
Forts: Donelson, 30, 49, 57-60, 62, 193, 195, 200, 224, 242; Henry, 30, 58-59, 235; Mackinaw, 65; Mims, 34; Patrick Henry, 16-17, 22; Sumter, 56; Warren, 62
Foster, A. P., 247
Foster, Ephraim, 47, 78, 175, 178, 227
Foster, Dr. R. V., 243
Foster, Robert Coleman, 20-21, 46-48, 61, 78-79
Foster Street Methodist Church, 148
Fowler, Thornton, 146
Frankfort, Ky., 82-83, 124, 132, 149, 171, 254
Franklin, Benjamin, 95
Franklin, Tenn., 40, 52-53, 68-69, 131, 136, 153, 163, 166, 233
Franklin College, 238
Freeman Dr. John D., 154
Freihammer, Rev. William, 162
French, J. S., 146
Freret, Carrie, 40
Frost, Dr. J. M., 152, 156-157

Gabhart, Dr. Herbert, 198
Gaiety Theater, 212, 214
Gale, Dudley, 224
Gallatin, Tenn., 29, 82, 93, 129, 149, 230
Galli-Curci, Amelita, 222
Ganier, A. S., 224

Gano, R. M., 159
Gans, Rudolph, 222
Gardner, C. S., 153, 202
Garland, Landon C., 98, 187-188, 191
Garrett, Mr., 121, 143-144, 249
Garrison, S. C., 185, 246
Garthan, Dr., 59
Gates, G. A., 193
Gayle, Rev. Peter, 150
Gazette, 209-212, 214, 234
General Methodist Conference, 239
George Peabody College for Teachers, 86, 182-185, 208
Georgetown College, 241
German Methodist Church, 167
Gernert, Dr. William, 168
Ghost Flower, The, 247
Gibbs, Gen. 38
Gibson, Dr. Foye, 208
Gibson, Dr. George, 167
Gibson, Maria, 208
Giers, C. C., 55
Gilkey, Dr. Landon, 245
Gist, Gen., 68-69
Glasgow, Ky., 23, 76, 81-82
Glen Leven Church, 137
Golden, Bella, 66, 215
Golden Cross of Honor, 97
Goldnamer, Dr. G. S., 168
Goodlett, Dr. Adam, 85
Goodpasture, A. V., 249
Goodpasture, Mrs. Henry, 116
Gospel Advocate, 243
Goucher, John F., 196
Goucher College, 197
Gower, Abel, 20
Gower, Dr. Herschel, 235
Grace Baptist Church, 156
Grace Presbyterian Church, 138
Graham, Dr. Billy, 220
Graham, Dr. Otis, 137
Graham, Rev. William, 164
Granberry, J. M., 188
"Grand Old Opry," 217-218, 222
Grant, Ulysses S., 57, 65, 70, 215, 226
Grantham, Dr. Dewey, 245
Gravath, E. M., 193
Graves, Rev. J. R., 152
Gray, Dr. W. D., 135
Green, Dr. A. L. P., 98, 126, 143-146, 186-187, 239-240
Green, Roy, 156
Green, Thomas Marston, 266
Green Mountain Boys, 215
Greenleaf, Prof., 96
Grimes, Green, 237
Gross, Dr. John O., 84
Grundy, Felix, 21, 53, 77-80, 83, 119, 140, 173-175, 178, 227
Grundy, Mrs. Felix, 131
Guide to the Study and Reading of Tennessee History, A, 249
Guild, Joe, 65

Haggard, W. G., 100
Hale, Dr. George L., 154